KEENAN

KEENAN

The High Times and
Misadventures of
Hockey's Most
Controversial Coach

Jeff Gordon

MCGREGOR
PUBLISHING

04 03 02 01 00 1 2 3 4 5

Library of Congress Cataloging-in-Publication Data

Gordon, Jeff, 1956-
   Keenan : the high times and misadventures of hockey's most controversial coach / by Jeff Gordon
   p. cm.
   ISBN 0-9653846-0-8
   1. Keenan, Mike, 1949- 2. Hockey coaches—Canada—Biography. I. Title.

GV848.5.K42 G67 2000
796.962'092—dc21
[B]   00-061272

Every reasonable effort has been made to obtain reprint permissions.
The publisher will gladly receive any information that will help rectify,
in subsequent editions, any inadvertent omissions.

Jacket design: Antler Design Works
Jacket photos: Bruce Bennett Studios
Design and typesetting: Sue Knopf/Graffolio

Published by McGregor Publishing, Inc., Tampa, Florida.
Canadian edition simultaneously published by Stoddart Limited.

Printed and bound in the United States of America.

To my father,

David Gordon,

for giving me the opportunities

to pursue my dreams.

CONTENTS

Acknowledgments

This chronicle of Mike Keenan's life and times would not have been possible without the outstanding reporting of the many journalists who followed his teams and his sport. I am especially indebted to Jay Greenberg, Gary Smith, Michael Farber, Austin Murphy, Pat Jordan, Kerry Banks, Rick Carpiniello, Larry Wigge, Barry Meisel, Dave Luecking, Tom Wheatley, Dave Dorr, Mike Kiley, Bob Verdi, Steve Rosenbloom, Brian Hanley, Jennifer Frey, Laura Price, Joe Lapointe, Larry Brooks, Mary Ormsby, Jim Matheson, Mike Beamish, Gary Mason, Tony Gallagher, Iain MacIntyre, and Elliott Pap. Also, thanks to my editor, "Iron Dave" Rosenbaum; the patient women in my life, Leigh Anne, Jennifer, and Cara; and my loyal miniature schnauzer Trixie, who stayed right by my side through the many months of writing.

Prologue

I have an intensity problem. Sure, I've gone over the edge too many times and probably am too harsh on them. And, yeah, I'm miserable when we lose. I can't help it.
—MIKE KEENAN, WHILE COACHING THE CHICAGO BLACKHAWKS

ON MAY 22, 1992, ALL WAS GOOD IN MIKE KEENAN'S LIFE.

His Chicago Blackhawks had made great strides during his four seasons behind the bench and his two years as general manager. This was his team, built in his fiery "Iron Mike" image. He had molded a stylish but lazy team into a forechecking buzzsaw. He banished to the hinterlands any player who refused to hustle. Even Denis Savard and Doug Wilson — two fan favorites adored by Blackhawks owner Bill Wirtz — had been exiled. Those players who remained rocked Chicago Stadium with their hard-hitting play. The beer-gulping, Behn Wilson-sweater-wearing fans were most pleased.

Chicago was very good to Keenan, his wife Rita, and their teenage daughter Gayla. Finally, Keenan was realizing that there was a world outside the rink. He had never seemed happier. He was riding high and enjoying the view after driving this long-woeful team to the Stanley Cup finals. As he prepared to lead his charges against the talented Pittsburgh Penguins, he seemed at ease. His gregarious side, previously obscured by his desperate quest for success, occasionally surfaced.

Long before reaching the NHL, Keenan manufactured his coaching persona from whole cloth. He began dressing like a CEO and speaking in the overblown language of an MBA candidate. He gleaned aphorisms from self-help books and applied them to hockey, stuff like, "Great players have needs that have to be satisfied, but needs of the team come first."

Starting in major junior, he borrowed heavily from the imperious manner of his hockey mentor, Scotty Bowman. Even his famous temper was often contrived: Early on, he learned to saw through sticks before breaking them in not-so-spontaneous anger.

In Chicago, though, the Blackhawks saw glimpses of the real Mike Keenan. His anxiety and insecurity finally seemed to ease.

"My wife told me the other day she can't believe how relaxed I am," he said on the eve of the finals. "I always felt earlier in my career that if I didn't win the next game, I would be out of a job. Now I'm to the point where if I'm out of a job, well, that's the way it goes."

He had spurred these Blackhawks to one of his trademark playoff runs. They made short work of the St. Louis Blues, Detroit Red Wings, and Edmonton Oilers, winning eleven straight games heading into the finals. The Blackhawks had blitzed their foes with all-out puck pressure and beat them down with physical play.

The assault continued in the Cup finals against the Penguins. The Blackhawks surged ahead, 4–1, in Game One before Mario Lemieux, Jaromir Jagr, Ron Francis, and the rest of the Penguins knew what hit them.

But the good times would not last. For Keenan, they never do.

The Penguins regrouped. They turned back the Blackhawks' assault. Gradually, the momentum shifted. Lemieux trimmed the lead to 4–3 with an end-to-end rush finished with a bad-angle goal against goaltender Ed Belfour. Keenan felt as if his team was suddenly falling asleep in the Stanley Cup finals.

With four minutes, fifty-five seconds remaining in regulation, Jagr intercepted Brent Sutter's clearing pass, worked his way through three Blackhawks, and rolled a backhanded shot past Belfour to tie the game. Keenan was livid. In his mind, Jagr's linemate, Shawn McEachern, had interfered with Blackhawks defenseman Igor Kravchuk and held defenseman Frantisek Kucera's stick. Keenan thought the goal shouldn't have been allowed and was enraged at one of his long-standing nemeses, referee Andy van Hellemond.

With time running down in the third period and Lemieux steaming down the slot, Blackhawks defenseman Steve Smith reached his stick into Mario's midsection. Lemeiux went down. The whistle blew and van Hellemond sent Smith off for hooking with eighteen seconds remaining. Keenan was furious with his veteran defenseman and accused him of relaxing on the play. Later, he accused Lemieux of taking dives.

On the ensuing faceoff in the Chicago zone, Sutter lost the draw to Francis. The puck was kicked back to Penguins defenseman Larry Murphy. Rather than hold up Lemieux, Blackhawks winger Steve Larmer rushed the point. Murphy's shot got through. Lemieux, left uncovered, lifted the rebound past Belfour to win the game with thirteen seconds remaining. It was more than Keenan could endure quietly.

During his postgame media address, Keenan ripped several of his players and blasted his team as a whole.

"There's no excuse to give up a three-goal lead in the playoffs," he said. "On Jagr's goal, we had a forward and two defensemen play the puck rather than the man. We can't expect to be successful playing the puck. They get the winning goal when nobody picks up the most dangerous player in hockey."

Such comments allowed Keenan to blow off steam. But he didn't cool off. At a team meeting, he went ballistic and yelled at his players for forty-five minutes more. Never mind that this was just one loss. Never mind that the team had played nearly flawless hockey in the second and third rounds of the playoffs. The blown three-goal lead pushed him over the edge.

"Andy van Hellemond did a very poor job and I was frustrated with him," Keenan said later. "And out of that frustration, I really leveled the team. It was way beyond what they deserved after going to the wall for me, for us, and going to the Cup finals. That was the only day, because that year I really made a concerted effort to change dramatically. And that was the one day I regretted because they didn't deserve it."

The next day, the Blackhawks kept a stiff upper lip about Keenan's public and private outbursts.

"Mike believes negative energy is better than none at all," said center Jeremy Roenick, one of the players singled out for ineffective play. "When he yells and screams, he gets you going. I guess he feels people can get kicked in the butt and they'll respond. Personally, I think our team reacts better to getting kicked than patted on the back. This team reacts better to adversity than praise."

But the demoralized Blackhawks never quite recovered from the Game One loss. The team had won all along with passion, energy, and belief. The Blackhawks had talent, but not overwhelming skill. Their tactics were blunt, their Xs and Os simple. They won with dedication, which dissipated after Game One. Chicago put up a fight, but lost the Cup finals to Pittsburgh in four straight games.

Once again, Keenan's extreme intensity had undermined his extraordinary work. Once again, he had failed to shoulder responsibility for defeat, deflecting blame to his players and the referee. And this time, his irrationality would change the course of his career and his personal life.

Keenan allowed himself to become demoralized. That, in turn, demoralized his team. He seriously considered quitting. He was angry at the officiating. How could he go on, he felt, when the National Hockey League didn't match his commitment to excellence? How could the NHL tear out his heart like this?

"I thought, we worked four years to get here and the officials did us in," Keenan said. "Somebody didn't prepare himself to call a big game. I said, 'What am I doing coaching?' I took it very personally."

The 1992 playoffs captured, in two months, the whole Keenan experience. He drove his team toward the top of the NHL, just as he had driven himself to the top of his profession.

These Blackhawks mirrored their coach. They worked harder than anybody. They were aggressive risk takers. Their passion fueled them. Once they got momentum, they were nearly unstoppable. But when they blew up, they blew up real good.

"That's probably where he runs into problems, intensity," said New York Rangers scout E.J. McGuire, who spent two seasons with Keenan in Chicago after assisting him in Philadelphia and Rochester of the American Hockey League. "Problems with players, problems with upper management. I'd joke around to him, to his face, that he doesn't burn bridges behind him, he fucking nukes them. Once you're over the bridge, it blows up. You'd better be running and staying up with him."

Keenan admits he invites conflict. He acknowledges that he has pushed teams and players too far. He concedes that his family life suffered because of his obsessive quest for success. He understands why people believe he is nuts. But he can't stop pushing. Even in Chicago, where he appeared to be the picture of contentment, he couldn't stop pushing.

"I gave up sanity to chase the dream," he said long after moving on from the Windy City. "That's why I win, I guess. I'm willing to pay the ultimate price. Whether it's worth it or not, it's my choice. You preserve your integrity when you do that. You have to have that purity to be a champion."

◄ 1 ►

One of the Nice Guys

The reason he was a force in the band in college is that he had this ability to take over the audience. He wasn't a good singer or anything. He was almost a rapper, long before anybody thought of that.

— GARY WEBB
A FOUNDING MEMBER OF THE COLLEGE BAND
NIK AND THE NICE GUYS

LONG BEFORE HE EARNED THE NICKNAME "IRON," MIKE KEENAN was one of the Nice Guys. As in Nik and the Nice Guys. Gary Webb, Keenan, and other members of the St. Lawrence University hockey team formed the band in 1971. They played the fraternity party circuit in the role of "Otis Day and The Knights" long before the movie *Animal House* gave toga parties and the song "Shout!" mainstream acceptance.

"He becomes entranced when he listens to good music," Webb said. "He really wishes he could play something."

But he couldn't. And he couldn't really sing, either. But he could lead a party just as well as he could lead a hockey team. He would grab the microphone and take over. He could read his audience like he would some-day read his players. He would feel the ebb and flow of the show the way he would later feel the flow of hockey games from the bench. He had an uncanny feel for when to crank it up.

"Mike didn't play an instrument and he sang in this incredibly flat voice, but he wanted so badly to be center stage," Webb said. "He would sing that Sly and the Family Stones' song 'I Want to Take You Higher.' He'd get everybody in the room down on their knees, then wiggling their rear ends, then flopping like fish on the floor of some beer-soaked frat-house basement. It was hilarious! He'd compensate for his lack of ability by bullying the crowd into doing what he wanted."

Ottawa Senators coach Jacques Martin played hockey with Keenan at St. Lawrence and later was Keenan's assistant coach with the Chicago Blackhawks. The mild-mannered Martin wasn't part of the band, but he found his way to a few of the beer blasts where Nik and the Nice Guys played.

"They did a lot of bubble-gum music," Martin recalled. "They were really big at St. Lawrence. After the games, the fraternities would have dollar parties. You'd pay a dollar to get in and they'd have draft beer on tap, and lots of rock and roll. They had their own song called 'Peanut Butter.' They'd always get a guy up on stage with them, some guy from the audience. The guy would have a jar of peanut butter and he would start putting it all over himself. That really got the students going."

Hmmmmm . . . Mike Keenan? In a college band that smeared peanut butter on audience members? Somehow, that image doesn't match the image of a glowering Keenan standing behind a bench like a field marshal, arms folded, looking down his nose at his troops. Some twenty-five years later, a St. Louis radio station would offer a cash reward for concert videos of Keenan. At a time when Blues fans were starting to turn on their team's dictator, the community wanted proof that he really was a Nice Guy.

Boundless ambition and his relentless drive overshadowed this side of Keenan. His teams would see only glimpses of his playful side. Keenan's friends find him a charming, warm, gregarious, and generous man who can be ceaseless fun. His players, on the other hand, often want to choke the life out of him with their bare hands. How could the same man evoke such contrasting reactions?

A lot of writers have tried to psychoanalyze Keenan over the years, a job made easier — but, in some ways, more difficult — by Keenan's willingness to openly examine his past and probe his psyche.

Keenan grew up in the 1950s and '60s, a time when people buried their emotions and soldiered on through adversity. Families kept their problems to themselves. Counseling and therapy were absolutely the last resort. These days, family therapy has become a televised sport, an endless freak show for morbid daytime viewers. Trauma and tragedy are big sellers. Dysfunctional families slug it out for the amusement of others on *Montel.* Keenan's generation dealt with family strife by not dealing with it.

Keenan was born on October 21, 1949, in Toronto. He grew up just east of there in Whitby, Ontario, a city of 45,000 off the shore of Lake Ontario. The General Motors plant in nearly Oshawa employed his father Ted, his two uncles, and his grandfather. Mike would get his taste of factory work, too, enough to reaffirm the benefits of higher education.

Ted was a fun-loving man who enjoyed carousing with friends. Mike's mother Thelma was far more serious. Sparks flew when he ambled in from the bar. Mike and his sisters, Cathy and Marie, saw more domestic disputes than they cared to remember.

"It wasn't always a good situation at home," Marie said. "It wasn't the Nelsons, Ozzie and Harriet. And it wasn't the Cleavers."

The Keenans had their share of tragedy, too. When Mike was four, his infant brother Patrick died of pneumonia. The baby, born prematurely, was just two months old when he died at the hospital. The family had no phone, so police went to their home with the grim news. This traumatic scene would haunt Mike. So would the funeral for the little brother he would never know.

"I can see my father and me kneeling at the casket," Keenan recalled. "I can relive every minute of it now."

A beloved grandmother, Helen Chatterton, was stricken with multiple sclerosis. Her slow, painful, and ultimately fatal decline left a mark on him. He would later describe Helen as the most influential person in his early life. Another grandmother, May, lapsed into alcoholism after her husband left her. The disease killed her.

"She died of a broken heart," Keenan said.

Keenan was a good Catholic lad who wasn't afraid of the nuns who taught at his school. His knuckles got rapped many times. When the nuns would ask who was talking in class, Keenan never cowered.

"I'd always say, 'Me,'" he recalled. "After a while, she'd say, 'That's enough. At least you're honest,' and not strap me anymore."

He was an altar boy for eight years. He attended the 7:30 A.M. mass at St. John's Catholic Church daily from first grade on. "Just a likable, easy-going kid," said Marie, who is younger by two years. "Never controversial. Everyone wanted to be his friend."

Keenan fit right in with the neighborhood kids.

9

"I used to hang around with seven Italian brothers when I was a kid," he said. "I was the only Irish kid. If they got a beating from their mother, I got a beating too."

He had his rebellious moments around the neighborhood. He once described his younger self as "an Irishman trying to fight his way out of a bad situation."

Hockey provided the perfect outlet. His father built him a backyard rink and hung lights on clotheslines so the neighborhood children could play past dark. He took Mike down to the frozen marshlands along Lake Ontario. He brought along a jug of hot chocolate and helped the other fathers sweep off the snow so the kids could play.

A couple of cousins, Tom and Ted O'Connor, helped him master hockey. Both had played on the Whitby Dunlops Senior A team that had won a world championship in Oslo, Norway. Tom would come home from the night shift at the GM plant and tutor Mike on the empty Whitby rink.

Mike became an excellent player. He scored fourteen goals in a game as a nine-year-old. He became a solid junior hockey player and a star at Dennis O'Connor High School in Whitby. In 1965, he was named Athlete of the Year among ninth-grade students. He could play forward and defense with some skill and was tough in the corners. He was only 5 feet 7 inches, though, and he didn't skate like Rocket Richard.

Off the ice, Mike was industrious, too. He was always willing to work for the things he wanted.

"The first thing I started working at was cutting lawns," he said. "I was fourteen years old and I hired other people to work for me, work with me. Then it was paper routes, [selling] *The Globe and Mail* of Toronto. That was 5:30 A.M., up and running." When he was sixteen, he went to work as a bottler for Coca-Cola.

All the while, life at home was bleak. Mike's mother and father were always fighting. "They separated a lot," Marie recalled. "Mum would stay and Dad would go. He'd stay away from the house for a long time. We never talked about it outside the house, Mike and I. It was awkward, not something that you told your friends about. It hardened Mike. He kept his emotions hidden. I never saw him cry as a child. Not once."

Ted and Thelma divorced in 1968, when Keenan got the break of a lifetime: a scholarship offer from St. Lawrence University in upstate New York. Another player, Jimmy Adair, had declined the scholarship offer given to Keenan. The home Keenan left behind was in disarray. All the

ONE OF THE NICE GUYS

battles and all the separations had finally taken their toll.

"You know, sometimes I wish I could have done what Ted did, just drink a couple of beers, let go, relax, party time," Thelma said years later. "But I had to be the ogre. I'd say to Mike, 'You could have done better,' no matter what he did. Our family doctor said he'd never seen a son turn out to be more like his mother."

Thelma was obsessive. If the kids got up early to go to the bathroom, she'd make their beds before they got back. She set curfews and made the movie house off-limits on weeknights.

"She pushed the kids," Ted said. "At times, she might have gone overboard, but I had to back her up."

One time, Thelma held Mike out of an all-star hockey game because of poor grades. The men in town were furious, but Thelma wouldn't budge. "It was her decision," Ted said. "My choice would have been that he play hockey. She was right. She set the ground rules and I'd agree to them."

Years later, Keenan's players would see Thelma's personality come through in their coach, from his fanatical devotion to order to his reluctance to lower his guard. "I just wish I could let my emotions out and hug somebody, and I know he feels the same way too," Thelma said.

As a young man, Mike wanted to let his emotions spill out. But you just didn't do such things in those days, lest you be considered a weakling. "That was my shortcoming from the beginning, I was oversensitive," Keenan said. "I'd keep it all in. I was the stiff-upper-lip oldest son, but inside, I kept thinking, *I'm way too soft.* I knew I'd get chewed up if I didn't change."

Mike also inherited his father's personality as a charismatic fun-lover. He made friends easily and could party with the best. But while Ted and Thelma remained locked in conflict, Mike felt conflicted. Was he Iron Mike or was he a Nice Guy? Or maybe he was both.

At the height of the Keenan's domestic struggle, Mike couldn't find comfort in his faith. When his grandmother, Helen Chatterton, died at age fifty-four, the nuns wouldn't let him out of his tenth grade classes to attend the funeral next door. He would never forgive the Catholic Church for this and he later renounced his religion as hypocrisy. He felt betrayed.

"The nuns went crazy," Keenan said. "Here I'm supposed to be a role model and I've just announced I'm never going to church again." Later, even in his most introspective moments with the media, he would never talk about religion.

The hockey scholarship to St. Lawrence was Keenan's ticket out of Whitby, out of the shadow of the GM plant and the battleground back home. "I had to get the hell out of that environment," he said. Suddenly, each day presented myriad options. The hockey was fun. The class work was stimulating. The coeds were pretty and the social calendar filled up in a hurry.

"It was a good school, academics, a good small school, like only 2,000 students, in the North country," Jacques Martin recalled. "A little town. Canton, New York, was only about 5,000 people if you take away the university and there is a New York state college, too. It's kind of a small environment, close to Canada. You weren't just a number there, you were a person. I met some friends that stayed friends to this day. For a lot of Canadian boys at that time, it was a great opportunity to pursue education and pursue hockey."

Keenan and fellow Canadian kids like Gary Webb were in awe of their opportunity. They had escaped the working world for utopia. Their fellow students arrived on campus with skis to use at the school's ski lodge, or with horses in trailers. There were no smokestacks or grime-covered men with hollow eyes walking out the factory gates, as there had been back home. Here, there was hope. The good opportunities seemed endless.

"The second our feet hit the ground, we absolutely loved it," Webb said. "Mike and I would just look at each other and say, 'Double A!' It was our signal word. It meant all-American. Every time we got excited — it would be a blonde walking across the quad, or a great party — we'd say, 'Double A!' It meant, this country's great! Let's go for it! A place where you either made it on your own or you didn't, where you could go as far as your creativity and convictions could take you. No more socialist crap, no government to bail you out or unions to protect your ass, no laid-back approach to life like we'd both grown up with in Canada. For people like him and me, St. Lawrence and America was paradise. Double A!"

Keenan's grades, however, were not Double A. He ambitiously enrolled in the pre-med program, but flunked out after one semester, done in by too much America too soon. Just like that, he faced a watershed moment in his life. Was he headed back to Whitby to do fifty-one years at the plant, like his grandfather? Or was he going to pull himself out of trouble and move on to greater things?

Keenan met with his dean. He asked if there was anything he could do to earn a second chance. They struck a deal. He had to sit out a semester, then pay his own way for the following semester while regaining good academic standing. Do that, the dean told him, and he could get back his scholarship.

This was a reality check. To make sure he would never forget what was at stake, he asked his father to get him a job at the dreaded GM plant. Figuring his boy needed to learn a lesson, Ted arranged for him to get an awful assignment: spot welding in a unit known as the jungle line. The job was grueling and monotonous, and left Mike sweat-soaked and singed after each intolerable shift.

"Is this how you want to spend the rest of your life?" Ted asked him after a few weeks.

"No bloody way," Mike said.

Keenan returned to St. Lawrence, eager to achieve. Ted cashed in a life insurance policy to help pay for school. Mike took his second chance more seriously than anything he had ever done.

"Here I was, this poor Canadian country kid," Mike said. "Did I belong here? I felt I owed it to the school to fit in, to survive. They had given me my chance."

He made the honor roll. He whipped himself into top shape. The good hockey player became a good student as well. He studied education. He decided he wanted to teach some day. He wanted to coach.

"It was the lifestyle I wanted," he said. "I knew simplicity would be lost. But I didn't care what adaptations it would take. I was going to do it."

Keenan was a 5-feet-10-inches, 185-pound right wing who could also fill in on the blue line. In 1969–70, he played 10 games for St. Lawrence and had 4 assists. In 1970–71, he played 22 games and scored 4 goals with 12 assists. In 1971–72, he scored 13 goals and added 16 assists in 25 games.

"A pretty steady, methodical type player, nose to the grindstone," Webb said. "Very steady, conscientious, a smart type of player. He had quite a high level of tenacity. He played the policeman role, too. I was a smaller guy. He took care of me."

Martin played goal for one season with Keenan. "He played both defense and forward and was one of the captains," Martin said. "He's a kind of an aggressive player. Kind of outgoing player, outgoing person."

The hockey was good, but not great. "We were a pretty ragtag bunch," Webb said. "It was a few years later that St. Lawrence began developing some really good players."

Along the way, Keenan's coach, George Menard, subjected him to the sort of acid test Keenan would later give his own players. After watching Keenan play halfheartedly in a game during his junior season, Menard accused him of throwing the game.

"I'm not going to tolerate it," Menard said. "You did that on purpose. You threw the game. You won't suit up for any more games."

After serious self-examination, Keenan decided to work even harder and prove his coach wrong.

"He was in a total fog," Webb said. "Looking in the mirror, thinking, *I couldn't have thrown a game, but . . . but maybe I should have been stronger so I don't even give off the appearance of weakness again.* The mind games Mike plays on his players today, some of that stuff has to come from Menard."

Keenan worked many jobs during his school years and summers, but he never went back to the GM plant. "I worked at construction, digging ditches," he said. "I worked on a railroad line, putting in rails, ties, and lived in a boxcar. I worked at the university in a number of jobs, shoveling snow, in a restaurant cleaning floors, in a kitchen. I worked as a lifeguard. I had quite a few experiences."

During his time at St. Lawrence, soldiers began returning from the Vietnam War and enrolling in colleges. Living with these physically and emotionally wounded young men was an eye-opening experience for Keenan. "I was living with vets who had just come back from Vietnam at a time when there was, really, a transformation of America," he said. "I remember sleeping in rooms with those vets and waking up to their screaming nightmares."

When Keenan arrived, St. Lawrence had strict rules of conduct designed to maintain its pristine campus image. But the veterans didn't want to hear about those rules, not after their hellish Vietnam ordeals.

"When I started school, there were classes six days a week, no women allowed, no alcohol, shirt and tie to school," Keenan recalled. "Within two years, vets would say, 'I got my leg shot off and you're not going to tell me I can't have a beer and you're certainly not going to tell me I can't have a woman in my room and I'm not going to school on Saturday.'"

Keenan once introduced a drunken vet to the dean. The vet grabbed the dean in a headlock and said, "Have a beer, Dean."

"No, no," Keenan said. "He is the dean."

Despite being surrounded by comely coeds at St. Lawrence — and singing in a popular campus band — Keenan found love back home in Ontario. His future wife, the former Rita Haas, was a farmer's daughter and the granddaughter of a Hungarian Jew killed at Auschwitz. Rita and her family offered the nurturing so clearly lacking in Mike's upbringing in Whitby.

"Maybe because we didn't have a nice family situation at home, that was one of his center focuses," Marie said. "He was trying to achieve that in his own married life."

Mike and Rita married in 1972. Keenan graduated with a Bachelor's of Science degree in physical education. To teach in Ontario at that time, he had to earn his certification from the University of Toronto. While continuing his higher education, he played for the school and added a Canadian university championship to his resume.

"He could skate and shoot," said Tom Watt, who coached the University of Toronto. "He had a lot of enthusiasm. We had a very good team. We won the national championship in 1973. If that wasn't the best team I had there, it was the second best. We had a good group. We had no trouble winning the national championship. Mike was a very good college player."

Keenan saw himself as a future teacher and coach. But the Vancouver Blazers of the World Hockey Association had drafted him. He went to the Blazers' training camp in 1973 and came away with a pair of the team's colorful skates, as well as a roster spot with the Roanoke Valley Rebels of the Southern Hockey League. Feeling obligated to give professional hockey a try, he spent the 1973–74 season playing in the minor leagues.

If you have seen the move *Slap Shot*, you have a pretty good idea about what life in the Southern League was like. Some rinks were enclosed with chicken wire. Cheapshot goon tactics were the norm and fights were commonplace.

The general manager of the Rebels was a colorful character named Colin Kilburn. During his earlier days as coach, Kilburn had pulled his share of stunts. One night, he grew disgusted with his team's listless play. Rather than merely switch goaltenders, Kilburn strapped on the goaltending equipment himself and made a mockery of the craft. But his startled team came to life and won. In another game, an opposing player skated past the Rebels bench and slugged the coach. Kilburn grabbed a hockey stick and swung it at the transgressor like an axe, just missing the guy's head. Playing in the Southern League was an exercise in civil disobedience. And the rewards were modest; the highest-paid Rebel was Claude Piche, who earned a $17,000 salary and another $12,500 in bonuses.

Keenan scored 25 goals, 36 assists, and had 94 penalty minutes in fifty-eight games for the Rebels, who won more than fifty regular season games and then swept through the playoffs to win the league championship. Though he played for the Rebels just one season, Keenan was later inducted into the Roanoke Express Hall of Fame as part of the city's thirtieth anniversary celebration of pro hockey.

"He was a good all-around player," Piche recalled. "He played defense and right wing for us, all around. You could tell he knew the game really well. A good team guy, definitely a good team guy, no question about it. He hung around with the boys. When the chips were down, he'd be there. He wasn't a fighter, but he was a real physical guy."

In the semifinals, Keenan scored the winning goal in Game Seven to eliminate Winston-Salem. In the decisive game of the championship series against the Charlotte Checkers, he set up the game-winning goal by Michael Plante.

"Oh man, we had a heck of team," Piche said. "We had six guys the following year who would go on to the NHL."

Could Keenan have made it to the WHA or the NHL? Watt noted that college players of that era had little chance to advance because of their age. Keenan was five years older than junior players entering NHL camps. Piche had been to camp with the Minnesota North Stars and also belonged to the Boston Bruins organization.

"I'd say he [Keenan] was about halfway [there]," Piche said. "I think he could have been a good solid player. Not enough speed. He was a little slow on his skates."

Webb saw Keenan lose some of his jump because of knee injuries. "He might have had some opportunities if his knees were a little better," Webb said. "He got pretty banged up. He might have gotten a shot at playing in the NHL."

Rebels coach Greg Pilling was a lot like Menard, or the coach Keenan would become.

"Pilling was nuts, absolutely," Piche said. "He made everybody play that way. I think Mike learned a lot from Pilling."

Among the lessons Keenan learned was this: It was time to fulfill his destiny as a coach.

"It didn't take me long to realize that I wouldn't play in the National Hockey League," he said. "After evaluation, it was very difficult to face the facts — and it always is for players to stop playing when they love the game — but I realized that when I was twenty-three years old. Basically that's when the decision was made."

◂ 2 ▸

Becoming Scotty Bowman

His best attribute as a coach is he hates to lose.

—VETERAN NHL COACH SCOTTY BOWMAN,
WHO HIRED KEENAN TO COACH
THE ROCHESTER AMERICANS

MIKE KEENAN'S PLAYING CAREER ENDED IN 1974 AND HIS COACHING career began. He landed a job at Forest Hill Collegiate Institute in Toronto. This could have been the start of a sane teaching career, one that would have allowed him and Rita to settle down close to home, raise a family, and enjoy the nine-to-five stability celebrated in the television show *Leave It to Beaver.*

But Keenan couldn't lead that life. He was not Ward Cleaver. The hunger that had brought him back to St. Lawrence University and revived his collegiate career kept churning. He could not sit still. The daytime teaching job did not exhaust his energy. He still wanted to play. His uncles had played for the Whitby senior team that won a world amateur title in 1958, but the franchise had become dormant. Keenan wooed McDonald's as a sponsor and revived the team in the fall of 1974. He scored 20 goals in his second and third seasons with Whitby and won an Ontario Hockey Association Senior A title as a player-coach.

"He's always working," said Tom Watt, his coach at the University of Toronto. "Whether that's drive or just hard work, I don't know. When he was teaching, he was building cottages in the summer. He's a guy who continued to work hard and succeed at whatever he did."

In 1977, he took the helm of the Oshawa Legionnaires of the Junior B Ontario Hockey Association and won two straight Metro Toronto Junior B titles. His first star player was Dale Hawerchuk, who was just a youngster at the time.

"He taught me a lot when I was fifteen years old," Hawerchuk said.

Keenan quickly distinguished himself as an instructor of the game. "He was head and shoulders ahead of any coach I'd had to that point with his professionalism, his preparation, his presence," said Mike Pelino, another Legionnaire. "You could tell he was a knowledgeable hockey person."

The relentless Keenan drove from Oshawa at 5:30 in the morning, coached the girls' swimming team at Forest Hill at 7 A.M., taught at the school, coached the boys' hockey team in the afternoon, then drove back to Oshawa to coach the Junior B Legionnaires. His teaching and coaching career melded into one. He even coached the Don Mills Collegiate lacrosse team for a spell.

"I've been very fortunate in my profession because my educational background was in teaching, and that translated into coaching hockey and a number of other sports," he said. "There was always something to be learned, even from running a girls' swim team. I guarantee the things I picked up in those days, in the pool and on the lacrosse floor, are useful to me."

He was always looking for an edge. He would attend the University of Toronto's training camps and find a few players who weren't quite ready to make the school team, but had the ability — and the eligibility — to play junior hockey. Keenan would round up a couple of them for his team, let them crash at his place after practices, and get them back to Toronto in time for their classes. Whatever it took to win, Keenan would try to do it.

He was just twenty-nine years old when the Peterborough Petes of the Ontario Hockey Association hired him as head coach in 1979. This was a chance to coach full-time at the major junior level, just a step below the NHL. Keenan left Forest Hill and whatever hopes Rita may have had for a normal life.

"I enjoyed teaching, and I had tenure," Keenan said. "I went to the principal and said, 'I'd like to try this, and if it doesn't work out I'll come back to my teaching job.'"

This was the first of many jarring changes Rita would endure. "How far do you have to drive to get home?" she asked her husband.

"You don't get it," Keenan said. "Peterborough is our new home."

The Petes had one of the elite franchises in junior hockey, a spawning ground for future NHL stars and coaches.

"Peterborough is an organization that has a lot of tradition," Jacques Martin said. "A lot of it had been established by Roger Neilson. He's the one that put in a lot of the things, as far as kids in school, keeping track of their education. They're well known for being one of the best junior teams to develop players. They had a lot of great hockey people work there. When Mike became the GM and coach in Peterborough, he hired me to scout in the Ottawa area. I was coaching Tier II at that time in Ottawa. The year before he went there, Gary Green was coaching there and they won the Memorial Cup."

As he settled into his new job at the Peterborough rink, Keenan noticed a photograph of a former Petes coach who had won a league championship in his first year there. That coach was Scotty Bowman, a commanding figure who had taken the expansion St. Louis Blues to three Stanley Cup finals and directed a Montreal Canadiens dynasty. Soon, the student was studying the master. How did Scotty carry himself? What were his bench mannerisms? What about his coaching philosophies? How did he manage his bench and his players?

Keenan became a young Bowman. In his one year at Peterborough, the Petes went 47-20-1 and reached the Memorial Cup finals. Bowman, then the general manager and coach of the Buffalo Sabres, got to chat with Keenan and follow the Petes. The two met at a Peterborough game in Niagara Falls and hit it off immediately.

"He dropped down to say hello," Keenan said. "I was respectful. I can't say I was in awe. I certainly knew who he was."

Bowman was so impressed with Keenan that he hired him to coach the Rochester Americans, the Sabres' American Hockey League affiliate, the next season, 1980–81. The New York Rangers and the Washington Capitals were also interested in Keenan, but Keenan couldn't say no to Bowman. The proximity of Buffalo and Rochester to Toronto helped make his decision easier. Once again, he and Rita packed up and moved on to a new adventure.

Bowman credits Neilson, who temporarily replaced Bowman as head Sabres coach for the 1980–81 season, with seeing Keenan's potential. Dick

Todd, Keenan's assistant coach in Peterborough, was close to Neilson. The Peterborough people knew there was something different about this young coach.

"We were looking for a coach for our minor league team and Roger had a pretty good connection in Peterborough," Bowman recalled. "We needed somebody we could work with. They had a good team."

At age thirty, Keenan arrived in Rochester. He wasn't coaching high school kids anymore. He wasn't coaching Junior B teenagers or nineteen-year-old hopefuls in major junior. The Americans had an older team, led by grizzled NHL veterans on their downside. There would be much for both the coach and his players to learn.

"When Scotty introduced him at that first press conference in Rochester, Mike was like a puppy dog following his master," Gary Webb recalled. "He siphoned every ounce of Scotty he could."

Bowman was a willing teacher. He saw Keenan's vast potential and appreciated his commitment. Bowman would often phone Keenan after games, sometimes from his car, and ask why Keenan had used players in certain situations.

"The calls often came after midnight, and they were always one or two hours long," Keenan recalled. "He'd ask me things like why in the third period I had Rob Mongrain out killing a penalty, or something like that. We would talk about every game that happened in the league and every move and every drill we did in practice."

Keenan, following Bowman's lead, developed a gift for shuffling player combinations to alter the game's flow. Bowman didn't roll out four set lines in a game and neither would his student.

"The biggest things I learned from Scotty were bench management and ice-time allocation," Keenan said. "Getting the right players in the best situations they're suited for. In a sixty-minute game, a coach is in control of three hundred and sixty minutes of ice time, since you've got six players on the ice. How you allocate that ice time is the key to success."

Bowman approaches hockey with a single-mindedness that borders on comedy. When he is preoccupied, which is often, he could walk through a meteor shower without blinking. He is often a poor communicator, leaving players to guess why their roles change, but he has unmatched insight into the game. His in-game focus is remarkable.

"What I learned from him is how insightful he is about the game of hockey and how inquisitive his mind is," Keenan said. "He teaches you to ask questions and seek out solutions to become a better team and how to make the players individually better."

Jimmy Roberts played for Bowman in St. Louis and served as both an assistant coach and head coach under Bowman at Buffalo. He saw the Bowman-Keenan, mentor-student relationship up close.

"Scotty was a guy Mike kind of looked up to, who he wanted to be as coach," Roberts said. "We had contact, either him coming up to Buffalo during the year or us going down to see games and talking to him after the games. I think the relationship between what Mike is and what Scotty is started before that Buffalo thing. I think it started in Peterborough, with Mike watching Scotty's success his whole coaching career, building his career with what he saw in Scotty. There are a lot of similarities in them. You go back to when Scotty was real young and he was in St. Louis, he was pretty erratic at times. He always seemed to be pulling the right strings and things worked for him. I think Mike had some success doing the same things, but when it doesn't work, it can really backfire on you."

Did Bowman see a bit of himself in the young Keenan? "I don't know if he'd ever admit it," Keenan said, "but I think he did."

Neilson had to chuckle watching Keenan develop into a young Bowman. He got to know both men very well. Both were a pain to work for and both were a chore to coach against.

"They're always looking for an edge," he would later say. "They're always one step ahead."

Though his first team struggled through a 30-42-8 season, Keenan started turning the team, the city, and the league on its ear. Keenan became an innovator unlike anything the minor leagues had ever seen. He took the Amerks to a fitness center for aerobics. The players were a bit skeptical, because they viewed aerobics as an activity for pudgy housewives. But this wasn't about working off a plate of cake or maintaining a dress size. Keenan measured and charted his players' body fat percentages and aerobic fitness levels. Having been a pre-med student at St. Lawrence, he thought he understood people and their bodies. Keenan monitored their water and nutritional intakes. He pioneered the use of circuit training and interval training at a time when some NHL clubs didn't even have weight rooms. He broke down scouting tapes and devised a computer program that analyzed the productivity of each line combination.

"He had a lot of ideas, different ideas about conditioning, off-ice stuff," Roberts said. "Certainly Mike was a student of what had to be done in the future of the game and the future of developing players. He started putting that in his teams and researched all the different ways that might help on the ice and off the ice."

Keenan added an assistant coach, a novel concept in the AHL, by convincing nearby State University of New York at Brockport coach E.J. McGuire to volunteer his time to the Amerks. The two had met at one of Neilson's summer coaching clinics in Peterborough, and Keenan called McGuire when he got to Rochester. The NCAA Division III hockey season was shorter than the AHL season, so McGuire was able to spend a fair amount of time around the team.

"I joined him, quote, full-time, at a time when there were absolutely no assistant coaches, barely in the NHL, let alone the AHL," McGuire said. "It was all for free or whatever, but it increased my experience and kept me busy in hockey. I learned quickly about not only pro hockey, but about Mike Keenan. Mike Keenan is the definition of intensity."

Keenan began developing his imperious bench demeanor. He began dressing like a chief executive officer, with classy suits and hundred-dollar shirts. He peered down his nose at players, as Bowman did. Rather than sip water from a cup during games, he chewed ice chips, just as Bowman did. He got the rest of Scotty's act down cold, too.

"The same facial expression, the same stare, with chin protruding, looking up at the scoreboard," McGuire said. "I'm not saying he copied that, but it could have been subconscious."

Keenan became just as unyielding as Bowman, too. Once he gave up on a player, that was that. He would spend no more time with someone after he deemed him hopeless. Coaching professional hockey is a tough job and Keenan quickly realized he had to be a tough coach.

"If winning is your goal, sadly people and things go by the wayside," McGuire said. "The weak fall by the wayside. It's 'If you don't want to win a Calder Cup or a University Cup or a Stanley Cup, I've got no time for you.' I never saw him be mean, just tough. Pretty soon it's the kiss of death, he gives up on you. For somebody who is weak, they might look for somebody to blame. They say he's unfair, he is this or he is that. No, he's just focused and if you happen to get in his way . . ."

His distinctive coaching philosophy began to emerge in Rochester. His system was essentially based on hell-bent puck pressure: all five players going all out after the puck and finishing their checks. If properly motivated, a team can exploit this approach to break down opponents with constant pressure. His system is the hockey equivalent of Buddy Ryan's blitz-happy "46" defense in the National Football League and Nolan Richardson's pressing "40 minutes of hell" in college basketball. He juggled his forward lines constantly, keeping players on their toes.

"It's constant switching, not only to get the right guys out there, but to cross up the opposition," McGuire said.

Keenan's teams practice power-play skills, but not the power play itself. He believes players are at their best when they operate intuitively with the man advantage. Rather than allow his team to fall into easily defended patterns, he expects his players to use their well-honed skills and natural instincts to create scoring chances. He wants spontaneity and creativity, not predictability. If his players are sharp, he believes they'll read each other and read the play correctly. Let others develop complicated X-and-O systems; he emphasizes making his players fit, focused, and fierce. To give his players that edge, he became their worst nightmare.

"You know, I was a hard-ass coach even in the minors," Keenan said. "I made my team leave on a bus Christmas night for a game two days away in another town. Two days! I acted like it was the most important game in the world."

Keenan inherited a war-weary Rochester team. Many of the players had seen their NHL time come and go. They were playing out their careers and did not want to be inconvenienced. They were about as far removed from the wide-eyed realm of junior hockey as they could get. The Amerks were not easily led. But he wouldn't let them drink alcohol. One time, Keenan stopped the team bus because he smelled cigarette smoke. Liquor bottles rolled to the front. Keenan threw a tantrum.

Because the Amerks were a disjointed team with several veterans older than the coach, Keenan knew he needed a strong leader as his point man in the dressing room. In Rochester, he eventually found that man in former Montreal Canadiens regular Yvon Lambert.

"The leader of that team didn't have a letter," Keenan said. "Yvon Lambert was our leader. He was the hardest working player, the most prepared player every game. It doesn't have to be the best student in the classroom. Maybe they don't have the personality. It could be an individual who has the qualities of leadership. In the classroom, it could be the kid who's an average student who is the best leader."

Lambert had won four Stanley Cups in Montreal, so he knew how to win. He had played for Bowman, so he knew how to cope with the demands of an autocratic coach. He saw a lot of Bowman in his new coach's style.

"They both didn't give a damn about anyone," Lambert said. "Mike wanted to be as tough as Scotty, but there was one problem. Away from the game, Mike was friendlier. He cared about what you thought of him."

McGuire saw, firsthand, how adept Keenan is at reading players. "He has a way with people that people don't know," McGuire said. "One of the characterizations of Mike is, 'He who is good with the hammer tends to think everything is a nail.' Yvon Lambert was a fading Buffalo Sabre. The Sabres couldn't fit him into their regime. They sent him to Rochester. It would have been easy for Yvon, who at the time was on a one-way contract, or whatever, to say, 'Who is this maniac? I've got four Stanley Cup rings. I'm in Rochester, New York, I'm playing out the string. I don't need to be excited.' Yet Mike had a way with Yvon that brought him into the fold. He pushed him hard. Probably a lot of days Yvon felt, 'I don't need to be in shape anymore, I'm playing in the AHL.'

"He gave him a bit of a role with a number of French guys who were on the team: Robert Mongrain, J.F. Sauve. As important as anybody, certainly more important than I was in a coaching role or whatever, was Yvon Lambert. To this day, when I go to Montreal to see Yvon Lambert, he goes, 'You know, I cherish that Calder Cup ring almost as much as I cherish my Stanley Cup ring.' For him to say that and half believe it is something."

Geordie Robertson, one of Rochester's stars during Keenan's tenure, said Lambert deserved plenty of credit for that team's title run in 1982–83. Lambert maintained order in the dressing room. He somehow kept the players from rebelling against the young tyrant who wouldn't let up.

"Yvon Lambert told him to back off, or he wouldn't be alive today," Robertson said. "It was clash after clash after clash. Each team Mike coaches needs a player who has won four or five Stanley Cups, like a Mark Messier or a Lambert, to tell him to slow down. He'd panic sometimes. He'd go into the coaching office between periods and pull into himself, go into a shell, and you'd be on pins and needles because you could feel he was ready to explode. But he was the greatest practice coach ever, ran the shortest and most productive practices you've ever seen."

Another Keenan trademark emerged in Rochester: the rookie test. Any young hotshot coming into Iron Mike's program faces a day of reckoning. Keenan wants to know, as soon as possible, if the prospect has what it takes to survive under his system. He figures it's better to find out early about a player than keep hoping for something that probably will never happen.

One day, Randy Cunneyworth, a petulant rookie, flipped all of the practice pucks into the stands at the practice arena. Keenan took out the puck bucket, handed it to Cunneyworth, and, before the team bus left, made him retrieve all of the pucks.

"I'm thinking, *Is the kid going to do it or is he going to challenge him back?*" McGuire recalled. "The kid did it."

Keenan also tested his assistant coaches. "Mike would ask you why you thought a certain way about something, then he would say, 'Aw, you're full of crap' and walk away," McGuire said. "But he'd continue to think about it and probably put that piece of strategy in the next game or the next week. He just wants to see how you think. He'll tease you with things you don't believe. Mike would say, 'We can't send him out on the power play, he gives the puck away.' I'll think, *I don't see that,* and go back to the videotape. And I would be right, but Mike just wants to test you."

The Americans went 40-31-9 in Keenan's second season and 46-25-9 in his third. A team that had been fractured and apathetic came together and won. Problem players were cycled out and guys with a future were brought in. He was doing the job he was hired to do. Keenan believed Bowman was grooming him for the Sabres coaching position. After coaching the Sabres in 1979–80, Bowman had stepped back from behind the bench to concentrate on his duties as general manager. Neilson coached the 1980–81 season and Roberts coached for half of the following season before Bowman returned to the bench. Keenan believed his chance was coming.

Perhaps the defining moment of his Rochester regime came during a so-called death skate in his third season. That day, Keenan discarded his cutting-edge fitness theories and became a tyrant. He put away the pucks and ordered his team to skate harder than they ever had before. This was a two-hour skate-puke-skate marathon without water. Several players cramped up. The trainer was running around in a panic. Such practices show players they can do much more than they ever thought possible. But they're mostly a way for coaches to kick some ass and remind everybody who's the boss. The death skate became another vital component in Keenan's coaching program.

After the death skate, the Amerks won twenty of their next twenty-four games. They rolled through the playoffs to win the 1983 Calder Cup championship over Maine, the Philadelphia Flyers' well-stocked AHL affiliate. When it was over, Keenan collapsed into bed with the Cup by his side. Once again, he had taken a team to the top. Once again, he had found ways to make a team do things it couldn't imagine doing.

"Early in the year, it wasn't that good of a team," Roberts said. "He added a player here and there and motivated some fairly skilled players that ended up doing a lot more than they thought they were capable of doing. That has a lot to do with Mike and his motivation and coaching. That team went from a team that probably wasn't that great at the start of the year to a team that just kept working and eventually won."

Keenan believed his apprenticeship under Bowman was complete. The Calder Cup was his diploma. He believed he was ready to become Bowman's assistant in Buffalo, or even head coach if Bowman again decided to focus on his general managing chores. Keenan's friends insist he had a handshake agreement with Bowman to move up. He was ready to answer the call from the highest level of hockey in the world, but it never came.

Bowman wasn't ready to promote Keenan. The Sabres had gone 38-29-13 in 1982–83 and Bowman thought things were fine the way they were. Bowman wanted to keep coaching and saw no place for his ambitious acolyte. Keenan was exasperated. He had done everything asked of him and more. If the Calder Cup couldn't earn him a shot at the NHL, what would? He wondered whether his mentor really want to see him succeed.

Feeling scorned, Keenan quit the Americans. He decided to take a professional step backward, hoping a move to the University of Toronto would eventually allow him to vault two steps ahead. Only an extremely confident man would have left the AHL to coach at the Canadian university level, where the players don't even get scholarships. Canadian university players aren't pro prospects, they are students. But Keenan felt he had learned all he could in the minor leagues.

"At that particular time, it was the best opportunity for me to grow professionally, to move to the University of Toronto, to try another venue," he said. "As far as the Buffalo Sabres organization was concerned, it was my objective to be a National Hockey League coach, a head coach at some particular point in time. Scotty Bowman was a very competent coach and a very young man. So there probably wasn't the room to move there that I would have liked."

As usual, Keenan won. The University of Toronto went 41-5-3 in the 1983–84 season and won all nine of its playoff games to win the national title.

"He took a good team and made them great," said athletic director Gib Chapman.

McGuire, who had moved on to the University of Waterloo, coached against Keenan that season. His recollections sounded pretty typical of Iron Mike's work.

"He overspent the budget, pissed off the athletic director, won the national championship," McGuire said.

Actually, Keenan toned down his act a bit for the college players, who were headed to jobs in the real world, not the NHL. But he wasn't afraid to challenge them.

"Everything you read about Mike now is how he was at U of T," said Dave McCarthy, a forward on that team. "He was demanding. He played some head games with us. But he always had a purpose with what he did. Nobody stayed in his doghouse for any length of time."

According to legend, Keenan would put his players on the bus after disappointing games and take them home without any dinner.

"That was folklore," Chapman said. "I think he only did it once. He was certainly intense on the ice, but the players enjoyed playing for him. He was a master motivator."

The university players learned to expect the unexpected, just as the Amerks had.

"Mike's philosophy was to keep everybody on their toes, so he'd do little things," recalled Paul Titanic, Keenan's assistant coach at Toronto. "If we were up, he'd bark down at me, 'How many lines are we using? Who's up next?' just so you don't lose your focus. He's an unbelievably driven person who was willing to work as many hours as it would take to be successful. And he expected that kind of commitment from everybody else on the team, or else."

Late in the season, Keenan boasted about how every player had been benched at least once. Trainer Norm Calder corrected him. Defenseman Mark Euteneire hadn't been benched. Sure enough, the next game, Euteneire was benched after playing a solid first period.

"He told Mark he wasn't doing anything out there," McCarthy said. "Mark couldn't figure out why and he probably still wonders why he was benched."

Mike Pelino, who had played for Keenan in Oshawa, saw Keenan at his best in Toronto. "He was very much a people person, which is certainly not the way he might have been perceived in the NHL," Pelino said. "He was very demanding. But what allowed him to be successful is that he made everybody feel integral to the team's success. We used four lines and six defensemen all through the season, until push came to shove."

Keenan understood that his players were, for the most part, headed for professional careers outside hockey. He realized he was dealing with good, team-oriented guys as opposed to two dozen individual businesses, as recent NHL rosters have become. The University of Toronto was more a team, in the pure sense, than what a coach encounters in the pro ranks.

Pelino had seen the teaching side of Keenan at Oshawa. By the time Keenan reached Toronto, he had evolved into a master motivator. The Xs and Os were still important, of course, but Keenan put his emphasis on getting the most out of each player's potential. He used many of the same tactics he had used at Rochester, although in a milder form. He kept the players guessing. He kept them on edge. He raised their expectations.

"He was less concerned with the hockey aspect than making sure he was getting the most out of every single player," Pelino said.

These university students saw how Keenan felt the flow of the game and read how each player was performing from shift to shift. They saw how adeptly he moved players in and out of the mix to provoke a response. How would a lesser player react to more responsibility? How would a better player respond to losing responsibility?

"He wasn't afraid to experiment," Pelino said. "He was very composed, very composed and very good with his decision making behind the bench."

Many of the University of Toronto players took Keenan's lessons and put them to work in the business world. Pelino went on to coach at the university level before joining the Canadian national program.

"The main thing I got from him is how important it is to work hard, how important it is to be totally honest with players," Pelino said. "He was very, very honest with us. I saw how important it was to be prepared and to give the team confidence. I learned that different people respond in different ways."

Keenan counts the University of Toronto as one of his favorite coaching stops. He allowed himself to become close to his players. These students saw more of the old Mike Keenan than the Amerks did. Keenan and his players stayed in touch over the following years. Every now and then, one of the old university players would stop by one of his games for a chat.

"This was a really great group of people in my life," he said. "We won a national championship together, which was the last men's hockey championship at U of T. This was a close-knit bunch. I remember one time our captain, Mike Todd, showed up in Edmonton one night [several years later] and told me he was bunking with me. He flew down from the game from the Northwest Territories where he was studying dentistry."

Alas, one year of being a Nice Guy was plenty for Keenan. The university realm was a nice break from the professional grind, but it could hardly satisfy his ambition. He was way too intense for that level of competition and much too eager to reach the NHL. His success at the University of Toronto, on the heels of his success at Rochester, had made him a hot commodity. Several NHL teams began regarding him as a coaching prospect, including the Vancouver Canucks and New Jersey Devils.

But the job that really intrigued him was in Philadelphia, where the Flyers were eager to regain the passion of their "Broad Street Bullies" days from the 1970s. It certainly sounded like a job for Iron Mike.

◄ 3 ►

Philadelphia Story

He knocks you down with his right hand and picks you up
with his left. Everyone has taken their turn on the pine. But
he knows I need it. He reads all that stuff about how to handle
people. He wants to be the smart one, the intellectual.

— FORMER PHILADELPHIA FLYERS TOUGH GUY
ED HOSPODAR

AS THE WASHINGTON CAPITALS ELIMINATED THE PHILADELPHIA
Flyers in the first round of the NHL playoffs, the chant "Bob must go!"
echoed through the Spectrum. Bob was the Flyers' general manager and
coach Bob McCammon. His team wasn't awful, but it dragged its skates
in the playoffs, when teams are supposed to be at their best. The Flyers
were good in the 1983–84 season, finishing with 98 points, but got swept
out of the playoffs for the second year in a row. The lovable ruffians
who once ran roughshod over the NHL suddenly looked meek.

One of their bulwarks, Bill Barber, was sidelined by a career-threatening knee injury. Another, Paul Holmgren, finally wore down after many
years of hard battle. His remnants were shipped to Minnesota. Flyers captain Bobby Clarke skated into the twilight of his career and clashed with
McCammon for much of the season. The coach reduced Clarke's ice time
to save his legs, but lost Clarke's heart in the process. Young goaltender
Pelle Lindbergh wasn't yet ready to save the day.

These Flyers were an unhappy mix of fading veterans and green youngsters. The team became indifferent to the crusty McCammon. The team

often appeared sloppy and undisciplined on the ice. Attendance at the Spectrum fell below capacity. The fans who continued coming expressed their restlessness by booing and chanting derisively. This once-dominant franchise was in a funk. Owner Ed Snider and his son Jay concluded that changes had to be made. They listened to their fans and decided that Bob, indeed, had to go.

"I don't think the players had respect for McCammon," Jay Snider later said. "I don't think we had a game plan for discipline. I thought we were clearly outplayed two years in a row in the playoffs because we were predictable in our behavior."

The Sniders wanted McCammon to concentrate on his managerial chores. They gave him a list of exciting coaching prospects to consider. On the list was thirty-four-year-old Mike Keenan, who had won the Calder Cup and the Canadian collegiate championship in consecutive years. The Sniders were intrigued by his potential. But McCammon didn't see the need to make a change. After giving the ultimatum some thought, he agreed it would be best to leave his general manager post, too, and let the Flyers start over.

The Sniders took bold action, asking Clarke if he would like to retire and become the team's new general manager. Clarke believed he still had some hockey left in his battered body, but couldn't pass up this extraordinary opportunity to move into management. The concept had intrigued him for some time and he couldn't expect the chance to be there for him in another year or two. He told the Sniders he would think about the offer during a vacation in the Virgin Islands with teammate Dave Poulin and others. But the more he thought about it, the more excited he got. He phoned Jay Snider from the airport on his way out of town and said he would take the job. He was ready to don a suit and work the phones.

Poulin was surprised to hear Clarke's big news while on vacation. The two were extremely close. Poulin considered Clarke his mentor and the two were roommates, too. During the trip, Clarke and Poulin took a walk to the end of a dock.

"The day we get home, I'm going to retire," Clarke told his friend.

Clarke's new challenge was large. The Flyers needed new players, a new coach, and a new attitude. The Sniders had already been examining coaching prospects from a variety of backgrounds. Jay Snider had conducted a preliminary interview with Keenan before Clarke took his new assignment, and gave him a philosophical questionnaire to fill out and return after their meeting.

While on a Florida vacation with Rita and their four-year-old daughter Gayla, Keenan sat down and crafted his response, explaining why he should get that job. The treatise was filled with pretentious managerial prose. A typical passage in Keenan's nineteen-page position paper read:

> My approach in motivating the athlete is to maintain an imbalance of unpredictability in incorporating incentive, fear and attitudinal methods employed in a very dynamic environment. I would emphasize, however, that within this framework of discipline and team organization . . . the players must be kept loose, their creativity unstifled and their intrinsic enthusiasm for the game maintained. It is important that the practice year be well-planned. Practices must be creative, interesting and challenging.

Keenan poured himself into his job quest. He couldn't give himself a week off in Florida to splash in the pool with his family. While Gayla learned to swim, Mike hunched over his typewriter. He was consumed with professional advancement. He could not sit still until he reached the top. As for his family, he thought he was doing his very best to provide for them. This is what good men did.

"I come out of that macho, stoic school of manhood," Keenan said many years later. "Thirty years ago, as a young player, I was in a world of negative reinforcement. Do this or you're out. A one-way street. Twenty years ago, when I started coaching, the subject of family never came up. Men went on the road, women stayed home and had babies. Now, families have a much more dominant role and the relationship of men in the family unit has changed."

Gary Webb, Keenan's teammate at St. Lawrence and cohort with Nik and the Nice Guys, built a successful accounting career in Rochester, New York, after college. They hooked up again during Keenan's time in Rochester and Webb became his financial adviser. Webb accompanied Keenan to meet with Clarke about the Flyers job. The session couldn't have gone better.

Keenan explained how he had painstakingly prepared himself to coach in the NHL, winning at each level and polishing his skills in every imaginable situation. He was ready for the ultimate challenge. He wasn't an old NHL player just looking to stay in the game. He had made himself into a top-notch coach. He was a striver.

"I'm not one of those guys who started on third base and thought all he had to do was steal home," Keenan said. "I had to start at home and make sure I got around all the bases."

Bowman weighed in on Keenan's behalf. He called Clarke and gave his pupil a solid recommendation. "I told him he's a guy who won't let his players lose," Bowman said. "If they tolerate losing, they won't be there. He wants to win and wants a winning program and he'll come in very organized. And that's what he did."

Keenan came with a warning label, too, Bowman said. "I told him, 'He gets upset sometimes, like we all do, but he'll cool down. You just have to bear with it.'"

The candidates sorted themselves out. Finalist Bill Laforge, who had built intimidating junior teams, went to the Canucks. Finalist Dave King, a teacher and a tactician, stayed with the Canadian national team. The choice came down to Keenan or Flyers assistant coach Ted Sator, an innovator who had worked in Sweden. Keenan won.

"Everybody I talked to said that his style would cause some problems with players, but that he had always won," Clarke said. "I thought we needed discipline."

The Flyers had become stale under McCammon. Keenan brought to the job a hard-nosed reputation and a creative mind. In many ways, his program at Rochester was more advanced than the Flyers' program he was inheriting. He would push the players as they had never been pushed before. His maximum-pressure style of play was a perfect fit in Philadelphia, where the notoriously surly fans expected their heroes to be the aggressors. Flyers fans were accustomed to seeing monstrous hits and flying snot. Keenan was clearly the right man at the right time.

"In Mike, we've obtained the type of coach the Flyers want and the city will like," Clarke said. "He's young, innovative, and very dedicated. He'll provide the leadership and discipline the Flyers are going to need as we pursue our goal of the Stanley Cup."

To some, Keenan seemed too young for the job. He cut a boyish image, with his round face and a full head of hair. "There were players in the American League who were older than me," he told reporters during his get-acquainted session. "It's not a matter of age. It's a matter of respect. I don't anticipate any problems. As far as being a disciplinarian, I think discipline is very important in terms of your performance on the ice."

He explained how he had built his coaching philosophy from components learned from several mentors. At the University of Toronto, Peterborough, and in the Sabres organization, he had learned from some of the masters of the sport. He also attended hockey clinics religiously, taking copious notes. He sought out new ideas and absorbed them.

"Earlier in my coaching career, I was very fortunate," he said. "I worked under outstanding people such as Tom Watt, probably the man to influence me the earliest, Scott Bowman, Roger Neilson, Red Berenson, and Jacques Lemaire. I viewed what made these people outstanding and developed my own coaching style."

Sator stayed aboard as an assistant coach. McGuire reunited with Keenan after his stint at the University of Waterloo. McGuire quickly saw that Keenan was the perfect fit for a franchise that had to start over with hungry, resilient young players.

"The time was right for a new coach to come in and sort of kick ass," McGuire said. "The Flyers hadn't won in the playoffs. They had made the playoffs, but they hadn't won in the playoffs in three years. The atmosphere was right."

The Sniders were thrilled to have an energetic trendsetter in charge of their team. Keenan was an avid student of fitness training, sports psychology, and managerial science. From these disciplines, Keenan fashioned a "whole person" approach that most NHL players had never seen before. Hockey players were used to cheeseburger-and-beer lunches. They read the sports section, not motivational books. Their idea of fitness training was a few weeks of skating with the boys before camp. Keenan arrived in the NHL to challenge all of that.

"It was a program founded on nutrition and the right psychological attitude and the proper physical conditioning," Keenan said. "It includes everything from how the players approach the media to how they approach their families."

Keenan was the anti-McCammon, the new-school mentor replacing the classic old-school coach. No other coach was measuring heart rates in practice. No one else was charting the amount of water players consumed. Together with strength coach Pat Croce, another man who was well ahead of his time, he would set new standards for a staid industry. The players were thoroughly impressed. Though they often bristled at their new workload, they bought into the new program wholeheartedly. They soon realized they were gaining the upper hand on opponents. Life on the forefront was good. Fans picked up on the Flyers' new energy. The Spectrum was buzzing again.

"He came on at the right time, when the game was changing," McGuire said. "Maybe he had a hand in accelerating these changes. Everything from stuff like computerization. Ed Snider bought the Flyers, but prior to that he was a partner in the Philadelphia Eagles. When Clarkie hired Mike, Mr. Snider said, 'Why don't you use a football model, use seven coaches or whatever?'" Keenan opted for a more traditional model with only McGuire and Sator as his assistants. He wasn't big on delegating authority.

To make this a totally fresh start, Clarke and Keenan elected to feature younger players into the lineup. Prospects Rick Tocchet, Derrick Smith, and Peter Zezel became integral right away. Aging Darryl Sittler expected to be named Clarke's successor as captain of the Flyers. On the day it was supposed to happen, he got traded to the Detroit Red Wings. It was Clarke's first big move as general manager and it caused quite a stir. Sittler called Clarke a liar, among other things, and refused to report to the hapless Red Wings for a week. The youthful Poulin became the new captain.

"I had a weird situation going on," Poulin said. "My second year in the league, Mike comes in and he's a rookie coach. All of a sudden, he and Bob Clarke name me captain. Mike hasn't been in the NHL, he doesn't know Dave Poulin, so it's not necessarily him that's doing it. But he's picking a twenty-five-year-old captain. He's got veterans at the time."

Keenan felt secure with Poulin as his on-ice leader, even though Poulin was obviously Clarke's guy. "We had a very, very strong relationship and Mike knew that," Poulin said. "So it was kind of a weird threesome."

The young general manager, the young coach, the young captain, and the young team quickly melded and became a powerful combination. Clarke was one of the most ferocious competitors the NHL had ever seen and he transferred that intensity to his managerial role. Keenan's thirst for success was insatiable. Poulin was fiercely competitive, too, and smart. He would have been on a fast track to corporate upper management had hockey not intervened. Sator had lured Poulin to Sweden to continue playing after his career at Notre Dame, then recommended him to the Flyers. His interviews with blue-chip corporations were put on hold, forever as it turned out.

Croce was a fascinating character. Keenan fancied himself a visionary, but Croce really was one. In his day job, he worked with both the Flyers and the 76ers, Philadelphia's NBA team, on their weight training. But he had bigger dreams. Though he didn't invent sports medicine, as he occasionally boasts, he was among the first to exploit its business potential. He later parlayed his technical knowledge, high profile, promotional zeal, and keen business instincts into a fitness empire. He amassed a fortune and later bought control of the 76ers.

All of these hard chargers were able to set a high standard for the veterans who remained. The veterans, in turn, set a lofty bar for the young players entering the program.

"It's assimilation," Poulin said. "When a kid comes to camp and sees what's expected of him — and remember most of these guys were stars of their junior teams and probably weren't used to being pushed — he thinks, 'I've got no choice.' It's a lot easier to assimilate somebody than to start from scratch."

Expectations for the 1984–85 Flyers were not high elsewhere in the NHL. The team had three rookies and seven second-year players in its lineup. Only one player was older than thirty. A team so young couldn't realistically have been expected to take a run at the Stanley Cup. Or could it?

"Really, the only pressure I felt was developing the team, not winning," Keenan said later. "Now there was no Clarke, Barber, or Sittler, so nobody expected anything."

Keenan kept his players guessing. There was no predictability in his coaching approach, except that he was unpredictable. Rookies and newcomers got a harsh test early on, allowing him to judge their worthiness for the long haul. He didn't want to invest time in guys who lacked heart and perseverance.

"Mike had a way — he was a master psychologist — of getting to the players, the key players," McGuire said. "The fringe players, he'd test. If they cracked under pressure, the cruel side of Mike said, 'Let's get rid of them or use them as a fourth liner.'"

Leaders like Poulin were constantly tested, too, to see if they were worthy of the responsibility Keenan gave them.

"One of our first practices when I was captain, Mike didn't come on the ice," Poulin recalled. "Say it's an eleven o'clock practice. Mike didn't come out on the ice. So it's about ten after eleven, he comes out on the ice and he comes flying right over to me. He said, 'Let me get this straight, if I don't come out, you're not going to run practice?' From that point on, I had a full practice prepared every day of my career. Sure enough, a couple weeks later, Mike doesn't come out. At eleven o'clock we start practice. About eight after eleven, Mike comes out. He just joins in and runs it from there."

Intimidation remained his prime motivational tool. "He would get Zezel in the stick room and motivate the heck out of him," Croce said. "Zezel would come out crying and all the sticks would be broken. He'd break everything in the dressing room. That table with all the Gatorade on it? That would be on the ceiling. He was nuts. This guy, he'd call a team meeting, we'd all be there, and then he would change his mind. He just played with your head. I loved him. He was crazy. We called him The General. He looked like a general with that little Hitler mustache he was wearing."

Indeed, his players called him "Hitler" behind his back and mocked him with Nazi salutes. The people around the Flyers got some laughs out of this, but Rita wasn't amused when a cartoonist depicted her husband as Hitler.

"I'm Jewish and my grandfather died at Auschwitz," she reminded people. "We were both very upset. Mike was very sensitive to how that would affect me and my family."

Croce said the Flyers wrestled with mixed feelings toward their coach. "The players hated him," he said. "They loved him because he got the best out of them, but they hated him. His organizational skills were second to none. They loved the winning, but they hated him."

Even Keenan's favorites grew weary of his tactics. "I never really hated him," Tocchet said. "But there were some days and nights when I went to the rink when I didn't like him. I really disliked him. But he made me the player I am today."

Keenan would skate straight at players and turn away at the last instant. He would hover over them while brandishing a stick. He turned optional practices into surprise skating marathons. He set a practice for 11:59 A.M., just to give the players something else to think about.

"I remember one practice in which he wanted us to go to the net harder," Zezel recalled. "And when I stopped short, I heard him yell and then I turned around and had to duck because there was a stick flying at my head. Believe me, I got the message."

Not everybody assimilated. Defenseman Tommy Eriksson, a member of the 1983–84 all-rookie team, freaked out. A few weeks into his first season as coach, Keenan berated Eriksson. Later, Eriksson was crying when he went to Clarke's office.

"I want to go back to Sweden," he said. "I hate it here. Keenan's going to kill me."

Eriksson lasted two seasons under Keenan before returning home.

A high attrition rate was just part of Keenan's program. McGuire had watched Keenan run off many players in Rochester, and the pattern continued in Philly. Keenan didn't sell his program, he simply implemented it. Players either bought into it or bought homes elsewhere. He knew he was right and he expected the players to figure that out.

Keenan's desperation to succeed fueled some of his over-the-top behavior. All of his outward confidence couldn't quell the nagging self-doubt he felt inside. "I felt I owed it to the owners to be that way," he would explain. "I came into the NHL as a complete unknown. They'd given me an opportunity."

Despite Keenan's considerable success in life to this point — high grades and a degree from St. Lawrence, post-graduate work at the University of Toronto, championships as a college, pro, and senior player, and championships at every previous coaching stop — he always felt he had more to prove. Most people would have been content to experience a fraction of this success, but not Keenan. That disastrous first semester at St. Lawrence had marked him. Poor grades had knocked him off the hockey team, banished him from campus for a semester, and sent him back into the bleak blue-collar life he longed to escape. Since his stint on the "jungle line" at the GM plant, he had been working at a manic pace. He didn't want to win, he had to win. He wasn't just eager, he was anxious.

"Mike was a desperate man in those early days," Clarke recalled. "He partied with a sense of desperation. He coached with a sense of desperation. Everything in his life was done with a sense of desperation."

Keenan believed it could all end at any time. Every loss wounded him. For all of his apparent cockiness, he was actually quite insecure. Fear of failure drives many successful people, but sometimes he seemed haunted.

"I carried this fear every game, the fear that this would be the last game I'd ever coach," he said. "The media read me all wrong. They thought I was arrogant. I was really just scared. It's a great way to hide fear."

Another shield was the pseudo-intellectual prattle that left players rolling their eyes. What other hockey coach used the word "intrinsic" even once? He had manufactured his coaching persona step by step. This was the coach his players would see. "With all those words, half the time I don't know what he's saying to me," winger Tim Kerr once said.

But there actually was a real person under the façade. Sittler saw this before the season even started. He was devastated when he got traded to the Red Wings. He was supposed to be introduced as the team's new captain at a public function, but the ceremony was scrapped. Instead, Sittler learned he had been traded to a horrible team. Keenan lived in the same suburban New Jersey neighborhood as Sittler, so he gave him a lift home. Sittler didn't have his keys and his wife wasn't expecting him home so soon, so he sat out on the porch with Keenan. Here was a rookie coach, fresh in the league, trying to comfort a fading star.

From time to time in his career, Keenan sat down and spoke heart to heart with players in crisis. He was capable of connecting on a highly personal level. But he preferred to keep his genuine side in the background and let "Iron Mike" do the heavy lifting.

Sports Illustrated profiler Gary Smith compared Keenan to Jay Gatsby from F. Scott Fitzgerald's *The Great Gatsby* and Benjamin Siegel, a 1940s gangster who was the subject of Warren Beatty's movie *Bugsy*. Wrote Smith, "Bugsy, like Gatsby, was an extravagant criminal who staked his life on a long-shot dream, to construct a posh casino in the Las Vegas desert that would eventually blossom into Las Vegas. To steel himself, to suffocate any remorse after killing someone, Bugsy repeated over and over a phrase: *Twenty dwarves took turns doing handstands on the carpet.* Mike memorized that phrase and recited it to friends."

Poulin considers the Gatsby comparison a stretch, but he agreed that Keenan constructed his coaching persona. "He definitely decided what was necessary to be a coach and took pieces of all those different elements, a piece of Scotty Bowman, a piece of Tom Watt, a piece of different people," he said. "When it came down to it, I don't know if Mike could find himself in that coach that he created. He is an extremely, extremely bright man. He had built, almost like an Orwellian, a construction of a perfect coach. That's fine. The best thing about coaching is that you have to be yourself at some point. Mike had created this whole Mike Keenan. In a way, Mike's strength, his perceived strength, is that people don't know who he is."

Keenan always pushed himself as hard as he pushed his players. Keenan mined motivational books, managerial treatises, and inspirational biographies for material. At the team's suburban practice facility, his modest office became a gallery of upbeat platitudes framed and displayed on the wall. One message read: "Some athletes compete against others. Champions compete against themselves." Some visitors found these self-help phrases corny, but Keenan lived off of this psychological nutrition.

The 1984–85 Flyers blasted off to a 16-4-4 start. Their blitzing style and relentless effort beat teams down. They fired the puck into the offensive zone and hustled in hard to make big hits. Shift after shift after shift, the Flyers skated hard and attacked. The style became Keenan's trademark.

"Our teams have always tried to play dynamically and use their skating skills as a big asset," he said. "With all the teams I've coached, I've felt responsible to the ownership and also to our fan base. We should play dynamic hockey and high-tempo hockey. You have an obligation not only to win, but to entertain the fans as well."

Flyers fans demanded robust hockey for their money and loved their new coach. Keenan believed in tactical intimidation. He had to have players who could hit and he had to have players who could fight. One of the quickest ways to change a game's flow is to tap the tough guys on the shoulder and send them out onto the ice to start trouble. Nothing had to be said. These men knew their job and knew when to ply their trade.

"My teams are aggressive," he said. "Physical. They intimidate with passion. Hell, it's an aggressive sport. Let's get it on!"

The Sniders were thrilled. Energy had replaced lethargy. Clarke, who would later become a first-class meddler with his coaches and players, usually didn't interfere. The Clarke-Keenan-Poulin triumvirate worked beautifully.

"Because Mike had success early, it was a good situation that Clarkie wasn't around looking over our shoulders and Mike was able to run with the football," McGuire said. "That was the personality they hired on purpose. They knew that reputation. Give the Flyers credit, they knew they had a group coming in that had to be led, forcefully, rather than get behind and push from behind."

The signature event of Keenan's first year was his Christmas Eve death skate. It was an experience Poulin would never forget. The Flyers were on a hot streak, so Poulin approached Keenan with a request.

"We played on the twenty-third," Poulin told Keenan. "Could we skate early in the morning on the twenty-fourth so the guys can catch an eleven o'clock flight? Guys can get home Christmas Eve, have Christmas Day, and come back late Christmas night."

"Sure, no problem," Keenan said.

That morning, before practice, the Flyers had their Christmas party. The players had pizza and beer delivered to the rink at nine o'clock in the morning. Then they raced through a productive forty-five-minute practice, eager to eat some grease, drink some suds, and celebrate the holiday.

"At the end, Mike would have an aerobic skate, six minutes each way," Poulin recalled. "He brings a big boom box out, he's got Christmas carols playing. We skate six minutes each way. Guys are turning an aerobic skate into an anaerobic skate, they are flying. At the end, he lines everybody up at both ends, half at each end, and we skated for forty-five minutes. Just down and back, climb the mountains. Guys were sick. At the end, he calls everybody together and said, 'Expect the unexpected. Merry Christmas.' And he skates off the ice."

Keenan insisted there was a method behind such Yuletide madness. "I had pre-identified it as a conditioning day," Keenan later said. "But we were starting to get noticed and I also wanted to reinforce the idea that expectations had been raised."

Such unsettling events were essential to Keenan's coaching style. He insisted he wasn't being mean just for sport. He believed he had to constantly jar his players to keep them from getting complacent.

"It's part of keeping the interest of your club high," he explained. "You try to create challenging situations for them, individually and collectively. That way they stay out of grooves and ruts. Individually, you ask them to do things they might not think they're good at. It's uncomfortable for some people. There's a lot of anxiety, but anxiety isn't the creative tool, it's seizing the opportunity to do something you're nervous about. Try it. So what if you fall on your face. No harm in that. Many of us do. It's getting up and trying to do it that breeds success."

The Flyers fell. They responded to the death skate with a 6–0 loss the day after Christmas. But then they got up. Just as the Amerks had gotten hot after passing their most painful physical test, so did the Flyers. Pelle Lindbergh became outstanding in goal. The moose-like Tim Kerr became an unstoppable force in front of the net.

"Pelle and Tim Kerr are stars, no doubt, the way they've played," Poulin said at the time. "But they're stars as part of the overall structure. They're not set off by themselves. They're all within the framework of the team."

By attacking in waves, the Flyers wore down opponents night after night. "We win by outworking the other team," defenseman Brad Marsh said during the Flyers' hot streak. "By no means are we an intimidating team anymore. Other teams know they'll be pushed to the limit because we work hard."

Keenan never seemed satisfied, no matter how hard his team worked. The victories made him want to win more. Other coaches would have been content with the team's progress, but not Keenan.

"Mike and I would sit and talk," Poulin recalled. "I understood a lot of what he was doing. That year we were unbeatable at home. We won every game in the first period. We would be up 4–0 after the first period. He'd grab me going up the walkway and he'd say, 'If they're not ready to play in the second period, it's your fault.' And he'd walk away and I'd say, 'Okay.'"

Success earned Keenan credibility in the dressing room, as did his personal work ethic. The players knew he was working around the clock. He would try anything that might help his team win. He even tried to talk Clarke out of retirement to play down the stretch. Clarke was flattered, but decided to stay in the press box. But the offer proved Keenan was always searching, always striving, for ways to win.

"You owe it to yourself and your team to give yourself every chance to win, and to do that you should cover all the bases," Keenan said. "If you look after the details, you are better able to deal with the big problems. I'm a perfectionist, but I also am aware that you can carry that too far, so I try not to create undue pressure on the players. I try to teach them and give them confidence."

The Flyers hit full stride as the playoffs neared. They won 16 of their last 17 games, including 11 straight, and stormed to the division title, finishing first overall in the NHL. They won their last 14 games at home and finished 32-4-4 at the Spectrum, outscoring teams by a two-to-one margin. Still, Keenan didn't gloat.

"We're not drinking champagne tonight because this is just one step toward a larger goal," he said after the division title was clinched. "Beer would be okay."

Keenan expressed satisfaction in the growth of his team. He paused for just a moment to praise his players. "This team has responded in every key situation," he said before the playoffs started. "It hasn't been one thing. It has been a case of constant growth and maturation on the part of the players."

But were they ready for the playoffs? The Flyers entered their first-round series against the New York Rangers carrying a nine-game post-season losing streak. Keenan was alarmed by his players' lack of confidence. He urged them to forget the past. But those failures haunted the team.

"They were being reflective," he said. "I wanted them to be passionate, angry, assertive. I could feel the nervousness. After all we had accomplished, as strongly as we had finished, they weren't sure they could win. I hadn't gone through all those negative experiences with them, so I was really taken aback by it."

But the Flyers carried their regular-season momentum into the post-season. Philadelphia attacked New York and the Rangers broke down. They never got a chance to catch their breath.

"We know not to let them throw the puck from defenseman to defenseman," Kerr said. "They used to outskate us, but not anymore. Today we're much faster and better prepared — the best preparation I've seen since I've been playing hockey."

The Flyers swept the Rangers. Their next opponent was the New York Islanders, who had been to the finals five consecutive seasons and won four Cups in a row from 1980 to 1983. Again, Keenan implored his team to forget the past and the Islanders' daunting recent history. The Islanders had beaten the Flyers to win the Stanley Cup in 1980.

"Who the hell is Mike Bossy?" he kept asking his players, referring to the future Hall of Famer, and then another: "Who the hell is Denis Potvin?"

Sure enough, the Flyers beat the Islanders, four games to one. The kids proved they were more than all right. The Flyers took apart the Islanders.

"It doesn't seem to matter who's out there for them," Islanders center Bryan Trottier observed after the series. "Every line keeps coming at you at the same pace."

Even Flyers defenseman Mark Howe was amazed by his team's dominance in the series. He had lived through Philadelphia's previous post-season disappointments. He knew what an impressive team the Flyers had beaten.

"I admire the way the Islanders work, the way they have always found ways to win," Howe said. "It's one of the best teams of all time. And we beat them."

The third-round series against Quebec turned into a vicious battle. Kerr hurt his knee. Poulin suffered cracked ribs, but played on. Brad McCrimmon suffered a shoulder separation. The series seesawed, with the teams splitting the first four games. After two periods of Game Five, the Flyers trailed the Nordiques, 1–0, and seemed to be fading.

Keenan flipped out in the dressing room. He swatted juice bottles off the table with his stick. Then he got up on the table and reminded his team that they were only a goal behind. There was no reason to quit. Glory was still within reach.

"They were thinking if it ended here, they had still had a much better season than anybody expected," Keenan said later. "The injuries were piling up. I could see the kids saying, 'Enough already.' But they could do more than they thought they could. We were in the twenty-first mile of a marathon. We needed the emotion to get through it."

The Flyers rallied for a 2–1 victory and took charge of the series. They won Game Six easily. Somehow, they had tapped into an emotional reserve they didn't know they had.

"By the third period, we would have been beating anybody," McGuire recalled. "Edmonton, the Soviets, anybody. It was a coach's dream."

The Flyers were in the Stanley Cup finals against the Edmonton Oilers, the defending champions. The Oilers were in their prime. They had Wayne Gretzky, Mark Messier, Jari Kurri, Paul Coffey, and more. They were the fastest team in the league. The Flyers carried their Game Six momentum into the first game of the series and dominated from start to finish for a 4–1 victory.

But the Flyers ran out of adrenaline. Their hearts remained strong, but their bodies were breaking down. When Kerr's knee gave out again and Lindbergh tore a quadricep, the out-manned Flyers were finished.

The Oilers won the next four games, winning Game Five, 8–3, and hoisted their second consecutive Stanley Cup. Edmonton was a superior team, a dynasty. The Flyers had exceeded expectations by miles and earned the admiration of the entire NHL. But Keenan cried on the flight home to Philadelphia. His team had come so close. He could not accept defeat, not after he had come so far.

"They had a better team, but I thought we were cheated by all the injuries of a chance to play them on an equal basis," he said. "Most clubs that reach the finals for the first time are pleased and proud and don't know what it takes to win. Maybe I was naïve. I guess I expected the impossible at all times."

Keenan felt indebted to his team for its fearless run and let his key players know just how he felt about them.

"I have a note from him, a very simple note, on a Flyers card," Poulin said. "In 1985, we beat Quebec. I had broken my ribs in the second game. I came back and played in games five and six and we beat them. He wrote me a note afterward about my leadership and how we couldn't have attained success without it."

Poulin doesn't consider himself a sentimental sort and doesn't keep a lot of stuff from his playing days. But he keeps that note close at hand and wonders why Keenan didn't express that side of his personality more often.

"It meant a lot, it meant a terrific amount," he said. "Can you overkill that part? Probably. Could you do it more? Absolutely."

The Sniders were thrilled with their coach's stirring debut season. The team awarded Keenan a new Mercedes and a new three-year contract. He earned the Jack Adams Award as the NHL's Coach of the Year.

"When Mike came, we'd been knocked out of the playoffs in the first round three straight years," Jay Snider said. "We had the youngest team in the league. We were picked to finish fourth in our division. Instead, we made it to the Stanley Cup finals. It was an incredible accomplishment. It was enormous. Clarke retired. Barber retired and Darryl Sittler was traded. We were thinking five years down the road. It's amazing, sometimes, how fast the future gets here."

The Flyers had their share of quality veterans, like Marsh, Howe, McCrimmon, Kerr, and Brian Propp, but the kids had made the unlikely Cup run possible. They kept the team playing well over the normal speed limit.

"All those guys were coming from major junior, kids who easily bought into the intensity system," McGuire said. "They were somewhat intimidated. They were still nineteen years old, still able to be sent back to juniors. Believe me, Mike used that trump card. 'You want to go back today to Peterborough?' That type of thing. Out of that came the right type of mix, the right kind of intensity to get us to the Stanley Cup. Pelle Lindbergh got us to the finals. Without that early success, who knows if Mike's act, Mike intensity would have worked."

This success convinced the Flyers, at least for a while, that there was a method to all of Keenan's madness. "My word for Mike would be control," McGuire added. "When you speak of great coaches, intimidation has to be there. And I've read a lot about coaches, good coaches. I remember reading about Vince Lombardi, and Jerry Kramer said he could tear you apart with the things he said, but he could also pat you on the head to bring you up. More than intimidation, it's respect with Mike."

Before the 1985–86 season, Sator left to coach the Rangers. Paul Titanic declined an offer to join the staff, so former Flyer Paul Holmgren returned to Philadelphia as an assistant coach after retiring as a player in Minnesota. The coaching staff's challenge was to keep the team hungry after a taste of success. They were up to the challenge. The Flyers got off to a 12–2 start.

"We didn't make believers out of too many press people last year," Keenan said early in the season. "I wasn't worried that we might be a flash in the pan, but it seems everyone else was. This team is made up of traded players, late-round draft picks, and free agents. The common thread — and I know this sounds corny — is hard work. Every one of them has had to work hard to play at this level."

Marsh became one of Keenan's notable disciples. He saw what hard work did for himself and the team. He could see himself becoming a much better player.

"I was twenty-three when I came here [in November 1981] and I had a lot to learn," he said. "I guess I was a reliable defenseman, but my years here changed my game tremendously. I grew up as a player here. I was lucky enough to realize that the game had changed. It had become a twelve-month job and you had to be in top shape. Every hockey player always gives a hundred percent, but you can control what that hundred percent is by being in shape."

Keenan's mind was already racing ahead. He wanted to build a dominant organization and he wanted to do it his way. Early in the season, he requested an audience with Ed Snider, vice president Keith Allen, Clarke, and the coaching staff. He arrived dressed like a board member and referred to a stack of notes during his presentation. Recalled Clarke, "He told Mr. Snider, 'This is what I need. This is what we have to do.' And Mr. Snider said, 'Mike, Clarke's the GM of this team, not you.' Mike was trying to take right over."

Flyers fans had every reason to believe their team would get back to the Cup finals and maybe win. These were giddy times for this proud franchise. Perhaps Philadelphia could have what Edmonton and Long Island had, a team that would contend for titles for years. Perhaps these would be the Broad Street Bullies, Part Two. The Flyers would rule the league again.

But tragedy struck on November 10, 1985. The Flyers, with a five-day gap in their schedule, arranged to meet at a suburban nightspot. Lindbergh wanted to stay home with his wife-to-be, who was in from Sweden with her family, but decided to join his teammates. He drank his share of beer, but he didn't appear to be drunk as the night wound down and the players headed home or out to breakfast.

Lindbergh was notorious for driving his Porsche 930 sports car like a race car driver. Not all of his teammates felt comfortable riding with him, even though he was a skilled driver. After leaving the team party, Lindbergh missed a turn and crashed into a retaining wall. He slammed on his brakes at the last second, but it was too late. The resulting wreck was horrific. Lindbergh and two passengers were badly injured.

Paramedics revived Lindbergh at the crash site, but he had suffered grave head wounds. Within a few hours doctors found no signs of brain activity. A respirator kept Lindbergh alive while his family and the Flyers struggled to comprehend the unthinkable: The popular young star was gone. Lindbergh was taken off life support. He died at the age of twenty-six. The team and the entire Philadelphia sports community went into mourning.

Keenan was unflappable during the crisis. He suppressed his own grief so he could help his players deal with theirs. Just as his own family had tried to remain stoic in the face of disaster, so did Keenan. Many of the Flyers were barely adults and they hadn't lost their sense of invincibility. Zezel wept on Keenan's shoulder. They had not seen a lot of death in their lives. They had not lost a lot of friends. They could not believe Lindbergh was gone.

"I couldn't let these people down no matter how much pain I felt," Keenan would later say. "I probably needed to let myself go, but I didn't."

With the players devastated, Keenan skated them hard at practice the next day, hoping they could work through their grief.

"My instincts told me the only thing we knew was to work," he said. "We had to take the pain out in physical exertion. I don't know if it was good or bad or right or wrong, but the reality was we had no choice."

Later, the players met and started sorting through their emotions. The players and wives had group discussions at the homes of Keenan and Poulin.

"People were encouraged to talk about their feelings and most of them did," Keenan said. "I think all those things helped. There was anger aimed both at Pelle's carelessness and the general randomness of death, like families unable to reconcile members' contracting incurable diseases. And because there were so many players at an age where they hadn't experienced much death, some felt vulnerable to their own immortality. Some felt guilty because they hadn't interacted with Pelle as well as they could have, had never told him how much they thought of him. It's limitless, the emotional response you could have."

Players who had tried to remain brave finally broke down as the enormity of their loss sunk in. "This was the first time I wept for me," Howe said. "I've cried at deaths, but always because I felt bad for somebody else's loss."

Remarkably, the Flyers threw themselves back into their work and returned to the task of winning. Bob Froese had the unenviable task of replacing Lindbergh, although prospect Darrin Jensen played the first game after the crash because Froese was injured in practice. That game, at home against Edmonton, served as a memorial service for Lindbergh. The dasher boards were stripped of advertising. The souvenir stands were closed. Fans attending the game received a small photo of Lindbergh, surrounded with a black border. On the back was this message: "In loving memory of Pelle Lindbergh, Our Goalie, Our Friend." The Reverend John Casey, the team chaplain, was among those who spoke about Lindbergh's life during the pre-game ceremony.

The Flyers won that game, 5–3, and kept going. They stretched their ten-game winning streak to thirteen games, a franchise record.

"Four days gave us some time to regroup," Keenan said. "And the fact we were going for the record for consecutive wins gave us a focal point mentally. But I can't tell you that we kept winning through the whole thing for any bigger reason than we were on a roll coming in and that it proved self-sustaining. It's almost like we went back into our bubble, the games, to escape our troubles. Our refuge was just how well we were playing."

Keenan admired the courage of his players and wasn't afraid to tell them. They had pulled themselves together and moved on as best they could.

"The way they've faced the tragic loss of someone they loved and respected has been an inspiration to everyone in the community," he said at the time. "The tragedy didn't really add to this team's character. The character was always there. The only difference is that now it's public."

On a later team flight, he played flight attendant and served food and drinks. "I guess I was saying, 'Hey, I'm thankful for you guys.' I care for these people more than they could ever know," he explained. "I do have a heart. I was just showing my appreciation for them. I probably don't do that enough."

The Flyers had to be a close-knit group to deal with Keenan's demands. The bond held after Lindbergh's death. The players needed each other more than ever.

"We knew the character of this team," Poulin said. "We knew how we felt about one another. But a lot of those feelings had never been expressed, not just because we're athletes, but because we're males. As much as Pelle's death pulled us together, I think it showed us how close we already were."

Replacing Lindbergh was a daunting challenge for Froese. Keenan would pull Froese from games, single him out for criticism, and rip him in the papers. He didn't believe Froese measured up to Lindbergh and he let everybody know it.

"He can make life unbearable," Froese said. "You hate him. He won't talk to you. He doesn't even acknowledge you. You feel like two cents. You shake your head at the time, but then later, you say, 'There was a master plan.' A lot of times I thought I was doing pretty good and he brought me down. Looking back, I see what he was doing, trying to make me stronger."

Keenan began to unravel as this taxing season wound down. Losses affected him greatly. He berated players in private and ignored them in public. He pushed for the trade to get goaltender Chico Resch in March 1986 because he had no faith in Froese. He went to his motivational whip again and again and wore down his players.

"I have no idea what he's thinking," Kerr said during one of Keenan's dark periods. "One day he says hello, the next day he doesn't say anything. He doesn't get close to his players, that's for sure. I don't think he has respect for me. Total intimidation is how he runs this team. On this team, you're only as good as your last shift."

Keenan shrugged off any criticism of his hard-hearted approach. He believed he was doing what he had to do to win.

"He has his personal opinion and he's entitled to it," Keenan said of

Kerr. "If that's the way Tim feels, that's his prerogative, that's his view. He might be a particularly sensitive individual, I'm not sure. All I know is, there have been a tremendous amount of excellent coaches who have been feared, from time to time, by their athletes."

But maintaining this posture was difficult. Being the tough guy left Keenan conflicted. He really did care for many of his players, but he figured he couldn't let them know it. He doesn't believe coaching in the NHL is a touchy-feely job. How could he be their friend when he might have to bench them, demote them, or have them traded?

"There's a fine line you walk as coach," he explained. "Sometimes you have to develop a feeling for a player who needs compassion. But how far do you go? If you develop that kind of relationship, what happens when you have to fire that person? He'll feel betrayed."

He lost some players' respect by belittling them in private and ripping them in front of support staff or in off-the-record chats with the media. Every insult made its way back to the players and made them furious. "It's like the guy who takes his wife out and tells everybody how wonderful she is, then goes home and treats her like dirt," Froese would later say. "How much does that praise mean to her?"

Keenan's outbursts were planned as often as they were spontaneous. After losses, he struggled to control his rage. But as often as not, his practice-day outbursts were pre-planned and calculated to trigger a certain response.

"My temper is a tool," he said. "I lose my temper for the right reason, to make players better. My assistant coaches would tell me that I had to give in on some of the little ones to win the bigger ones. But I could never find one to give in on."

The Flyers finished the season with fifty-three victories and faced the Rangers, coached by Sator, in the first round of the 1986 playoffs. During the Flyers' pivotal Game Three loss, Keenan called a time out for the sole purpose of lecturing them. He ordered the team off the bench and onto the ice so he could browbeat them from his perch. But his harsh words fell on mostly deaf ears. The players didn't want to take any more of his crap. They were spent. Keenan could yell and scream all he wanted, but it didn't matter anymore. They had no emotional reserve left.

"It was a mistake," Keenan would admit. "I should have been a calming influence."

Keenan would say that many times in his career. He knew he should back off more often, but he couldn't help himself. He just pushed and pushed and pushed.

"Mike was sort of a football-type coach mentality in hockey coaching," McGuire said. "The Iron Mike moniker isn't bad because he has the Mike Ditka persona on the sideline, not the Tom Landry persona of cool, calm collected, calculating. Mike is calculating. Sometimes it doesn't show on the bench. Sometimes he boils over in the walkway. Or he leaves the coaching door open and you see it brewing in his office. It's that kind of intensity. It's a flame that burns bright. You could argue that it doesn't sustain. That why he is labeled as coming in winning, winning right away, and then . . ."

During a meeting at the team hotel after Game Three, Keenan backed down and allowed the players to drink beer as they tried to relax and hash out their problems. The Flyers had one more spasm of life, bouncing back for a 7–1 victory to force a decisive Game Five, but that was it. The Rangers won the final game, 5–2, and eliminated the Flyers.

"We were mad that we lost," Tocchet recalled. "But I remember also thinking, 'At least it's over.' There had been a lot of pressure on us for a long time. I think it caught up with us."

Keenan looked back on the season and wished he had given the team a bit more breathing room as it worked through the Lindbergh tragedy. "I probably should have let them falter a little bit and learn their own lessons," he said after the season. "They were a tremendously strong group. They deserved the opportunity to learn that on their own."

The Sniders supported Keenan and upgraded his contract once again. After calming down over the summer, Keenan promised to take it easy on the 1986–87 Flyers. The boys were men now and could be treated as men. The playoff wars had toughened them.

"The players are mature enough now that the coaching staff can throw the ball to them and say, 'Let's have some fun,'" he observed before the season began.

Fun? With Keenan? Trouble started right away. After the 1986 playoff fiasco, Keenan had time to scout the Flyers' farm team in Hershey, Pennsylvania. He became smitten with feisty goaltending prospect Ron Hextall. Keenan saw Hextall as the solution to Philadelphia's biggest problem. When Keenan moved Hextall into the starting role early in the 1986–87 season, Froese asked to be traded. He sat and he stewed and he thought some very unkind things about his coach. Finally, Clarke liberated him by trading him to the Rangers in December.

That wasn't the only crisis. Injuries sidelined Propp, Howe, Zezel, Tocchet, Ron Sutter, and Ilkka Sinisalo. Keenan expressed contempt for many of Clarke's additions. He hounded young power forward Scott Mellanby, who he dismissed as a spoiled prep school kid. He told Mellanby the only reason he still was on the team was that his dad, *Hockey Night in Canada* producer Ralph Mellanby, was friendly with Clarke. Keenan had no use for him and told him so. Keenan screamed at Mellanby. He humiliated him in front of the team. He mocked him and worked him and tried to break him down.

"One day Mike really tested him in practice," McGuire recalled years later, after Mellanby had played in his one-thousandth NHL game. "When I saw the one-thousandth game by Mellanby, through everything, through all the other challenges, I thought of that day. That day, I wouldn't have bet on a thousand periods, let alone a thousand games. A thousand minutes. I thought he'd quit right there. He didn't."

Mellanby survived Keenan's wrath, but his first two NHL seasons were a nightmare. Keenan never let up. "If not for your father's friendship with Clarke," he kept telling Mellanby, "you wouldn't be here. You have earned nothing."

"There's been some bitterness between us," Mellanby said at the time, measuring his words carefully. "Maybe it's improved me, I don't know."

Keenan made no apologies for his approach. Mellanby owed his job to Clarke, not Keenan, who wanted every Flyer to prove himself. There was no place for tourists and hangers-on in his dressing room. And once Keenan dug in on a player, he never let up. He could not be proven wrong.

"I may have been hard on Scott Mellanby, but I thought he was handed a spot when he should have been at Hershey," Keenan later explained. "The rap on me was not playing the kids, but I didn't think the kids were ready to play for us."

The Flyers rolled through Keenan's third season until a series of injuries sent them into a 12-13-2 midseason slump. They pulled out of it, but their tenacious coach punished them in the final week of the regular season by conducting brutal practices. A season-ending 9–5 loss to the Islanders left Clarke growling. Was the team setting itself up for another first-round exit?

"There are no excuses for that kind of effort," Clarke said. "The coach has to share some of the blame."

Marsh didn't believe the team was on the brink of a mutiny with Keenan, at least not yet. The team was prepared for the playoffs. "I still maintain it wasn't that bad of an environment," Marsh said. "A lot of guys had their best years. But the expectations were higher and Mike hated losing so much that things became that much more tense."

The Flyers, 46-26-8 in their up-and-down season, again met the Rangers in the first round. Circumstances made the matchup easier for the Flyers. Rangers general manager Phil Esposito was one of the greatest players in NHL history, but he was an impetuous executive and an ineffective head coach. After a series of trades failed to inspire better play, he put himself behind the bench as the playoffs neared. Nobody was surprised when Keenan led the Flyers past the Rangers in six games.

One of the highlights of the series was the beating Dave Brown gave Rangers pest George McPhee in Game Two. When Keenan sent any of his tough guys into the fray, they knew their job was to stir up some trouble and change the game's direction. Keenan had made deft use of strategic fights throughout his Flyers tenure, but Esposito was aghast.

"He sent Brown after McPhee, plain as day," Esposito whined. "It makes me think that a lot of rumors I've heard about him are true." Rumors? It was obvious from the day Keenan took the Flyers job that he was going to put the bully back in Broad Street.

A tense series with the Islanders was next. The Flyers won three of the first four games, but struggled to put the Islanders away. After New York won twice to tie the series at three games each, Clarke suggested that Keenan take his obviously uptight players to a comedy club to loosen them up. He did, and it worked. A comic mocked Keenan, who actually smiled. The Flyers finished off the Islanders with a 5–1 victory in Game Seven and moved on to face Montreal in the semifinals.

Once again, the Flyers rolled to three victories in four games before losing Game Five. The most intriguing subplot of the series was a pre-game ritual involving Montreal's Claude Lemieux. At the end of each pre-game warm-up, Lemieux tried to shoot a puck into the Flyers' net. Each time, the Flyers tried to thwart him. Finally, before Game Six, Lemieux came back onto the ice with Shayne Corson after everybody had gone to their locker rooms. He wanted to score. Tough guy Ed Hospodar, who had barely played in the series, came back onto the ice with Resch and resolved to stop him. Words were exchanged, tempers flared, and Hospodar did what he was paid to do: He pummeled Lemieux.

Players from both teams streamed back onto the ice in various stages of undress. Because the officials weren't on the ice, the players had to sort out the mess themselves. The teams went toe to toe for fifteen minutes, with Flyers ruffian Dave Brown battling Montreal's Chris Nilan in a marathon bout. A furious Ed Snider implored Keenan to do something, but Keenan told his boss to beat it. He knew this appalling free-for-all would fire up his team, and it did. The Flyers rallied from a 3–1 deficit to win the game 4–3. Canadiens Coach Jean Perron refused to shake Keenan's hand after the game, and Keenan became livid when the media harped on the brawl in post-game questioning.

Keenan never ordered Hospodar to punch out Lemieux. Big Ed knew his role and knew that the free-for-all would fire up the team. "Intimidate with passion," as Keenan put it, was job one for all his enforcers. This was hardly a revelation. Keenan was a hockey coach, not the captain of a debate team. Goon tactics had always been part of his program. He couldn't manage the shift-to-shift flow of games without setting up the odd sock exchange.

For the second time in three years, the Flyers met the Edmonton Oilers in the Stanley Cup finals. The speedy Oilers stormed ahead of the Flyers, winning the first two games and skating to a quick 3–0 lead in Game Three. All appeared lost for Philadelphia. But the Flyers would not quit. They somehow rallied to win the third game 5–3.

"You can't give up in a situation like that," Tocchet said. "We always knew we could beat them. At one point, we wondered when the heck we would ever get a break. Then, finally, it came. We were pretty close to the grave, but this is a character team."

The Flyers battled on despite suffering a debilitating array of injuries. Kerr's shoulder came apart. Poulin was trying to play despite broken ribs. Doug Crossman pulled a groin muscle. Sinisalo had a twisted knee. Both Murray Craven and Lindsay Carson were playing with various injuries. Keenan had to call on his reserves.

"It's always a collective effort here, more so than other teams," Crossman said at the time. "We put personal statistics aside and just play offense and defense to the best of our ability. We sacrifice individual accomplishments and put the team first. And our depth goes right to Hershey and the juniors. It makes jumping into our lineup so easy, it doesn't look like anyone is missing."

Edmonton won Game Four decisively, 4–1, at Philadelphia, to take a three-games-to-one lead. Again, Keenan reached into his bag of motivational tricks. The Stanley Cup was in Edmonton for Game Five, in case the Oilers closed out the Flyers, so Keenan had it wheeled into the Flyers' dressing room before the game. This was the ultimate visualization exercise.

"I got permission to bring the Stanley Cup into the locker room," Keenan said. "It really made an impact on our team, because it was a visual experience that identified the ultimate goal that we were striving for. There really wasn't anything to be said at the time. Just the fact they had walked into the room and the Cup was there was motivation enough for them."

The Flyers won Game Five 4–3, and Game Six 3–2, setting up Game Seven in Edmonton. Keenan was moved by his team's unwillingness to quit. Before the championship game, he reflected on the Flyers' remarkable playoff run.

"I'm even in awe of some of the things they've done," he said. "It's been the most exciting aspect of the entire playoffs as a coach, learning a great deal about each of our players. The neatest thing is watching them grow. Over the course of the last fifty-two days, I've seen young men grow up — as people, not just as hockey players. It's been a subtle improvement in players you didn't expect it from. I'd rather not name names because of the inference that it wasn't expected before, but there's been a maturation process. To learn something about yourself is a really neat experience."

But the Oilers finished off Philadelphia with a 3–1 victory in Game Seven at the Northlands Coliseum. The Flyers were devastated.

"I've never been shot with a bullet," Howe said after the loss, "but it couldn't hurt any more than this."

Keenan earned his place in international hockey lore by directing Team Canada to victory in the 1987 Canada Cup. This tournament paired Wayne Gretzky and Mario Lemieux, on the Canadian side, against the last of the truly great Soviet Union teams. It may have been the finest hockey we'll see in our lifetimes.

The selection process created controversy. Keenan made certain the team was ready to go by wedging key Flyers Rick Tocchet, Ron Hextall, and Brian Propp into the mix. Among the players left off were Patrick

Roy, Steve Yzerman, and Wendel Clark. Two of Keenan's bitter coaching rivals, John Muckler of the Edmonton Oilers and Jean Perron of the Montreal Canadiens, joined Keenan and his ally, Tom Watt, to direct this extraordinary group. Among the support staff was Mike Finocchiaro, the Flyers' videotape expert who performed a similar role for Team Canada.

"The most fascinating thing I've ever done in hockey," he said. "During a season, these guys hate each other. Now it's like they've been working together all their life. It's like watching General Motors, Ford, and Chrysler getting together to build a car."

Keenan didn't treat these tournaments as all-star events. Nor were they working vacations. They were work, period, and he hurt feelings right off the bat. For instance, the players groused when they didn't get much cuddle time with their wives during a stint in the spectacular mountain village of Banff, Alberta.

A post-game curfew after a 4–4 tie with the Czechs didn't go over well, either. Who wants to drink beer in his room? A committee of players went to event organizer Alan Eagleson and complained. Eagleson sent the committee to Keenan, who eased up when Gretzky and the others reminded him that they were volunteering their valuable time to the cause. Keenan listened and relented a bit.

"Things are 100 percent better around here," one player reported after the summit.

"Part of the regimen was to develop team discipline and togetherness," Keenan said. "I think the meeting opened up communication and turned into a very positive thing."

The coach was smart enough to give Gretzky the considerable respect he had earned by dominating the sport through the 1980s.

"Coaching against him, you just see him go out and play, but coaching him you see a different dimension," Keenan said. "He has a great deal of ability in terms of concentrating and focusing on what's going on around him during a game. His awareness is very acute. If a light were to go on in the corner of the stands, or the clock missed a second, he'd be aware of it. He's provided great leadership on the ice in terms of working hard, and if you tell him once what you want done he does it. It all adds up to why he's a special athlete."

The Canadians weren't dominant early. Besides the tie with the Czechs, they had a 3–3 tie with the Soviets in round-robin play. But in the semifinals, Keenan was on top of his game. He shuffled line combinations constantly, sending twenty different units into battle. The players groused, but Keenan was able to sustain shift-to-shift pressure by riding hot players and rebuking those who slipped. Team Canada rallied from a 2–0 deficit against the Czechs to earn a rousing 5–3 victory.

"To a lot of these guys, this was a new style of coaching and they had trouble adjusting," Keenan said. "They're used to set lines, like in Edmonton, I suppose. Finally, they came to me about it and I explained it. They seemed to go along with it. I know we've played outstanding hockey ever since."

Line shuffling has always been a Keenan staple. He prefers to keep his players on edge. He loves managing the flow of the game. He wants his players going full speed and improvising offensively on the fly. He despises patterns and predictability.

"The other argument against keeping the same lines together in a short tournament like this is you give the opposition an opportunity to scout you and take note of what you're doing," Keenan said. "I don't think anybody could figure out what we were up to. Some of our players were complaining that even they were stumped."

Keenan may not have had to mix a few grinders and muckers into his mix. On this team, the stars were all willing to do the dirty work.

"If you examine the work ethic and level of all our players, then you know why it's been tough for a grinder to stand out," he said. "If some guys with talent are not working that hard, then the grinder, who knows he has to work hard, has a better chance of standing out."

By beating the Czechs, Team Canada got its date in the finals with the Soviet Union. The Soviets had entered the tournament fired up about their loss to Sweden in the World Championships a few months earlier. This was this nation's last big go-round with its top players and the team knew it. A sense of urgency prevailed in the Soviet camp.

In Game One of the finals, Keenan used twenty-two line combinations as the Soviets squeezed out a 6–5 victory. Keenan just about exhausted the mathematical possibilities of line combinations in Game Two, using twenty-nine as Team Canada won, 6–5. Lemieux's goal in the second overtime, off a Gretzky feed, decided the game.

"Wayne is the best player in the world and playing with him is an honor," Lemieux said. "You see what kind of hockey player he really is when you play with him."

Keenan was a bundle of nerves after that game. He didn't get to bed until 4:30 A.M.

"I couldn't get to sleep," he said. "I finally went for a walk by myself. I needed a breath of fresh air."

All of Canada was abuzz before the decisive Game Three. "The fans are caught up in it now," Keenan said. "We've got a country behind us. Maybe that'll be the difference. Maybe that will be our fourth line."

The Soviets wanted to make a firm stand. The World Championships had gotten away from them. Now they had a chance to right that wrong against the very best, the Gretzky-led Canadians. For many of the Russians, this would be the biggest game they would ever play.

"Like us, the Soviets are looking for new challenges," Perron said. "They've been playing the same teams over and over. This is the best thing that's happened to this game. The third one is going to be even better."

Sure enough, it was. The evenly matched teams battled to a 5–5 tie through fifty-eight minutes. Overtime loomed. But then Gretzky and Lemieux got a break and The Great One fed The Magnificent One for the game-winner with one minute, twenty-six seconds left in the third period. Team Canada's 6–5 victory may never be topped in international play.

"We won it on guts and desire," a beaming Gretzky said.

Canada celebrated. Philadelphia celebrated, too; five thousand fans poured into the Spectrum to watch the game on big-screen television.

"It seems like a long time ago that we started traveling up this road," said defenseman Doug Crossman, another of Keenan's selections from his Flyers team. "And when you come to the end of the road successfully, it's very satisfying. I've spent the best six weeks of my life — my hockey life — here with these guys."

Looking back on that 1987 series, Keenan raved about Gretzky's dominance. "Wayne would probably admit that was the best he has ever played the game," he said. "I never knew that he had that kind of intrinsic motivation. I knew he was exceptional, but I saw an ability to take his game to heights I had not seen before in any athlete. I remember he would turn to me and without saying anything would be asking me to put him out there again, and that was on every second shift. To me, that epitomized what an athlete of his caliber is capable of doing."

The bonding of Gretzky and Lemieux — who, to that point, had not earned the reputation as a champion — was an historic event as well. Lemieux learned how to win during the Canada Cup. He later used that knowledge to lead the Penguins to two Stanley Cups.

"I had a feeling Wayne was showing Mario anything and everything for two reasons," Keenan said. "One, he wanted our team to win. But just as importantly, I think he needed a challenge. It was never stated, but I think Wayne was saying, 'All right, Mario, I'm giving you the goods and that will give me the challenge to drive to another level.'"

Each summer, Keenan went back to school at hockey clinics and seminars. During the summer of 1987, he heard sports psychologist Dr. Cal Botterill speak at York University in Toronto. They chatted after the lecture and Keenan suggested he might give him a call sometime. Botterill was a former player and the aggressive Flyers program intrigued him.

"He has a feel for the game," Keenan said. "When you're preparing a team for competition, I think that developing the mental skills is as important as developing the physical skills."

Botterill would come to the Flyers midway through the 1987–88 season, when the team hit a rut. Ed Snider wanted Keenan to be more upbeat and Clarke demanded he start making better use of the young players. Clarke was fed up with how Keenan rejected his draft picks and acquisitions. When Clarke would add a player, Keenan would ignore him, forcing Clarke to trade the player. When Clarke would recall youngsters like Glen Seabrooke from the minors, Keenan would deem them unusable.

After three seasons of Keenan's browbeatings, the players quit listening to their coach. Carson asked for a trade, saying he just couldn't take Keenan anymore. Clarke was alarmed at his team's declining morale. He wondered if the team could regenerate its enthusiasm. On the team flight back from Edmonton after the Stanley Cup finals, several players, after drinking several beers, had lobbied Clarke for Keenan's dismissal. Clarke wasn't ready to fire a coach who had won his conference two times in three years. But he was getting concerned.

"For as good a job as he did with some players, he ruined others," Clarke said. "Tommy Eriksson was on the all-rookie team one year and next year he wanted to go home. Keenan just about drove him crazy. Kerry Huffman came in as an eighteen-year-old who looked like he'd be an all-star, and the next year he couldn't even get on the ice. He's never been the same, really. We lost lots of good, young players."

Ed Snider remembered how Mike blew him off him during the

Montreal brawl. He remembered how Keenan showed up late for the owner's post-season party after the Edmonton series. Clearly, Keenan was down in the count with his bosses. Issues well outside his control compounded matters. McCrimmon had another contract skirmish with Clarke and got traded for draft picks. Kerr was sidelined by serious shoulder problems. Hextall was suspended for the first eight games of the season for a vicious slash on Kent Nilsson during the Cup finals. Brown got a fifteen-game suspension for cross-checking Rangers nemesis Tomas Sandstrom in the back of the head early in the 1987–88 season.

"I don't even blame Brown," Rangers goaltender John Vanbiesbrouck said. "He's only doing a job assigned him by Keenan. Keenan pats him on the head and says, 'Good job tonight. We'll put you in a cage and let you ride home on the team bus.'"

When the team went into a 1-8-2 tailspin in late October, Snider reiterated the need for his coach to be more positive. But each loss insulted Keenan. Clarke gave Keenan a vote of confidence, which meant nothing because coaches are frequently fired after getting them.

"I'm not firing the coach," Clarke insisted. "Some of the players are trying to put the blame on the coach, and that's not right. They are professionals. Where does it say they have to like the coach?"

Doug Crossman, who had never been Keenan's type of player, became unresponsive during this slow start. He had seen all of Keenan's tactics and heard all the abuse. None of it registered anymore. Crossman just didn't care. He showed no since of urgency and nothing Keenan did was going to change that.

"I think it was just the cumulative effect of four years of playing for Mike," Poulin said. "Dougie was down on Mike for the way he treated other players more than for the way he was treated himself."

Even Keenan's warriors, like Poulin, Ron Sutter, and Rick Tocchet, had seen enough. Tocchet was benched during a 5–2 loss at St. Louis on November 10. Tocchet said it was because he didn't instigate a brawl when he was supposed to.

"There are players who have their personal priorities ahead of the hockey club's," Keenan said. "They are thinking about their own needs instead of the team's."

Responded Tocchet, "I'm not going to go out and just fight."

During a team meeting the next day in St. Louis, Poulin was ready for a major confrontation with Keenan. He expected something big, like a physical challenge. But when Keenan took a non-confrontational approach to the session, the players decided not to follow through on their much discussed rebellion.

Tocchet had a long talk with Keenan on a subsequent flight and tried to put the episode behind him. "Mike and I have been through a lot and I didn't want it destroyed in twenty minutes," Tocchet said. "We're a lot alike. Sometimes we butt heads." Poulin also had a discussion with Keenan and came away satisfied — for the time being, anyway.

At their low point, the Flyers were at 6-13-3. Several players would have enjoyed stringing up Keenan by his feet and letting him bleed to death through his eyes. But Keenan plowed ahead, undeterred by the mounting sentiment against him.

"The pressure was very extensive," he recalled. "I myself didn't feel any true despair or major amount of discomfort. But there was so much psychoanalysis about what was wrong and we had more than a few genuinely young guys." Flyer fans demanded a lot of their team and some of the less experienced players were nervous. "They were turning street corners in their neighborhoods worried about who would confront them next," he said.

Just when it seemed hopeless for Keenan, Botterill arrived to provide positive reinforcement.

"He's been too tough, by his own admission," Botterill said at the time. "Too irrational, too abrasive, too perfectionistic. Not able to let it go and relax. And yet the bottom line is that he has a special nose for which players have character and which don't. If you want to be among the elite in the NHL, this is the guy you want to be with."

Botterill would become a key component in Keenan's programs in Chicago and New York, too. Mark Howe became one of Botterill's prize pupils. The psychologist talked to him, identified the roots of his anxiety, and recommended ways to relax. Usually a few choice suggestions did the trick.

"He was responsible for something that kind of turned my career around," Howe said of Botterill. "The mental part of hockey was becoming difficult for me in those years. After the game, I'd lie awake until seven in the morning, sort of replaying it over and over. It got to be, like, 'How long can this continue?' I was terribly uptight about the whole thing. It was getting to me. Keenan directed me to Botterill, who taught me how to keep everything in the right perspective, to be serious about my job, you know, but not to the point where I was obsessed. I've been fine ever since. He just relaxed me and put me in a little trance or got me relaxed, and I guess put a lot of positive reinforcement within me. I had been feeling tired every day, and when I left, I felt like I could have skated forty-eight straight hours and never get tired."

The team getaway became another staple of Keenan's program. With his team sinking, Keenan took his team to the Olympic facility in Lake Placid, New York, to isolate his players from outside distractions. All they had were each other, so they finally started to relax and work through their collective frustrations.

"Nobody knew we were there," Zezel said. "We ate, drank, had a bunch of laughs. For me, the mental pressure had really hurt. It was my first time going through it. You don't know how pulling yourself out of it is done. But over those three days, our lines began talking, the blaming began to stop. And we began to cross our fingers."

The Flyers reeled off a fourteen-game unbeaten streak to salvage their season. But Botterill's presence and the unbeaten streak didn't change Keenan completely. He still tested his players. Paul Lawless, who arrived midway through the season in a deal for the disgruntled Carson, quickly got a taste of the Iron Mike routine.

"Mike Keenan 'Flyerized' me," Lawless recalled. "Rick Tocchet, Derrick Smith, and Peter Zezel warned me. After the first game, sure enough, Paul Holmgren told me to go see Mike. He tore a strip off my backside like you wouldn't believe. In Toronto, Mike told me to come in again. We went at it. Boom, boom, banged it out. After that, we got along great. There was no bitterness."

But Lawless lasted just eight games with the Flyers. Clarke traded him to Vancouver. Such was life for the Flyers' supporting cast.

The team finished with a 38-33-9 record and reached the playoffs. They drew the Capitals in the first round and moved out to a three-games-to-two lead in the best-of-seven series. Before Game Six, Keenan asked Clarke for some input on who to start in goal, the ailing Hextall or backup Mark LaForest. Clarke suggested LaForest. Naturally, Keenan went with Hextall. Hextall got rocked, 7–2.

"I wondered why he had even asked," Clarke said. "It was like that a lot with Mike. You never felt like you were working with him, only for him."

The Flyers took a 3–0 lead in Game Seven, but lost 5–4 in overtime.

The down-and-up-and-down season was finally over.

Keenan termed the season "disjointed." His players agreed. The players, Clarke, and the Sniders agreed on something else after the final loss: Keenan had to move along. The relationship between the coach and the players had deteriorated beyond the point of reconciliation. If Jerry Springer had had a television show back then, the Flyers would have starred in the "We Can't Live With Our Abusive Coach" episode.

"Each and every guy's taken a lot from him," Ron Sutter said. "It got to the point where the players couldn't take it anymore. You can whip a horse only so long before it quits on you."

Few professional sports coaches can last as long as four years and maintain a strong rapport with their players. After a while, their message grows old and the messenger is ignored. An aggressive coach like Keenan is even more susceptible to flameout. Clarke faced the prospect of massive player turnover if he didn't change coaches. Something had to give.

"In watching him through this year, I thought we weren't playing with any emotion," Clarke told reporters. "And I think he worked himself to the bone. When a team plays with no emotion and he got as much as he could out of them, he did a good job. Even when we played well, I sensed no happiness there. There was nothing left between Mike and the players.

"I think we have good hockey players. Still, I didn't think we played with a zest for winning. I think this year we played with very little emotion, very little enthusiasm. As hard as Mike worked, as hard as he tried, the players didn't have any enthusiasm. I thought we were going downhill. Sometimes a team gets tired of playing for a coach. Maybe four years was too long for them. It seems that in professional sports, coaches have a time limit for their success. And then changes have to be made."

Jay Snider believed everybody was ready for a change, including the front office.

"We wanted hard work and discipline and a lot of great things that Mike brought," he said. "But we also wanted an atmosphere that showed he cared about them as people."

Despite all the turmoil he went through during the 1987–88 season, Keenan was devastated when the Sniders fired him. Clarke summoned him to his office at the team's practice facility and quickly summed up the situation: The team was no longer playing up to its capability and a change had to be made. Keenan disagreed, but he couldn't change the decision. Clarke left the office and allowed Keenan time to compose himself. Later, as he left the facility, he saw Keenan standing alone by the boards, staring at the rink.

"I couldn't stop crying," Keenan recalled. "I couldn't talk."

The players, on the other hand, were overjoyed that Keenan was gone.

"The biggest thing is a lot of guys lost respect for Mike a while ago," Howe said. "Mike was good to me and showed me respect, but I can honestly say he showed no respect to other players. Mike's favorite saying was, 'They may not like me, but they respect me.' There were a lot of deep wounds and the players ended up not respecting Mike. That's a bad situation and it shows up emotionally. Guys would be out working and trying, but without emotion it shows up. At the start of the year, a lot of guys were hoping Mike would get fired, but the owners stood by him. We had a meeting and said we had to get ourselves out of this, forget about our problems with Mike, and just do our jobs."

Keenan differed with Howe's view. "Mark is entitled to his own opinion. I didn't see it," Keenan said. "I don't agree with him. I think you have to look at the record and it speaks for itself. Winning is a very important part of the National Hockey League. Everybody would love to be well-liked and loved by everyone in your profession, but does that make you a winner? I don't know of any coach being successful over a long period of time that demonstrated that."

Keenan was successful. His record in Philadelphia was 190-102-28. He became the only coach in NHL history to win 40 or more games in his first three years. He won 150 games faster than any coach in league history.

"The Flyers decided that winning wasn't enough," Keenan sniffed. "They wanted to win and have fun at the same time. How much happiness is there on any team? If that's the number one priority, we could have the happiest team in the league, but not be as successful as we were. On all the great teams in the history of the game, there were always unhappy players. You can't tell me those Montreal teams were happy."

McGuire didn't believe the situation was hopeless. Perhaps some players could have been switched instead of the coach.

"There is a healthy amount of turnover that both a Keenan and a Bowman need to have," McGuire said. "Even Glen Sather in Edmonton in the dominant years, he always tweaked the fourth line or whatever. I don't think his time was up in Philadelphia. I think there would have had to have been a healthy bit of recycling or whatever, but I think Mike was willing to pass on some of his dictatorial style to Poulin, to Tim Kerr, to the guys who developed under him."

But how long could Keenan and Clarke really work together? In retrospect, it's somewhat amazing they lasted together as long as they did.

"I think they coexisted," Poulin said. "Bob was in his first year out of hockey, first year in any sort of leadership role with management. He was in a whole new thing as well. It was a relationship that just had a certain time amount to it. In this business, I've always likened hockey to dog years. Four years is a long time."

The firing forced Keenan into a period of introspection. Rita Keenan saw her husband leveled by the first firing of his career. Mike took individual losses very hard. How could he cope with a dismissal? He was nearly inconsolable. "It hit deep and sent a big message," she said. "He realized he had to make some changes."

When Keenan looked back on his Flyers tenure years later, he realized he could have let up on his players from time to time. He didn't have to ride them day after day, month after month, year after year. He had instilled a winning personality and that personality could have sustained itself with some nurturing.

"If I had expressed to them that I trusted them, it probably would have worked out a lot better," he said. "But at the time, I didn't think I could afford to change. If you are a nice guy, you can't get tough all of a sudden. If you're tough, you can occasionally be nice, but you can't be something you aren't."

Years later, Keenan would finally understand that his approach didn't have to be quite so manic. He had proven himself. He was in no danger of going back to the jungle line at the General Motors plant in Oshawa.

"I never coached as well in Philadelphia as I did my first year," Keenan admitted. "I see that now. I recognized I had to change if I was going to continue to be successful. I'm a very intense individual and I had to bring more composure to my approach. I grew a great deal as coach and would probably handle another situation differently."

When looking back at those Flyers years, Clarke wonders if the franchise couldn't have harnessed Iron Mike Keenan and have gotten more out of him.

"He's got the Darth Vader side to him as well, but I think with more experience we could have controlled it a little better," Clarke said. "He ran a little roughshod, but that was more my weakness. If I let him do it, that was my fault.

"In hindsight, I should have changed some of the players instead of Mike."

◄ 4 ►

Blowing through the Windy City

There's more to life than hockey, even though Mike Keenan may not believe that right now.

— FORMER BLACKHAWKS DEFENSEMAN DOUG WILSON,
SHORTLY BEFORE BEING EXILED

AGENT ALAN EAGLESON HAD HIS HANDS ALL OVER HOCKEY IN 1988. He represented coaches and players, ran the players association, and counted key NHL owners as his favorite bedfellows. It was a cozy setup and he made it pay handsomely with some brazen double-dealing — at least until the authorities closed in and sent him to the Big House.

After Keenan was fired by the Flyers, Eagleson represented him in his job search. One of Eagleson's closest business associates was Bill Wirtz, owner of the Chicago Blackhawks and the de facto president of the league. One of his long-time clients was Bob Pulford, general manager of the Blackhawks. So he routed Keenan into the Blackhawks job, even though Keenan's autocratic tendencies made him an extremely poor fit in the Wirtz family store.

The Blackhawks haven't won the Stanley Cup since 1961. Whatever frustration this drought brought Wirtz was more than offset by the millions of dollars hockey had made him and his family. Wirtz is a throwback, a classic sports baron who saw his franchise as a means of keeping his arena seats filled and his beer taps flowing. Hockey was just like the circus or an ice show — another event on the arena event calendar — except that its run lasted for months instead of weeks. "Dollar Bill," as

Chicago pundits referred to him, wouldn't think of putting home hockey games on television. Why should he give away his product when there was beer to sell at Chicago Stadium? He embraced the potential of pay-per-view playoff broadcasting. He was willing to allocate some of his vast revenue to retain a core group of fan favorites, such as Denis Savard, Steve Larmer, and Doug Wilson, but he wasn't about to endanger his profit margin for silly free-agent spending sprees.

Wirtz's front office was filled with loyalists, lackeys, and family members. Bob Pulford, Tommy Ivan, and Jack Davison had all been great hockey men, but their conservative mentality allowed the franchise to sink even in the rugged but vastly underskilled Norris Division. Pulford was notoriously inert as a general manager, loathing to make major moves even in the face of sustained failure. He sat still on the job, like a man posing for an oil painting. The Blackhawks went 29-37-14 in 1986–87 and 30-41-9 in 1987–88 and their prospects for a turnaround seemed bleak. Eagleson suggested to Wirtz that he hire Iron Mike to replace the mild-mannered Bob Murdoch, who had been on the job just one season. Murdoch wasn't going to take this franchise anywhere, so the Wirtz family, which had grown a bit weary of its laughingstock role in Chicago sports, decided to take the plunge.

Wirtz admired Keenan's sterling record in Philadelphia and his determination to make the boys work for their paychecks. He appreciated the old-time work ethic. Not only did Wirtz hire him to coach, he promised him the opportunity to graduate to general manager. Keenan wouldn't have signed on without that promise, not with the passive Pulford impeding progress. In a couple of years, Wirtz would ease Pulford into a peripheral role and let Keenan run the show.

"It sounds like a good idea to me," a gracious Pulford said at the time. "But I've got some years left in me."

The hiring took some pressure off Pulford. Keenan's impeccable credentials brought instant credibility to a beleaguered front office.

"He's a winner," Pulford said after the hiring. "He's a proven coach. He wins. We feel that, more than anything else, is what he's going to bring to us. It's an innate thing, but we feel that with Mike Keenan, our team will improve. We believe our teams have been underachievers for the last few years. His teams have been achievers."

Those words sounded great, but they rang hollow. The Blackhawks family didn't fully embrace their new coach. Conflict was inevitable. Gary

Webb, Keenan's long-time friend and business associate, felt the front office chill when making his periodic trips to visit Keenan in Chicago. There was a Blackhawks way of doing things — with much deliberation — and the impetuous Keenan didn't fit. Pulford put on a brave public face when Wirtz hired Keenan, but he clearly wasn't thrilled. Other staffers felt the same way about this interloper.

"He was getting no support off the ice," Webb said. "Pulford couldn't give a shit about Mike's image, Mike's relationship with the people in Chicago, the media, and all that stuff."

Webb, a master marketer, saw many small indications of trouble. For instance, the publicity photo of Keenan distributed by the team did the coach no favors. His eyes were bloodshot and his tie reached only halfway down his shirt.

"He looked like Bozo the Clown," Webb said. "And this is the picture they were sending to media. Here's Mike the Clown. It was so blatant I couldn't handle it."

Keenan wasn't concerned about public relations. He was fixated, as always, on the activity on the ice. He vowed to make Blackhawks fans proud of their team. He couldn't wait to get busy with his new players. He would make them understand what it took to win.

"I'm proud if people associate my name with discipline," Keenan said. "You can't be a successful club without it. I'm going to use a hands-on approach in Chicago. I always thought it would be interesting to coach in Chicago when I was just starting out in coaching in junior and it's so exciting that it's finally coming true. I've always loved the building and the fans here."

McGuire followed Keenan to Chicago as his top aide. Jacques Martin, an old college teammate who had just been fired as head coach of the Blues, came to the Windy City as well. It didn't take long for the coaches to realize just how enormous their task was. The Blackhawks were a horrible team. Though Keenan implemented the same program that made the Flyers great, he got nowhere at first. His words sailed past the blank faces of his players and bounced off the walls of a lifeless dressing room.

The Blackhawks tried to work hard, but they showed no spark at all on the ice. They won just six of their first twenty-nine games under the new regime, leaving Keenan aghast. He had won at every level of coaching. Every one of his teams had eventually met his demands. These

Blackhawks, however, appeared hopeless. This became the most punishing stretch of his career. Never before had he coached a doormat.

Keenan realized the team's confidence was low because so few players had been successful in the past. The team needed constant reinforcement. The Blackhawks suffered from miserable team leadership. Keenan couldn't get Savard and Wilson to make the all-out commitment needed to win. Game after game, practice after practice, he dug into Iron Mike's Bag of Coaching Tricks hoping to jar a response from his veterans. During a particularly galling loss at Boston, for example, Keenan ordered Larmer and veteran center Troy Murray to hit the showers after two periods. But the losing atmosphere could not be washed away.

"We used to be a tight, nervous locker room every day," center Mike Hudson recalled. "And he was a coach who would hold a meeting just to decide when our next meeting was."

Keenan had won with a graybeard leader, Yvon Lambert, in Rochester, and he had won with a young leader in Philadelphia, Dave Poulin. Neither Savard nor Wilson would or could fill such a role in Chicago. They just didn't have it in them. Savard, in particular, was much too sensitive to play for Keenan. He had an artist's mentality toward the sport; Keenan could coach only warriors. Savard didn't need long to become an emotional wreck. In fact, early in that first season, he admitted his head was a mess.

"I can't get excited about playing the games," he moped. "I know my attitude is hurting the team, but I don't know how to shake it. I want to be myself, be the player I am, play with excitement."

Keenan used hard practices to work Savard out of his haze. Quick-tempo drills are a building block in Keenan's system. Most of his practices are short, but all of them are intense. Savard didn't get it.

"I never have been a great practice player," he said during the early struggle. "I always thought I knew when it was time to push it, but I treated practice as fun. But Mike has asked me to be more consistent in my approach to practice and I'm trying. I'm trying to be a leader and practice hard every day."

One week, Keenan subjected the Blackhawks to not one but to two death skates. Each session was fifty minutes of hard skating with no pucks. Each skate left players cramping up and nauseated. During the second skate-athon, Savard simply stopped skating and headed off the ice. Wilson and fellow defenseman Keith Brown fetched him and brought him back. The next day, Savard apologized for trying to skate out on his teammates.

"I totally lost my mind that day," Savard explained. "I never had any real problem with Mike. We're both emotional and intense, and we both want to win, and he's made me learn how."

Two brutal sessions in one week might have seemed like overkill, but Keenan didn't think so. "Teams get too cozy," he said. "I don't like cozy. You can't win with flat-liners, not even with self-motivated flat-liners. You go first-class in everything, you give them charity, cleanliness, and comfort . . . and then you introduce confusion if need be. If you feel a sigh of relief on your team, even for a moment — bang! — you've got to shake them up. There must be a dynamic. If I'm completely unpredictable, the players have to stay focused. They have to always be thinking, 'When is the sonofabitch going to call on me?' I learn instantly who can be rocked."

The approach was harsh, but in the grand scheme of things, the life of a Blackhawk wasn't all that horrible. This was just hockey, after all, and the employees were well compensated.

"I've seen a lot of human failure, a lot of suffering," Keenan said. "We have to go on the ice and work for one or two hours? Are we really suffering because we have to come down here and exercise? Let's get real, boys."

Winger Rick Vaive didn't see it that way. He collapsed from leg cramps during one of the death skates. His relationship with Keenan was not good. Vaive, then twenty-nine, had scored 43 goals the year before for the mild-mannered Murdoch. But Keenan would not stroke him. During a 5–5 tie with Quebec on November 13, 1988, Vaive had two assists in the first two periods, but was benched in the third period. He was furious. After the game, his wife, Joyce, had to talk him out of quitting.

"I never really told anyone, but I mentioned it to my wife," Vaive said. "I was miserable. I don't like being miserable. The thought [of retiring] crossed my mind. After ten years in the league, it was ridiculous. I was very upset after the Quebec game. I got home that night and told my wife, 'That's it, I'm not going to practice tomorrow.'"

Joyce wisely told Rick to think about it for a few days. She said she would support him, but she wanted him to cool down before acting. Upon further review, he resolved not to let Keenan defeat him.

"I've never been a quitter," he said. "I thought, Why let one person do this to me? Why let it bother me and ruin my life? Forget it. I tried not to let it get to me."

Before long, Keenan suggested that massive changes could be in order. He doubted that the team's old core group could meet his standards. He pushed Pulford to acquire goaltender Tom Barrasso from the Buffalo Sabres. As a teenager, Barrasso had been one of the NHL's elite netminders. Though his play had slipped in recent years, he was still regarded as the cornerstone goaltender the Blackhawks needed. Of the team's remaining goalies, Ed Belfour was still a lightly regarded prospect, former number one pick Jimmy Waite wasn't ready for the NHL, and Alain Chevrier and Darren Pang weren't capable of stealing games for this team.

Ever cautious, Pulford couldn't make a deal and Barrasso went to Pittsburgh instead. Keenan stewed. His battle with Pulford had begun in earnest. Wirtz and Pulford talked a good game about wanting to win. Whether they had the resolve to make any move necessary to thrust the franchise out of its doldrums was another story.

"I told them when I came here the team had to change philosophies and, if they didn't want to, then they shouldn't have hired me," Keenan groused.

McGuire found those early days sobering. He had become accustomed to winning in Rochester and Philadelphia. He left the potentially strong Flyers to come to Chicago. He realized turning the Blackhawks around would be a big job, but the challenge was nearly overwhelming. His faith in Keenan was put to a stern test.

"We were two periods away from winning the Cup in Philadelphia and we believe we can get back there in Chicago or we wouldn't have come here," McGuire said early in the wretched first season. "I could have stayed in Philadelphia as an assistant. There is no way I'd have come here and hung my career on Keenan's hook if I didn't believe he was able to take the broad perspective and do what needs to be done with the team. He's learned to adjust.

"He's managed to channel his frustrations so far, but I think he's a little disappointed at how far we are from the Stanley Cup. The optimism of July has given way to the reality of December."

Some changes were finally made. Pulford shipped defensemen Gary Nylund and Marc Bergevin to the New York Islanders for Bob Bassen and Steve Konroyd. Vaive requested a trade and went to Buffalo for big center Adam Creighton, who became a Keenan favorite.

Greg Gilbert, who would also become a true Keenanite, came from the Islanders later in the season for a draft pick. Those who remained were urged to play faster, stronger, and harder.

"Mike wouldn't tolerate one bad practice or one bad shift," winger Steve Thomas recalled. "That's what made him different. Not one. Not even from a superstar."

The Blackhawks knew they were horrible. They understood what Keenan was trying to do. But that hardly made their task easier. The transformation was going to be painful and they were the ones who were going to hurt.

"What Mike expects from us, we never expected from ourselves," Troy Murray said. "I realized how much more of an effort I had to put in. He's always challenging us to go to a higher level. When you reach that one, you get pushed to another."

Keenan's ladder is high and the climb is difficult. When Creighton arrived from Buffalo, his new coach's demands shocked him. Keenan was in his face. Every meeting, every practice and every shift of every game brought the potential for more verbal abuse.

"I thought, Why does he keep bugging me like this? Why is he on me all the time?" he recalled. "I was too young or too stupid to realize he was trying to get the best out of me. And I thought he was trying to ridicule me and bring me down."

Bassen was also taken aback when he arrived from the Islanders and saw his new coach at work. He had never played for such a confrontational coach. He grew by learning to listen to coaches, absorbing their lessons, and putting those lessons to work. Now he was working for a guy who seemed to enjoy shouting matches. Insubordination energized him. Keenan seemed to think that a bad response from a player was better than no response.

"He demands a lot," Bassen said. "It's a big transition for guys. Either you wake up or you're gone. We were getting blitzed all the time. You had to be alert, even around the dressing room. He would challenge you. You had to be alert all the time, which can be good — you never get complacent — but you don't relax all that much. It's definitely good in the short run. A good example is, if you're fourth line and you don't have a good first shift, you're pretty much done for the night. You have to be ready to play. That can be good for guys. I mean, you're definitely sharp, right from the beginning of the game. You have to adjust to it or else it buries you."

The pace of the Blackhawks' practices startled newcomers. There was no let-up. When the Blackhawks worked, they worked. There was no joking, no fooling around, no daydreaming about lunch.

"It's high tempo, you don't take any breaks," Bassen said. "He just explains the drill and you go. He explains it very fast. That's how you play, too."

The Blackhawks staggered to a 27-41-12 record in 1988–89, Keenan's first season in Chicago. Normally, such a pathetic showing would send a team straight to the golf course for the summer, but this, again, was the Norris Division. Toronto somehow managed to be more awful and finished with four fewer points, so the Blackhawks backed into the playoffs.

In those more primitive times, the first two playoff rounds were played within a team's division, rather than against the whole conference. The Blackhawks drew the division champion Red Wings in the first round, but Detroit wasn't exactly a powerhouse in those days. The Red Wings won the Norris with a 34-34-12 record and brought a history of playoff underachievement into the series.

The Blackhawks upset the Red Wings in six games. Next up were the Blues, a very ordinary 33-35-12 team. Chicago won in five games and got their shot at the big, deep, and very physical Calgary Flames. The Blackhawks had found the energy to grind down the Red Wings and Blues with tough body checking, but they bounced off the Flames. Calgary, a virtual football team on skates, marched on to win the Stanley Cup.

Still, the two series victories finally established Keenan's program. The Blackhawks learned to play at the same tempo that Keenan worked them in practice. They learned to take advantage of their small, intimidating rink in the raucous Chicago Stadium. They were finally creaming opponents into the Stadium's famous tight corners.

"We definitely had a hard forecheck game, right in everybody's face," Bassen said. "There wasn't much trapping out there. Most teams trap now. Especially there, we had that small little building. We just jumped on teams. It can be very intimidating because you don't get any time. In that style, when you jump on guys and especially in a small rink, you don't have any time to do anything. That worked in that rink."

This success, the addition of a few more key role players, and the development of energetic center Jeremy Roenick pushed the Blackhawks forward in the 1989-90 season. With a hardy new leadership corps emerging in the dressing room, this formerly apathetic team was feeling juiced.

Roenick, Chicago's first pick in the 1988 entry draft, was the perfect addition. He had the makings of a classic Keenan player. He had great wheels and he could really staple a defenseman into the end boards. He wasn't as shifty as Savard, but Keenan didn't want shiftiness. He wanted his forwards to skate, hit, attack the net, and score.

Even before he arrived, Roenick had caught Keenan's eye. On the eve of the 1988 draft, he happened to be eating at the same restaurant as the Blackhawks contingent. As luck would have it, nature called Roenick at the same time it called Keenan. They ended up in the men's room at adjacent urinals. It was an odd place for a job interview.

"He asked me what I wanted to do in my life," Roenick said. "I just said I wanted to be a National Hockey League player. I said, 'If you draft me, you won't be sorry. I won't let you down.'"

And he didn't. Roenick fell in love with Keenan's aggressive puck-chasing scheme. He delivered crushing body checks that made enemy defensemen skittish, and developed into a point-per-game scorer. This evolution wasn't entirely natural; at one point during the preseason of Roenick's rookie year, Keenan grabbed him by the throat and suggested that he might want to start finishing some checks.

"There's a little psycho-ness in him, an unpredictability," Roenick said. "You didn't know what to expect one day to the next. Sometimes between periods, you'd have to cover up for fear of getting hurt. He'd just go nutso. He'd be swinging sticks and throwing skates."

Roenick insists he wasn't an inherently berserk player when he arrived. He had always been more of a finesse player, a scorer. Keenan located the "on" switch to his angry side and turned him loose on the league.

"I have always said that Mike Keenan created the role that I play in the National Hockey League, in terms of grittiness, feistiness, physicalness," he said. "He kind of instilled that fear in me that if I didn't play like that, I wouldn't play. I was like a hundred and sixty pounds when I came into the league, by far not a physical guy, not a gritty player at all. But I found myself having to battle for a roster spot because of the way Mike Keenan runs his regime. And in a way, I kind of didn't like it at the time. I grew into it. It's what the fans enjoyed and it really created a lot of opportunity for me and I got to enjoy it. I pretty much owe a lot of my career to how he perceived me and how he tried to make me into the player I am today."

To win, Keenan needed all his lines playing maniacally. Holdovers like Gilbert sustained their energy from the 1989 playoffs. Jocelyn Lemieux, a vicious hitter, arrived in a midseason trade from Montreal. Creighton got busy, despite his glacial skating stride.

Creighton was an intriguing project, a towering 6-feet-5-inch, 220-pound grinder with decent hands and awesome size. Given his limited quickness, however, he had to work extremely hard to be effective. Somehow, some way, Keenan goaded him into scoring 34 goals in 1989–90. It was an extraordinary coaching achievement.

"Mike is what I really needed, someone to drive that work ethic into my brain," Creighton explained. "Everybody always said I had the tools and the size, so why couldn't I put it together out there? He's tough, but he's the best thing for me, whether I know it or not."

Keenan has a flair for molding muckers into above-average players. "Sometimes those fourth liners were the ones who were near and dear to him," McGuire said. "Bob Bassen, God bless him, he's still playing on heart, not skill. It wasn't with Bobby — you know him, he's very religious — it wasn't an F-you contest as it so often was with Mike. Mike could turn on a challenge with Bob Bassen without using the F-word and get the most out of Bob Bassen."

Bassen regrets lasting just part of one season under Keenan. He finished the 1988–89 season and opened the following season in Chicago, but spent the bulk of the season with Indianapolis of the International Hockey League before moving on to the Blues for 1990–91. He had the speed and physical toughness to flourish in Keenan's system, but his meek countenance in the dressing room doomed him. Iron Mike didn't want players who retreated, even from him. Bassen wishes he had returned fire just once when Keenan came after him.

"The thing I wished I would have learned a little bit earlier was just to challenge a little bit more," he said. "I'd just sit there. You're taught to respect everyone and I respected him. I saw some guys that challenged him that he really had more respect for. A lot of kids grow up thinking, 'Don't say nothing, respect your coach.' But he likes a little bit of a response at times. It takes a while to figure out where the whole system is coming from. Especially the way I grew up, it goes against everything I grew up getting taught. Don't talk back to the teacher, you know. He didn't have guys challenge him all the time, but he thought you were a better person, you were ready, if you challenged back a little bit."

McGuire insists that Keenan really did treat the Blackhawks as individuals. He found a lot of the players' "on" switches, and those switches weren't always in the same place. Lemieux, for instance, was a flighty kid who got distracted in both St. Louis and Montreal. Keenan was able to reach him in a way no other coach had. All of Lemieux's other coaches had yelled at him. Keenan connected with him one on one.

"There are examples like that where he didn't treat everybody as a nail to hammer," McGuire said. "If he saw value in you as a player, where it was fourth-line value or Mark Messier value, he has a master psychologist's way to nurture that."

Keenan still used a real psychologist to spur his troops. Dr. Cal Botterill provided positive reinforcement to some of the holdovers struggling to meet Keenan's expectations. Botterill liked calling himself a "stretch" as opposed to a shrink. He wasn't there to make problems go away. He was there to help players do more with themselves.

"I joke with the players about not seeing me as a psychiatrist," Botterill said. "I'm not qualified for that job. I'm not a guru. I want to take the players further within themselves, develop the individual attributes that complement their physical talents. By myself, what I do won't make a difference. When the team had a bad spell before Christmas [in 1988] and again before the end of the regular season, it was a struggle to build their confidence. But we used team highlight videos to show them positive aspects of what they've done, and helped to work them through it."

Chicago's playoff success was just the reinforcement the team needed after years of abject failure. "This year, we've seen more resiliency than last year," Botterill said. "Now, they have to learn how to be the favorite. That takes a special respect and preparation. You have to finish teams off and stay respectful. Do you support each other or not? A team has to know players aren't going to bail out on one another. That was an easy thing to do in the past, but I think now player support for one another in Chicago is the strength of the club."

Defenseman Trent Yawney, a product of the Canadian national team, provided a typical challenge. His introspective personality made him a poor fit with a coach who used coarse competitive tension to sharpen his team. His confidence evaporated when Keenan buried him after a bad shift. Yawney became one of Botterill's best customers. During their sessions, Botterill explained what Keenan was trying to accomplish and explained how Yawney could relax and play hard at the same time.

"I was trying too hard to make the team and wasn't playing well as a result," Yawney said. "Cal took me aside and talked to me about it. After you talk to Cal, any negative thoughts are erased."

Keenan didn't want to have Botterill around all the time, however, because some of the players might have used him as a full-time crutch. His players needed to learn how to become self-starters. They had to learn how to cope with his demands and take responsibility for their play.

"They could consider it a quick-fix approach," Keenan said of Botterill. "They might think, 'I have a problem today, I'll call Cal and away it'll go.' They need time away from him to think about what he has said and work through it themselves."

Maturity as a coach also made Keenan's second-year surge possible. In Philadelphia, he had one of the best teams in the NHL, yet he allowed defeats to unhinge him. In Chicago, he had to remain sane through a 1988–89 season of near-constant futility. He saw more bad hockey in four months than he had seen in four years in Philly.

Rita was pleasantly surprised that her husband didn't crack up. He never came close to throwing himself off the Navy Pier.

"He was amazingly good last year," Rita said during the 1989–90 upturn. "I was really impressed. I mean, Mike is still a terrible loser, but he's not totally in another world after a loss like he used to be."

Losses evoked the same emotions as ever. He just handled them better. His recovery time improved greatly.

"I can't remember a time when losing wasn't a personal affront to him," McGuire said. "In the heat of battle, he'll still do anything or say anything that he thinks will help garner a victory. The difference is, he's quicker to mend it. Like right after the game. And then again the next day to make sure that it's healed properly."

He could actually joke with players and even help them as individuals. "Of course there were times in Philadelphia that he didn't kick the doors down, but the players remember only when he did," McGuire said. "He got a reputation and the Chicago players may have braced themselves for the worst. The guys see him and realize he may not be as big a jerk as everybody said he was."

Roenick had some memorable heart-to-heart talks with Keenan, discussions that helped mold him as a player and a person. He learned that his coach really did care about players who cared.

"I was going through a difficult situation off the ice my first couple of years with some personal stuff," Roenick said. "Mike was the guy who was there, who always called me, who asked me to come in and brought me to certain people that could help me. He came to my house, picked me up, and made sure that I was emotionally stable. Not many people would go out of their way to make sure that everything was okay for a player off the ice as well as on. I know a couple different sides of Mike that other people don't. He's a stickler to play for, but he is a very caring man. He does care about people he loves and I think that's very important."

Keenan wasn't really a heartless martinet, he just played the part of one at Chicago Stadium. Inflicting psychological abuse never seemed to affect Bowman, an aloof coach whom very few people get to know. Keenan still had a gregarious side that had to be fed. Relationships meant something to him. Some coaches seem to enjoy bullying players for the sport of it, like kids frying ants with a magnifying glass. Keenan insisted that wasn't the case for him.

"I don't find it easy being difficult on people," Keenan said. "Some people can do that in a less confrontational way than I have. Don't think I haven't had a few restless nights. It's hard on me. It would be a hell of a lot easier for me to be a nice guy. But there is no comfort zone for me and there can't be for any of the people working with us."

The danger with this approach is that discomfort can wear down a team. Staying on edge is hard work during the course of a hockey season, which can span more than a hundred preseason, regular season, and playoff games. McGuire saw how the Flyers burned out even while making the playoffs four seasons in a row and reaching the Stanley Cup finals twice. A fragile team can't stay on edge forever.

"Negative energy is fuel, but it isn't the best fuel," McGuire said. "You need gas to get across the desert, and if all they have is leaded, you use it. But when you get across, you better get that carburetor clean or the car is going to break down. Over a season, the motivation has to be primarily positive."

Hence Keenan's willingness to lighten up at least a little bit. Goaltender Jacques Cloutier, who arrived in midseason, brought with him some harrowing horror stories. He had played for Keenan in Rochester during the Amerks' championship run when Mike's approach was much more raw.

"Mike is a tough man, but very, very honest with his players," Cloutier said. "He's more demanding than any coach I played for — and I had both Scott Bowman and Ted Sator — and he makes sure his guys work like dogs out there. But sometimes a work ethic like that wins games for you. I've known Mike for a long time. Study him? Forget it. Our job is to be able to handle what he gives us when he gives it to us. Otherwise, you go crazy."

The Blackhawks improved markedly in 1989–90. They opened with a 14-6-1 surge that trumpeted their re-emergence. But an 0-6-1 slump prompted Keenan to badger Pulford for more deals.

"We're the only team in the league that hasn't made a major trade in a year," Keenan observed.

But change was afoot. Savard's team was transforming into Roenick's team. His fierce forechecking became the team's trademark. Steve Thomas followed suit, blowing up and down the wing to score 40 goals. The earnest Larmer was also at his peak, leading the team in scoring with 90 points. The ferocious Dirk Graham followed his 33-goal season of 1988–89 with a 22-goal season and lots of big hitting. There was no place for Savard, at least not the Savard who wanted to carry the puck into the offensive zone and try his famed "spin-o-rama" move. The Blackhawks dumped the puck in, chased it, and banged on the defense.

The team built its intensity shift by shift, hoping to break down opponents piece by piece. Untimely Savard turnovers in the middle of the ice could have killed that momentum. Keenan rode him constantly about his playing style. Savard was about as far from Dave Poulin as a NHL forward could be.

"It was always down, down, down with Keenan, lowering your self-esteem," Savard said as his rift with Keenan widened. "That might work one year, maybe two, but when you work like that for many years it reaches the point where you can't take it anymore."

Roenick felt Keenan's wrath, too, but he handled it better than Savard did. He has a stubborn, strong-willed personality. He was more likely to clash with a coach than sulk about perceived mistreatment.

"He was verbally abusive, very," Roenick said. "Was it destructive? That would depend on how strong a person is. I've seen people wilt under his verbal wrath. I've seen people fire back, which I think he enjoys, because he wants to see a response. He doesn't mind guys telling him what he can do with himself. That's what he wants to see."

The evolving Blackhawks earned a 41-33-6 record in 1989–90 and won the Norris Division title. They beat the Minnesota North Stars and the Blues in the playoffs, winning each series in the seventh game, and took a two-games-to-one lead over speedy Edmonton in the Western Conference championship series.

The Oilers recovered, won the series in six games, and went on to beat Boston for the Stanley Cup. But the Blackhawks knew they were close. The program was in place and the regime was on a roll. It seemed inevitable that long-suffering Blackhawks fans would finally see their team play for the Stanley Cup.

During the playoff series with the Blues, Savard was sent home from the team's hotel in Chicago after he and Keenan had another blow-up. Once again, Savard responded badly when challenged by his coach.

"Mike had a list of all the older guys he wanted to see in private meetings and I wasn't on it," Savard explained. "He did that on purpose because he was trying to tell me I wasn't a leader anyway. Then he says he wants to see me in his room that night at nine o'clock. I was frustrated because it did no good to talk to him. He asked me for my opinion, then felt everything I said was wrong.

"I told him, 'If you want to talk, let's talk straight. What are you trying to do with me? If you don't play me more in games, we're not going anywhere in the playoffs. I'm willing to sacrifice and do whatever, but I can't do anything if you don't play me.' He got upset at that, and I said, 'Don't scream at me. Talk to me like a man. I'm old enough. You act like you want me to go home.' He said, 'Yeah, why don't you go home.' So I left because he told me to."

In a vintage Iron Mike move, Keenan asked the Blackhawks to vote on whether Savard should return to the team. Savard won the referendum, but irreparable damage had been done. Once Keenan gave up on a player, that was that.

"There was a feeling I wouldn't go to bat for the team," Savard later said. "He questioned my leadership, but I'm not one of those phony screamers in the dressing room. I don't lead that way. He put me to the wall so many times."

Later in the playoffs against the Oilers, Savard didn't get a broken finger frozen because he thought it was feeling better. When Keenan found out, he benched Savard for nineteen minutes. He figured Savard would inevitably struggle because of the injury. In Keenan's eyes, not freezing the finger was a selfish act.

"The point was if he wasn't going to get it frozen, he could have given the team a better alternative by having someone healthy in the lineup," Keenan said after the benching. "That was the only point of contention."

Though Savard hadn't bought into Keenan's program, the Blackhawks were on the right track. Though Savard, his favorite player, was in peril, Wirtz liked what he saw on the ice. Keenan had promised to build a winner and win. The Blackhawks were winning. For the time being, Wirtz stood firmly behind his tempestuous coach.

"We brought in Mike to do exactly what he's doing, to have a competitive club and change the culture of the club," Wirtz said. "We like everyone fearing us when they come into our building. We're moving in the right direction. That's the main thing."

Keenan's contract called for him to become general manager in 1990. Wirtz saw no reason not to give Keenan more control. Keenan had earned some trust by making encouraging progress. Step by step, he appeared to be building a winning operation. Eagleson's arranged marriage looked like it might last.

"Mike doesn't want to hopscotch around from job to job," Wirtz said. "He is looking for an organization he can make a long-term commitment to and that's the kind of guy we're interested in. Just look at his record. It's world class."

This confidence earned Keenan the right to trade Savard for defenseman Chris Chelios of the Montreal Canadiens on June 29, 1990. It was a defining moment in Keenan's career. He had won a battle with the most belligerent superstar he had ever encountered. He had gained real power in the Blackhawks organization, having traded Wirtz's favorite player. And he demonstrated some personnel acumen, too, acquiring a Norris Trophy winner for a finesse player who would eventually melt down in the high-pressure Montreal market.

Wirtz felt pained to okay this trade. "I won't sleep for three or four nights," he said. "Denis Savard is the most electrifying hockey player I've ever seen. I put him in the same class with Bobby Hull."

Wirtz still kicked himself for letting Hull go. Deep down, Savard didn't believe Wirtz would let him go, too. Chicago had become his home. He had become a sports icon there and was setting up a good life after hockey.

When he got word of the trade, he was playing golf at the Butler National course in Oakbrook, Illinois. Keenan's call didn't last long.

"Fifteen seconds, tops," Savard recalled. "I said, 'Mike, I appreciate the comments. I'm on a golf course. Goodbye.'"

But the news devastated him, even though the deal was sending him back home to Montreal. Savard shot a twelve on the next hole. Later, while discussing the trade with reporters, his anger and frustration became clear.

"I'm a little surprised that Keenan is running the whole show," he said. "I'm disappointed, but it will be the best thing. He pulled me off the golf course and told me I was gone. He gave me no reason. Maybe it was personal, maybe not. I don't know. For two years, I tried to read him. Keenan would tell me something one day, that he loved me and wouldn't trade me. Then he'd tell me something that's completely different the next day. Keenan told me a lot of things. I don't think he wanted me to do well. Now, I'll be able to play hockey again where they want me to do well. I don't have to read him anymore. I can't say that I dislike the guy. It wasn't like we were always fighting. Not everything he's done is bad. But he's just different. I've met a lot of people in my life, and he's just different.

"I couldn't figure Mike out. I could never do what I wanted to do. I'm a gambler. In the offensive zone, sometimes I'd like to try a move that is everything or nothing. That doesn't mean if I lose the puck I won't be back for defense. But if the move works, I might be clear to the net. I couldn't do that with Mike. If I didn't throw the puck in deep, he said I wasn't going to play. For his system and style, I was worth nothing.

"Also, it's important for me, as a person, to be liked. I know if I'm not liked, I don't feel good about myself. That's just the way I am. Not that I can't take criticism — I know sometimes I deserved it — but I felt sometimes he was trying to make an example of me. I'm a caring person, and when I get my feelings hurt every day, I can't respond."

The Savard deal signaled the end of the star system in Chicago. Everybody would play the same style of game and like it — or leave it.

"You know what an entertaining guy Savard was," McGuire said. "At the time, Michael Jordan hadn't won anything in Chicago, yet he was filling the old Chicago Stadium. The Blackhawks were filling it with Denis Savard. To trade him for Chris Chelios — albeit Chris was a homegrown Chicago, Illinois, product — was a tough sell for Mr. Wirtz. It was all about winning a championship."

Keenan's big regret with Savard is that he didn't get him out of Chicago sooner. He was never going to be a Keenan-type player. Trying to make him into one of his soldiers was just a waste of time. Savard, who had been a 40-goal scorer in his three seasons prior to Keenan's arrival, scored only 50 goals in two seasons under Keenan. And their public feud made for an unpleasant distraction, since many media members sided with the personable Savard.

"I wouldn't listen," Keenan said. "I kept believing I could change him. Instead, I challenged him and he challenged me in the limelight. And it was probably completely unnecessary."

The trade, and the bickering that preceded it, was big news in Chicago. Keenan took a major public relations hit with this trade, but the blockbuster deal began paying dividends quickly. The 1990–91 Blackhawks took off, with Chelios teaming with Roenick and Larmer to lead the way. Larmer had a career year, scoring 101 points. Roenick scored 41 goals and Chelios patrolled the blue line with a snarl, providing an element the franchise had sorely lacked. The Blackhawks outworked and outhit opponents on a nightly basis. Keenan challenged them to give even more and they did.

"There are no days off with Mike," Larmer said. "He never lets up on you, especially at a time when you think you've accomplished something and start feeling satisfied. He forces you up one level, and just when you're stuck he'll push you to the next. Any way he has to."

The Savard-Chelios swap reduced greatly the amount of whining heard in the dressing room. When the team's undisputed leader is unhappy, everybody feels free to grouse about the coach. The atmosphere he walked into didn't shock Chelios.

"Hey, this is a job," he said midway through the season. "It's the same thing everywhere. Everybody complains on every team. With the Canadiens in 1986, guys were lined up to get at [coach] Jean Perron's throat. We won it all anyway."

Chicago was a rugged team, with nine players earning more than 100 penalty minutes. Goon tactics were still a big part of hockey and Keenan was an enthusiastic proponent. He had no shortage of willing combatants on this team. Among his most irritable players was Ed Belfour, who emerged, Ron Hextall–like, as a bulwark goaltender and another piece of the championship puzzle.

Belfour was precisely what Keenan wanted in a player. Conversely, goaltender Jimmy Waite, the eighth overall pick of the 1987 draft, was the polar opposite.

"Eddie Belfour thrived under Mike," McGuire said. "Jimmy Waite, who has more potential to this day, is still a great textbook goalie or whatever. Mentally, Mike could jump on him and he said, 'I guess I still do suck.' Eddie Belfour said, 'Fuck you I suck. Put me back in there and I'll show you.'"

Sometimes, McGuire admits, Keenan simply pushed potentially good players too far. His impatience created some waste.

"There may have been people he didn't gauge right, he didn't guess right," McGuire said. "Maybe if Jimmy Waite, with all his talent, was handled with kid gloves, You're all right, kid, come on . . . but he didn't have time for that." A similar case was Dominik Hasek, a strange little goaltender who broke in during the 1990–91 season after a decorated career in Europe. Keenan had little use for him.

"Hasek drops his stick, picks up the puck with his blocker hand. It looked like he can't play," McGuire said. "Now we had Ed Belfour, so it wasn't like we were running with Joe Smith or someone else. But [Keenan] certainly wasn't always right."

Because Belfour was as combative as his coach, he had some notable run-ins with Keenan. One came during a 5–4 loss to the Flyers December 9 at Chicago Stadium. After the Flyers scored to take a 2–1 lead midway through the first period, Keenan pulled Belfour and sent in Cloutier. When Belfour got the signal to come out, he threw up his hands at Keenan. When he got to the bench, he ignored Keenan, who was trying to explain what he had done. Keenan grabbed Belfour by the sweater, put his face to Belfour's mask and screamed at his goaltender. The crowd immediately rallied behind Belfour, chanting "Ed-die, Ed-die." After fifty seconds, Keenan sent Belfour back into the game.

"I was mad," Belfour said after the game. "He yelled at me, I yelled back. We yelled at each other. He told me I have to be ready, that I shouldn't give up goals like that. He told me to stay ready."

Keenan denied putting Belfour back in to shut up the Blackhawks fans.

"I didn't even consider it," he said. "What am I supposed to do, let the crowd coach?"

With Savard gone, Keenan focused his attention on the recalcitrant Doug Wilson. He knew Wilson would never be his type of player. When the Blackhawks assembled for their team photograph, Keenan changed the seating chart to move Wilson into a secondary spot in the back row. This was one more way of telling Wilson he was no longer a cornerstone player for the franchise.

During practice on February 19, 1991, Keenan had his finest Iron Mike moment of the season. With the Blackhawks botching drills left and right, Keenan unleashed a stream of profanities at the team. He hurled his stick into the Chicago Stadium seats. He ordered the team off the ice.

Blackhawks captain Dirk Graham told the team to stay at the bench. He went nose to nose with Keenan.

"We're staying here," Graham said.

"You don't want to work!" Keenan shouted. "And I'm not talking about you. I'm talking about them!" He spread his arms in the direction of the team, implicating everybody else for their slothfulness. "You may as well go home. We're kidding ourselves."

The exchange continued and Graham got his way. The Blackhawks jumped back on the ice and resumed their drills.

"I was getting their attention," Keenan explained. "They stop listening when you're winning and everybody is telling them they are the hardest working team in the league. When you lose a few games, they start listening again."

Not all the Blackhawks were hearing him. "Too bad we didn't have a pacifier to throw him," one player told the Chicago *Tribune*. Others felt the scene at practice was staged. Former Calgary Flames coach Terry Crisp, in town as a scout, advised reporters to check what was going on behind the curtain. Coaches, he said, sometimes were terrific actors.

But Keenan was right about this team. The Blackhawks finished with a stellar 49-23-8 record, then soiled their sheets in the playoffs. The surprising Minnesota North Stars, who would eventually lose in the finals to the Pittsburgh Penguins, knocked out Chicago in the first round.

The Blackhawks were a mess. They were undisciplined on the ice, taking lots of penalties with needlessly dirty play, and they were dispirited in the dressing room. The players groused openly about a Keenan practice before Games Three and Four of the series. Then they tanked Game Five, losing 6–0.

"We're pretty down," center Troy Murray said after the debacle. "This was a 20-man disorganization out there."

Wilson suffered a lacerated jaw in the Game Five loss. He wanted to play in Game Six at Minnesota, but was left at home by Keenan. He flew to Minnesota on his own and volunteered to play. Keenan wouldn't play him and the team lost.

"Then for him to come out and say I couldn't play is incorrect," Wilson said. "If you say something, say it face to face."

Keenan and Wilson had come to the end of their road. Wilson had endured enough public spankings. "I told Mike how I felt about our relationship," Wilson said. "I don't think things should be handled that way."

The popular Blackhawks veteran requested a trade to San Jose and was sent to the Sharks before the following season. The Blackhawks got minor-league enforcer Kerry Toporowski and a second-round draft pick.

"Even if I could have shopped him to other teams, we wouldn't have gotten any more at his age." Keenan sniffed. "I'm pleased with the deal. Doug's at a point in his career where the league has changed. Defensemen are bigger and faster than when he came into the league."

The two continued to parry after the deal was made. "I'm probably the happiest hockey player in Chicago right now," Wilson said at his farewell news conference, held at the suburban offices of Coca-Cola, where he worked during the off-season. "I wanted to come here and thank everybody . . . well, not everybody."

Keenan fired back from Team Canada's Canada Cup training camp, where he was preparing to lead his country to international glory. "Doug's upset because he didn't play his final game here," he said. "He lets that fact cloud the fact we went to two conference finals since I've gotten here, we've come from the twenty-first team in the NHL to first place, his salary more than doubled under me."

But Wilson, like Savard, was miserable playing for Keenan. And Wilson, like Savard, couldn't play well when he was unhappy.

"Looking back, I probably should have made my decision after Denis left," Wilson said after getting traded. "It hasn't been the same without him. No one should have to go through what he went through. It would have been wrong to try and stick it out here. I've played hockey thirty years and to not go to the rink and enjoy it, have fun with it, I could never imagine that. I wasn't enjoying it. You can't play to expectations if it's not fun."

Keenan figured he didn't come to Chicago to run a recreation center or a resort. He came to Chicago to win, and neither Savard nor Wilson was able to play to his stringent standards. Like "Iron Mike" Ditka, the bellicose Chicago Bears coach who built his own NFL champion in the

Windy City, Keenan wanted to build a team that would use all means necessary to win games. Wilson and Savard weren't willing to turn their entire selves over to their mercurial coach.

"That's exactly why I traded them," Keenan said. "They didn't win. I feel I was loyal and patient with them. Our objective is to win, and it wasn't happening with this organization when I arrived."

After the Wilson trade, Keenan was in no mood to stage an Oprah-like discussion on the matter. He didn't want to examine why the relationship didn't work. So what if the two didn't get along? This sport was about winning and Wilson wouldn't take the steps necessary to win.

"The issue of our relationship is a distraction from what had to be done," Keenan said. "He didn't win here and Denis didn't win here and you have to accept the realities of the game. What's fun for guys like Wayne Gretzky is winning."

And winning is what Keenan did at the 1991 Canada Cup. This time, both the Czechs and Russians were shells of their former selves. The United States, Sweden, and Finland presented the biggest challenge to the reigning kings.

Once again, Keenan refused to build a pure all-star team. His coaching staff bid adieu to Steve Yzerman again, along with Adam Oates, Joe Sakic, and Mark Recchi. Lemieux and Ray Bourque were ailing. But Keenan imported grit by bringing Steve Larmer and Dirk Graham along from his Blackhawks.

"The idea was to pick people who would make the necessary sacrifices," the coach said. "We selected the lineup most likely to win the tournament, though not necessarily the most entertaining or thrilling one."

Graham defended his presence on this team of legends. "A team can't have all one kind of player," he said. "You need different aspects, and I try to play my game. A lot of what's here in this dressing room, we already have in Chicago. Good people like Larmer, Roenick, Chelios."

Gretzky's leadership would prove invaluable to Keenan again. "What we're trying to do in six weeks, basically, is what NHL clubs expect to accomplish over a period of years," Gretzky said. "And the frustrating thing, in a way, is that just when you start getting the perfect blend, the tournament's over and you go back to your regular teams."

Dr. Cal Botterill joined Canada as the team psychologist. He got quite a learning experience watching Gretzky ready himself for war.

"He mentally prepares for games probably better than any hockey player ever has," Botterill said during the tournament. "He anticipates the opposition, he goes over their lineup, he prepares himself to handle the kind of demands that's going to produce for him. He gets ready for the various conditions he may have to play through in terms of distractions or pressure. He prepares his responses in advance."

Canada cruised into the championship round, then dispatched Sweden to meet the United States. The Americans had beaten Finland to earn a spot in the finals, and seemed ready to finally follow up on their "Miracle on Ice" Olympic victory of 1980.

But Canada won Game One 4–1. Game Two was tied 2–2 after two periods, after Team Canada squandered a 2–0 lead. In the dressing room, Graham stood up and told the players to stop fighting themselves. He had made the same speech several times for Keenan's Blackhawks.

"We hit a rut and things were going in the wrong direction," Graham said. "We had to straighten things out between the players and the coaches."

Tocchet always respected Graham, but he really connected with him at that moment. "He basically stood up and said we have a lot of ten- and twelve-year veterans and we should relax out there," Tocchet said.

In the third period, Larmer scored the title-winning goal on a short-handed breakaway. And Graham, appropriately enough, iced the championship with an empty-netter. Canada won, 4–2. The blue-collar guys had led the way.

"Larmer taught me about being a two-way player," center Eric Lindros said. "He and Graham don't get the credit they deserve. Graham took some heat, some criticism, when he came here, so I'm glad he showed everybody was wrong about him."

This tournament might have marked the last time Canada would tower over international competition. "We are the first team in the history of the Canada Cup to go through the entire tournament undefeated," center Mark Messier said. "At this level, against this competition, that's unbelievable."

Gretzky loved the work ethic this Keenan-built team demonstrated after just a few weeks together. Perhaps this is the sort of team Canada should always take into international play.

"We didn't have a Guy Lafleur or Mike Bossy or Mario Lemieux," Gretzky said. "But we had four lines that just kept rolling over the boards, getting the job done. Mike never really had to shorten our bench, and that certainly wasn't the case in 1987 or in the tournaments before that. No question, this is the best Canada team ever."

The same could have been said about Keenan. He had never been better.

With Wilson gone — along with Troy Murray and Wayne Presley, two more veteran Blackhawks at loggerheads with their coach — the 1991–92 Blackhawks were truly Keenan's team.

"Mike has helped the club. That's evident from us going to 106 points last year from 88 points his second year and 66 points his first year," Presley said before being traded to San Jose. "But the way he deals with people, it's tough to handle. The pressure he puts on you is difficult. I hate to lose just like he hates to lose. But after a loss, I think positively about what I can do better next time. Mike dwells negatively on the loss and harps on us not being prepared. He's a hard man to figure out."

But Bill Wirtz didn't have a hard time figuring out the bottom line: Keenan was winning. He rushed to the defense of his coach with a sarcastic rebuttal.

"Wilson said he wasn't having fun playing in Chicago anymore, so we sent him somewhere where he can play golf year-round," Wirtz sniffed. "I hope he has a lot of fun doing that in San Jose. He can't play golf year-round in Chicago. I never understood Wilson's remarks. For the salaries players get today, I expect them to practice every day, play three or four games a week and get fun out of winning. Now Wilson can go back to golfing three days a week in San Jose. I don't even know what he's talking about when he says he wants to have fun. Wilson wants to play until he's forty-six. I guess he has a chance to do that with an expansion club."

As for Presley, Wirtz said, "Wayne could be a decent player if he would just shut up and play hockey, discontinue his attitude. I hope he and Wilson enjoy themselves and have fun in San Jose."

The season began with the usual controversy. Just three games in, Trent Yawney decided he was tired of being made an example of. He met with Keenan after being scratched from the lineup in the first three games and went home to await a trade.

"I know what Yawney is going through, I feel for him," Wilson said from California. "To me, it's obvious Yawney's too good a player not to play. But I'm just a Shark, here in sunny California. That other stuff is behind me."

Yawney walked away from the Blackhawks, having decided that he, like Wilson, could take no more. In retrospect, he regards the Keenan experience as a positive in his life. Just as joining the Marines can build character in a hurry, playing for Iron Mike can transform a young man.

"I think, when I look back on my career now, I think it was a good thing for me, but maybe not to some of the extremes," he said. "He definitely made me mentally tougher than I thought I was. You always think you are mentally tough until you run into some adversity. I grew from that. When I look at my career with him, he pushed me hard during the year, but I got to play in the playoffs, so it was all forgotten. In a lot of cases it did benefit me. There is a fine line and I think he'd be a guy who'd tell you as his career progressed, as time has gone, he's had to change. Scotty Bowman hasn't coached as long as he has without changing. Mike is the same. He's a pretty bright guy. He knows as the game changes, players change and your tactics have to change as well."

Yawney became a student of coaching and after his playing career was over became an assistant coach with the Blackhawks. He came to understand the components of Keenan's program and their origins. He especially appreciated how Keenan organized his practices and travel to allow his teams to focus on hockey.

"The thing with Mike — and I read different articles about different coaches — is that he was a lot like [former New York Knicks coach] Pat Riley," Yawney said. "He gave the player the opportunity to succeed because everything around him was taken care of for him. I know when he came to Chicago, they never really had a travel director. He brought that in. All those little knick-knacks that some teams don't have, he brought them in so the players couldn't concentrate on playing the game. That was important. There is no question, when he came to Chicago he changed the culture of the whole organization and brought in a winning feeling."

Yawney was traded to Calgary for Stephane Matteau, but not until two months later. Agent Herb Pinder wasn't pleased about that. His client had to go to Chicago's farm team in Indianapolis to skate off some rust while waiting for Keenan to do something.

"I represent players and I like to stay in the background," Pinder said before Yawney was finally dealt. "But enough is enough. Anybody can see what's happening. Keenan got rid of institutions in Chicago like Doug

Wilson, Denis Savard, and Troy Murray. Dave Manson questioned Keenan's ways, and Manson's gone. Now Yawney challenged Keenan and is being punished, which is all rather ironic.

"Everybody else — including the owner, Bill Wirtz, and the vice president, Bob Pulford — feels that Trent should be the number three defenseman on the Blackhawks, behind Chelios and [Steve] Smith. But Keenan said Trent wasn't assertive enough. So Trent asserts himself in the strongest way possible. Do you realize how hard it is for a young player to turn in his skates to make a point? And Keenan is trying to bury Trent when all Trent wants to do is play. Elsewhere.

"This is Keenan's history, though. He is so obsessed with what he thinks will win in the end, he doesn't win. Never has. It's corrosive to team morale. You don't think those other players who like and respect Trent don't see what's going on? They might be too afraid to talk, but they know. Keenan has debased an asset. He's taken a number three defenseman and made him no better than seventh, just to show everybody who's in control.

"Well, I talk with other general managers and they're fed up trying to deal with Keenan. I can't speak for Mr. Wirtz and Mr. Pulford, but I don't think it's any secret that there's been a lot of infighting for quite a while. It's all quite bizarre. Keenan doesn't tell the truth to other people in the league. I wonder if he lies like that to his own people. Where does this all end? You have a basically insecure man being a tyrant. Wirtz and Pulford have to be embarrassed."

Keenan decided significant change was in order. He sent Adam Creighton, a sudden former favorite, and Steve Thomas to the Islanders for Brent Sutter and Brad Lauer. Thomas had finally cracked. Like Wilson and Yawney, he had his fill of Keenan and couldn't function on the ice as a result.

"He pitted you against your teammates," Thomas said after leaving. "He always made you feel you were letting them down. Eventually, he drove us physically and mentally insane."

Yawney's exit created an opening for Igor Kravchuk, a veteran of the Soviet hockey system. He played lots of international hockey for Russian taskmaster Viktor Tikhonov, a man who kept an iron grip on his players during his heyday in the old Soviet Union. Keenan was hardly a shock to his system.

"I went through Tikhonov, who thought he was the god of hockey,"

Kravchuk said. "From the perspective of toughness, he was never happy. Win, lose, he was never happy. That's something [Keenan] had in common with him."

Another key trade was the acquisition of rugged Edmonton defenseman Steve Smith, who came from the Oilers for Dave Manson. Smith was a powerful blue liner who had won it all in Edmonton. He had excelled under the tough-minded Glen Sather and he quickly took to Keenan.

"When I got traded to Chicago from Edmonton, I called my agent and asked if this was something that was good for me," Smith would later say. "He told me to go ahead, that Mike would help my career. It was the best thing that would ever happen to me. He's always reading books about great motivators in history, leaders and dictators like Mussolini, trying to learn from them."

Keenan kept trying to add grit to his lineup. He believed he had a deal with San Jose to land checking center Kelly Kisio, but the teams didn't report the trade to the league offer until after the trading deadline. The NHL nullified the deal. The Blackhawks appealed, but the board of governors was unmoved.

An irritated Keenan accused the North Stars of blocking the deal. Minnesota general manager Bobby Clarke, Keenan's boss in Philadelphia, dismissed this claim and fired back at his old coach.

"Keenan lies all the time," Clarke said. "He just lies. I'm sick and tired of him blaming other people all the time. It's never Mike's fault."

The 1991–92 Blackhawks slipped a bit in the regular season, finishing 36-29-15, but caught fire in the playoffs. They won eleven straight games while dispatching the Blues, Red Wings, and Oilers to reach the Stanley Cup finals against Mario Lemieux's explosive Pittsburgh Penguins. Keenan was at one with his team. He had had some tremendous springs in coaching, but this post-season push ranked with the best. Almost everything he tried worked.

"He's a risk taker and I have always respected him for that," Rita said. "He realized he was taking a chance, but he goes with his instincts. He is very intuitive. For example, I might ask him, 'Why did you use Ed Belfour?' And he'll say, 'I just had a feeling.'"

Keenan was thrilled to face his mentor, Bowman, in the Stanley Cup finals. Scotty had come back to coaching in 1991, when Penguins coach Bob Johnson became gravely ill. Now the mentor would face his pupil in hockey's greatest showcase.

"I'm looking forward to it," Keenan said as Game One approached. "You're up against a guy who is regarded as possibly the best bench manager in the game."

The Blackhawks flew into the Cup finals. They built a three-goal lead in Game One against the Penguins, but the good times would not last. The Blackhawks blew a pair of three-goal leads, lost the game, lost their confidence, and never got it back.

Keenan unloaded on his key players, like Roenick and Belfour. He was shocked when the international hockey media made a big fuss about his behavior.

"I didn't say Belfour was a bad goalie or not a competitor or not a playoff performer at this level," Keenan said. "I said he had a bad day. I don't understand why you people are so critical of a coach who tells the truth. I don't know what you want from a coach."

Still rattled in Game Two, Keenan sat Roenick for much of a 3–1 loss. With media critics howling, Keenan sought to deflect criticism by trotting out Roenick and showing the world that J.R. had a cast on his right wrist.

"Questions?" Keenan asked.

Roenick really was hurt, as luck would have it, but media skepticism remained. Was this playoff gamesmanship by Keenan? Was he covering his butt?

The Roenick affair was quickly forgotten after the highly skilled Penguins deftly countered the Blackhawks' forechecking pressure and swept them off the ice. But Keenan would remember these Blackhawks as one of his favorite teams. Like the Flyers, they squeezed everything out of their talent. But also like the Flyers, they ran into a more talented team. The Wayne Gretzky–led Oilers were the bane of Keenan's existence in Philadelphia and Lemieux's Penguins kept him from winning it all in Chicago. Had the Blackhawks faced a lesser nemesis than Super Mario, they might have been able to regroup and win the Cup.

"The one great thing about that Chicago club was that the players understood my intensity and passion as a coach," Keenan said. "It was part of our whole personality. Our entire team thrived on it. We got great results from it. Disagreements with coaching decisions might be sensational, but they often get left in the room. Take Ed Belfour, for example. We had a confrontation on the bench in Chicago [Keenan grabbed him by the sweater during a nose-to-nose shouting match], but it in no way affected Eddie's play on the ice. We went on to the Stanley Cup finals with great help from Eddie."

But Keenan was spent. He says he had considered retiring after Game One of the Cup finals, after a blown three-goal lead and some unfavorable calls by referee Andy van Hellemond threw him into a two-day rage. The combined role of coach and general manager was exhausting, especially on a team making a Cup run.

Immediately after the finals, Wirtz wanted to know where Keenan stood on coaching. Was he ready to commit for the long haul? At the time, coaching prospect Darryl Sutter, a favorite of Wirtz and Pulford, was starting to attract job offers. The Los Angeles Kings wanted to hire him.

The Blackhawks didn't want to let Sutter go unless Keenan was going to coach their team for a long time. They wanted to sign him to a contract extension to ensure stability. If Keenan wasn't ready to extend his deal, they wondered if he would step aside, let Sutter take the helm of the team, and concentrate on his duties as general manager.

"I thought that was unfair," Keenan said. "I was exhausted, to put it bluntly, and Darryl had a contract. He wasn't going anywhere. It was unfair to ask me to make that decision six days after the Cup."

Still frustrated over getting swept in the Cup finals, Keenan must not have been thinking straight. He agreed to give Sutter the team for the 1992–93 season. He succumbed to pressure applied by a nervous management team.

"Mike knew that Darryl was going to have the opportunity to go and coach elsewhere," Blackhawks counsel Gene Gozdecki later recalled. "If Darryl goes and we can't renew Mike's contract, then we don't have a coach. We'd be left high and dry."

Keenan was briefly satisfied to be an executive. As general manager, he was at his best at the 1992 NHL Entry Draft. He wheeled and dealed. He believed he had a blockbuster deal completed with Quebec for Eric Lindros, who would have been a megastar in Chicago. But Wirtz blanched at the price tag and pulled back. That left the Rangers and Flyers as the two teams left in the Lindros sweepstakes.

Belfour would have been included in that trade, so the Blackhawks probably would never have traded Hasek later that summer. How good would the Blackhawks have been with Roenick, Lindros, Chelios, and Hasek to build around? Hasek went on to become the best goaltender in the world. Keenan probably would have won the Stanley Cup with that team.

Those robust Chicago hockey fans would have been in heaven with Roenick, Lindros, and Chelios on the same team. The Blackhawks' rivals would have been skating for their lives.

After the draft, Keenan unwound at his cottage retreat on Ontario's Georgian Bay. He went boating. He fished. He tried to catch up on his family life.

"At the cottage, it's a 360-degree difference," Rita said.

He began recovering from the emotional grind of the playoffs and started second-guessing his decision to step back from coaching. He began to resent the fact Wirtz and Pulford had put him on the spot.

Keenan agreed, in principle, to a contract extension as general manager. He would make $2 million over five years and would get to spend more time with his wife and teenage daughter. After the grueling run to the Stanley Cup finals, this career shift sounded like a good idea. But Keenan is a stress freak who lives off adrenaline rushes. Scouting rivals, charting the growth of minor leaguers, and watching Blackhawks games from the executive suite didn't suit his personality one bit. He had never sat still in his life, not in college, not as a junior hockey coach, not now.

He looked deep inside himself. Did he really want to quit coaching? Could he really do something else with his life? After all these years and all these games, could he really leave the battle behind?

"If he were to choose another career, I don't think he would be honest to himself," said Keenan's sister, Marie Garraway. "It's in his blood. He gives two hundred percent all the time and maybe that's a flaw on his part. Maybe that's a flaw that he gives so much to his job. Maybe he's been too dedicated. But that's the way he is."

He became restless during games, telling cohorts he couldn't take it anymore. He was in the building, at the game, but sitting so far from the action. He missed the preparation. He missed managing the ebb and flow of games. Early in the season he asked Wirtz if he could put off signing the new contract until March, when he would have a better handle on his emotions. Maybe it would be best if he went somewhere else and coached, too.

"I wanted to make a decision after sixty games, not after fifteen games," Keenan later explained.

The Blackhawks management team balked at that request. Either Keenan was with them or he wasn't.

"We had a lot of internal discussions," Gozdecki said. "Did we want Mike Keenan being the prime mover in trades, with contracts, with what we do in the minors, when he might get up and walk away in March? We decided there was no reason we wanted to do that."

He was frustrated as a general manager, too. He felt constricted by the lingering presence of Pulford, who remained Wirtz's key hockey adviser. He began having second thoughts about his five-year agreement. The Blackhawks brass was puzzled by the mixed signals their general manager was sending.

"We hugged when he agreed to a new five-year deal to be general manager," Pulford said at the time. "I can't really tell what happened."

Keenan wanted his power clearly defined in writing, and the power he wanted was sweeping. Keenan gave the Blackhawks a proposal outlining ten areas of authority he felt he deserved. He wanted to deal directly with Wirtz and he wanted Pulford out of the way.

"What I wanted was only one boss," Keenan explained. "But Mr. Wirtz wanted Bob Pulford to maintain his authority and responsibility until he decided to retire. I've been patient the last five years to learn from Mr. Pulford, but now it was time to make my own mistakes and errors. I had been a consultant to Mr. Pulford for player contracts. Now I wanted to have that authority. I wanted him to be my consultant. I was not happy with my role in the organization as it went, so I put the authority I wanted into a document for Mr. Wirtz to approve."

Wirtz wasn't ready to tell Pulford to pack up his stuff and move out of the Stadium. He still needed a right-hand man to keep an eye on hockey for him. Pulford had earned his trust and Wirtz was incredibly loyal to those in his inner circle.

"Bill Wirtz has a lot of other things to deal with besides the Chicago Blackhawks, believe it or not," Gozdecki said. "Bill Wirtz is a businessman with other businesses and is not available twenty-four hours a day for hockey decisions. Mike refused to report to Pulford. He didn't want him in the organization in any capacity."

After reviewing Keenan's written proposal, the Blackhawks management team countered with one of its own that kept Pulford in the loop. Keenan said his original contract called for Pulford to slide into a consulting role in 1990, when Keenan gained the general manager duties.

"He went from being my consultant to where I was going to answer to him," Keenan said. "I almost started to cry when I saw it. I was so disappointed and hurt I couldn't believe it."

The only true autonomy Keenan saw in this proposal came on small matters, like negotiating with team hotels. "Embarrassing and demeaning," he said. "I worked my ass off for four years to put myself in a position to pick hotels?"

Wirtz claimed the Blackhawks weren't placing any unusual limitations on their general manager. Every NHL owner has final say on major trades and Wirtz figured his consultations with Pulford weren't so unusual.

"If we're going to trade a major player, we want a say," Wirtz said. "That's the way we've always done it. Mike wanted more authority than the Blackhawks have ever given a general manager."

Gozdecki said the franchise had never set a timetable for putting Pulford out to pasture. "At all times, it was very clear to Mike Keenan that he was going to report to Bob Pulford," Gozdecki said. "There was never going to be any time that Bob Pulford was going to wander off into the sunset, and if Mike Keenan thought that, he never understood what he was getting into — and I feel sorry for him."

On November 6, 1992, Keenan's employment in Chicago ended abruptly. The Wirtz family decided it had bickered with him enough.

"I did not quit. I was fired," Keenan told reporters. "In my last seventeen years of coaching, I never have given my players the license to quit. I wouldn't give myself the license to quit on the team in Chicago."

Mike was devastated by his dismissal. Just a few months before, life in Chicago seemed ideal. Now it was over.

"You give a hundred and twenty percent of your soul, you give up your family life, and then they kick you in the balls," he said. "I was fired in Philadelphia without what I believed at the time to be just cause. I was fired in Chicago with even less cause. I have come to an understanding of why the people in Philadelphia would fire me, but in Chicago it was a complete power struggle, inexcusable.

"At least Bobby Clarke had the courage to face me and say I was fired instead of playing all those silly games. They pride themselves in being loyal. Yet in the end, that wasn't the case. First I was surprised, then disappointed, and finally I was hurt. Their perception may have been that I wanted autonomy. However, I know the owner always has the final say and that's what I expected."

Keenan and the Blackhawks sniped back and forth for several days.

"I wanted no more than my general manager peers have," Keenan said. "Since I wasn't coaching, I wanted full authority to initiate and complete trades and contracts, with the understanding I would require Mr. Wirtz's approval for all of it, and only Mr. Wirtz's approval. I wasn't power hungry. I didn't ask for anything more than Bob Pulford has now. I was a team player. I gave Darryl the job."

Gozdecki scoffed at Keenan's assertion that he wasn't power hungry. "Mike wanted to be an alternate governor in the NHL," he said. "He wanted the whole picture. For him to say he's not a control freak, well, draw your own conclusions."

Everybody in the NHL knew Wirtz would never forsake Pulford to give Keenan free run of Chicago Stadium. But Keenan doesn't look at professional sports the way others do. He figures if he works hard enough and wins often enough, he will smash all obstacles and get his way. All he cared about was results. Isn't this business about results? Weren't great results enough? How could people who weren't dedicated to winning keep their jobs?

Keenan wasn't willing to play the game the way others did. He didn't have the patience to build his power base gradually, gaining favor step by step. Early on, Webb had advised Keenan to get his own team of people to look after his overall interests. There were so many relationships to maintain as coach, so many peripheral aspects to master. The media had to be wooed. Staff members had to be politicked.

"I could never get him to agree with that stuff," Webb said. "I could never get Mike to understand the importance of that stuff, the importance of having a good team of people working with you, the importance of having a good relationship with Bill Wirtz."

Keenan finally saw the error of his ways, but it was too late to make a difference. Only after the ax fell did he go to Wirtz's home and offer a bottle of wine as thanks for their run together.

"I thought I got along with Mr. Wirtz," Keenan said. "I respected him a lot. But, obviously, I didn't know him as well as I should have. I spent all my time working instead of politicking. I know in my next situation, I will be a much better coach than I was even in Chicago."

The key Blackhawks were sorry to see Keenan go. The franchise had been transformed into a Stanley Cup contender and those who survived the purge were true believers.

"Nobody's going to say they're happy Mike's gone," Roenick said after the firing. "Mike got rid of the players he didn't get along with. That was the way he dealt with it."

Chelios tried to give his deposed boss a laugh, leaving Keenan a comical message on his answering machine. If he needed work, Chelios said, he could come over and clear the snow off his driveway.

Darryl Sutter praised Keenan's work as general manager.

"There was no Darryl Sutter–Mike Keenan controversy," Sutter said. "We had a great relationship. When we struggled with finding our game, I got as much support from Mike as anybody."

Eagleson admitted that perhaps Keenan was just a lousy fit with the Blackhawks. Keenan needed to go someplace where he could make things happen.

"Maybe everything is for the best," Eagleson said. "I've known Bob Pulford a long time and he's as slow and methodical as a turtle. Mike and myself are hares in the race. Pulford would never have traded Denis Savard for Chris Chelios. Mike gambled his career on that move."

Keenan vacationed for a while. He went to Aspen, Colorado, to run, ski, and lift weights. He lost twenty pounds and cleared his mind. Then he got a gig coaching Team Canada in the World Championships later in the spring. That got him back on the NHL circuit to scout players for the tournament. He appeared tanned and refreshed, although he was still bitter about what had happened with the Blackhawks. The more he reflected on his accomplishments, the more unbelievable his dismissal seemed.

"From a business and hockey point of view, I got the job done in Chicago," Keenan said. "At the halfway mark of my first season, we were twenty-first out of twenty-one teams. It was a situation where the franchise had really been run into the ground and we did a pretty good job of building it up."

The dismissal from Chicago prompted Keenan to do another round of soul searching.

"When he got fired from Chicago, I spent quite a bit of time with him," Webb recalled. "I remember jogging with him. He stopped and asked, 'Will anybody hire me again?'"

◄ 5 ►

On Broadway

I can deal with the devil as long as he wins.

— RANGERS GENERAL MANAGER NEIL SMITH,
ARGUING FOR HIRING KEENAN
AS HEAD COACH IN APRIL 1993

IF EVER A TEAM NEEDED TO BE CUFFED AROUND BY MIKE KEENAN, it was the New York Rangers.

They had sleepwalked through the 1992–93 season for reasons nobody could adequately explain. They had earned 105 points the year before and were loaded with offensive talent, featuring eight forwards who scored 20 or more goals. They had speed with Mike Gartner, Tony Amonte, and Darren Turcotte. They had grit with Mark Messier, Adam Graves, and Esa Tikkanen. They had elite puck-rushing defensemen in Brian Leetch, Sergei Zubov, and James Patrick. They had two cat-quick goaltenders in John Vanbiesbrouck and Mike Richter.

General manager Neil Smith had assembled a dream team, but the dream team had a nightmarish season. Injuries to Leetch and Patrick hurt, but these Rangers were shocking underachievers. Their indifference got coach Roger Neilson canned in midseason and their apathy doomed replacement Ron Smith as well.

Neilson and Messier never did make a love connection. Both were battle-tested veterans who knew how to win, but both were very set in their ways. Like Keenan, Neilson wanted his forwards to dump the puck into the offensive zone and chase it. But unlike Keenan, he preferred a passive trapping game. He had been coaching that system long before it became fashionable.

Messier figured he was obligated to challenge Neilson about these passive tactics. Within a month of his arrival in New York in 1991, Messier began to bristle. The passive system created passive Rangers, putting the team to sleep. From this philosophical difference, Messier's problems with Neilson became more personal. By the following season, their relationship had deteriorated completely.

"In my mind, I knew we couldn't win the Cup his way," Messier would later explain. "Should I have shut up, gone along for the ride, finished out my contract? Or should I have stood up and said what I felt and taken one for the team? At times, the price of winning can be very harsh. I felt the players had to be protected. My responsibility was to the group of guys who were good enough to win a championship."

At one point, an exasperated Neilson summoned Graves, Gartner, and defenseman Kevin Lowe for a meeting in his office. Neilson wanted their help because he didn't believe Messier was leading the team. He asked them to take the reins from the recalcitrant captain and steer the Rangers. Unfortunately for Neilson, the players were more ready to follow Messier than him.

"To me, there's no question superstars can pose problems for a coach, but that's part of coaching," Neilson said. "To be a successful coach, you have to be able to get along with your superstar."

Messier denied leading a dressing-room revolt among the Rangers. He was angered by speculation that he went into the tank to doom Neilson.

"Anybody who knows me or anybody who has seen me play cannot suggest I laid down on Roger. That's criminal," Messier said. "I'm not a quitter. I didn't fire him. We had our disagreements, but this was no mutiny like he makes it out to be."

As the Rangers sank lower in the standings during the 1992–93 season, their long-frustrated fans turned against them. They taunted the team with chants of "Nineteen-forty," reminding the players of how long the franchise had gone without winning the Stanley Cup. Madison Square Garden became an ugly scene. The unthinkable was about to happen. The Rangers were threatening to miss the playoffs.

"If they don't make it, something big will happen — either ten trades in the off-season or somebody will get fired somewhere," observed center

Doug Weight, whom the Rangers traded to Edmonton during the season. "That's New York. If you don't win, things don't stay the same. Paramount has too much money to be in last place."

The Rangers did miss the playoffs, despite Paramount's generous corporate support. The team stumbled to an inexplicable 34-39-11 record, losing its last seven games. Neil Smith tried to resist the notion that his franchise needed a taskmaster like Keenan.

"The New York scene has a history of chopping the head off of somebody if things don't go the way they're expected," he said as the season wound down. "I don't agree that the team needs a dictator for a coach. That's not where the problem lies."

Actually, that's exactly where the problem lay. After four seasons as general manager, Smith was feeling the heat. He had to protect himself. Paramount's other team, the New York Knicks, was having great success with the slick and autocratic Pat Riley as coach. Stan Jaffe, president of Paramount Communications, understood the value of a commanding coach. He was a big Scotty Bowman fan. Smith was wary of Bowman, who could have become the Rangers' general manager in 1989. Madison Square Garden president Bob Gutkowski was ready to make a bold move, but he wasn't championing a particular candidate. Smith claimed he finally came to the realization that Iron Mike, with his record of winning big at every stop, was the best possible hire.

"I went to my bosses and told them what I wanted to do and they agreed," Smith said at the time. "That was it. The critical element to me was this: Wherever Mike Keenan went, he won. And I said to myself, 'I want that guy on my side.'"

Members of the Keenan camp credit Jaffe for the hire, noting that the overtures toward Keenan started after an intermediary posed the idea to the Paramount president. Other observers believe Gutkowski cast the tie-breaking vote when Jaffe pushed for Bowman and Smith offered Keenan as a fresher alternative.

Neilson's lawyer, Rob Campbell, began representing Keenan in 1993, after Alan Eagleson's empire crumbled amid allegations of fraud. In January 1993, Red Wings owner Mike Ilitch had signed Keenan to a future contract after he left Chicago, a deal that would have made him general manager and coach after the 1992–93 season. Bryan Murray, who was both general manager and coach at that time, was understandably disturbed by this news.

Keenan and other members of the St. Lawrence University hockey team formed the band Nik and the Nice Guys in 1971. Keenan didn't have much of a singing voice, but he knew how to work a crowd, and he also knew how to have a good time.

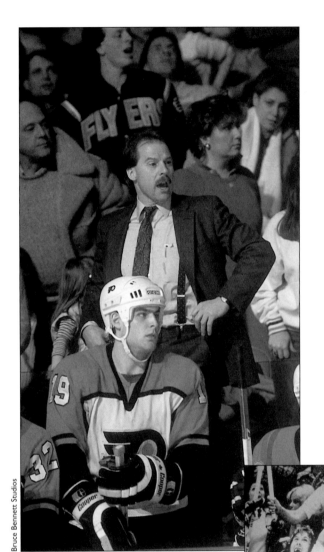

After winning championships in the minor leagues and college, Keenan's first NHL coaching job was with the Philadelphia Flyers (above). But Keenan ran into trouble when he tried to usurp power from Flyers general manager Bob Clarke (right).

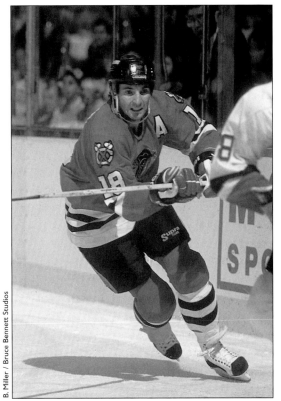

Future Hall of Famer Denis Savard (left) had scored over 40 goals in three consecutive seasons with the Chicago Blackhawks before Keenan arrived. Iron Mike's rugged practices, which included oppressive death skates, sent Savard packing after two years.

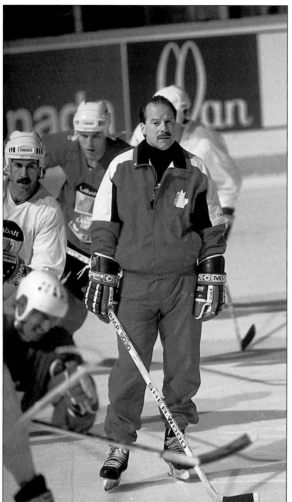

Scotty Bowman
(below) was the head
coach in Buffalo when
Keenan had his first
pro job in Rochester.
Keenan designed his
coaching style after
Bowman's, but he did
something Bowman
has never done:
win two Canada Cups
with Team Canada
(left).

J. Giamundo / Bruce Bennett Studios

"I can deal with the Devil as long as he wins," said New York Rangers general manager Neil Smith after hiring Keenan in 1993 (above). In the 1994 Stanley Cup playoffs, however, Keenan had to be bailed out several times by Rangers captain Mark Messier (below).

J. Leary / Bruce Bennett Studios

B. Bennett / Bruce Bennett Studios

Gayla Keenan, Mike's daughter (above), urged her father to concentrate on nothing but hockey as the Rangers struggled to win the 1994 Stanley Cup. Keenan raised the Cup for the first time on June 14 (below), but nobody suspected he'd be gone from New York a month later.

B. Winkler / Bruce Bennett Studios

Keenan insisted he was Iron Mike Lite
when he arrived in St. Louis to coach
the Blues, but his bench behavior was as
outrageous as ever. In retrospect,
Keenan realized his time in St. Louis
would have been more productive if he
had dealt better with Blues super
scorer Brett Hull (left).

The final blow for Keenan's stay in St. Louis was a series of run-ins with Wayne Gretzky, the greatest player in NHL history (above). Gretzky left after a half-season in St. Louis, and Keenan was soon sent packing, too. He ended up in Vancouver, where the Canucks were desperate to win (right).

Murray learned of the plan prior to a game at Joe Louis Arena and angrily confronted team executive vice president Jim Lites. "What's going on?" he demanded. "Is Mike Keenan coming here? I don't want to be strung along. Mike Ilitch can come and coach the game tonight. I don't give a shit."

Lites didn't know what was going on, either, but wasted no time finding out. He marched up to the Olympia Club in Joe Louis Arena, where Ilitch was hosting a dinner honoring former Red Wings great Gordie Howe, pulled aside a stunned and perturbed Ilitch, and asked him point blank, "What's going on with Keenan?"

None of the guests could hear what Ilitch and Lites were saying, but it was clear they weren't discussing the next family outing. Ilitch, who's not used to being confronted by his employees, didn't take well to this and exchanged some fervid words with Lites.

"It's my call," Ilitch reminded him.

Lites, who was married to Ilitch's daughter, Denise, at the time, dug in. So did long-time team executive Jimmy Devellano. They were leery of Keenan's take-no-prisoners managerial style, an approach that could have squeezed them out of the decision-making process.

"Ilitch waffled and breached my contract" is how Keenan recalled it. This decision created a rift within the Red Wings front office after Ilitch had second thoughts about letting Keenan get away. As a result, Lites moved on to the Dallas Stars in 1993 as president and governor of that franchise and later divorced Denise.

The Flyers seemed ready to bring back Keenan and offered him a five-year, $5-million contract. The expansion Mighty Ducks of Anaheim were interested, too. The Red Wings made another overture. Keenan had the Flyers' offer in hand before he took the helm of Team Canada at the World Championships in Germany. If the Rangers wanted Keenan, they would have to move quickly.

"I will be back in the NHL as a coach or a general manager or both," Keenan said as his suitors closed in. "I've never turned away from a challenge in the past and I can't see myself doing it at this point of my career. I feel I am at the height of my career, in terms of my experiences in coaching and managing. I have no fear."

Neilson was surprised that Smith wanted Keenan and that Keenan, his friend, would want to work for Smith.

"I can't believe that would be true," Neilson said. "I know Mike, and he's not going to be happy unless he's the general manager and the coach. Neil's in New York, and that's not going to happen there." After meeting with Keenan in Toronto, Gutkowski and Smith elected to match the general terms of the Philadelphia offer and throw in some nice perks as well. The Rangers wondered if Keenan could be satisfied with a coaching-only role. Keenan insisted that he could, noting how the twelve-month grind of being general manager and coach had taken such a toll on his family in Chicago. He wanted a longer summer vacation to spend with Gayla. Keenan also expressed an overwhelming desire to coach under the bright lights in New York.

During the swift, intense negotiations, Keenan's friend Gary Webb lightened the mood. He sent a courier into the negotiations in Toronto with a counter offer of $1 million for Keenan to rejoin Nik and the Nice Guys. Keenan's old college band was blossoming into a party band entertainment company. The pitch tickled Keenan, but he signed with the Rangers. When Gutkowski said the Rangers expected to play for the Stanley Cup, that's exactly what Keenan wanted to hear.

In his book *Losing the Edge,* author Barry Meisel spells out the details of Keenan's contract. It featured:

— a $660,875 signing bonus payable immediately, of which $160,875 was considered salary for April 15 through June 30, 1993

— a salary of $750,000 for the 1993–94 season, $850,000 for 1994–95, $900,000 for 1995-96, $950,000 for the 1996–97, and $1 million for 1997–98

— a $50,000 bonus for finishing first overall in the NHL standings in any season and $25,000 for finishing second overall

— a $40,000 bonus for finishing first in the Eastern Conference in any season and a $25,000 bonus for winning their division

— a $50,000 bonus for every first-round playoff victory, a $75,000 bonus for every second-round victory, a $100,000 bonus for every third-round victory, and a $200,000 bonus for each Stanley Cup

— a $25,000 bonus for winning the Jack Adams Award as Coach of the Year, $12,500 for each time he finished second in the voting, and $7,500 for each time he finished third

— an annuity that pays $50,000 a year from October 21, 2004, when he turns fifty-five, until his death

— a maximum of $5,000 a year for five years to purchase a life insurance policy of his choice

— a car phone, a computer with a printer, a fax machine, and a satellite dish for his home

— the club's choice of a fully insured automobile or a $850-a-month automobile allowance

— up to $50,000 to cover moving costs from Chicago

— all closing costs on the sale of his Chicago home and the purchase of a home in New York

— a $975,000 personal loan for the purchase of a $1.3 million home in Greenwich, Connecticut, payable within five years at 5 percent interest

The coaching profession had come a long way from the days of take-it-or-leave-it offers of $80,000 a season.

"I was able to maximize a situation that was unusual," Keenan said. "It worked out well for me. From the outside, it may look like a very opportunistic position to be in. But there was a certain price to pay in terms of stress, the aspect of going through that exercise."

It's no wonder Keenan became incredibly loyal to Rob Campbell.

"He's made me a lot of money," Keenan would say whenever his friends questioned his agent's tactics.

Keenan was thrilled to be hockey's best-paid coach by a large margin. The opportunity to coach at Madison Square Garden in New York City also excited him. St. Lawrence had played at the Garden during his college days and Keenan had long considered the job a coaching plum. This was America's most demanding sports market and he was his sport's most demanding coach.

"It was Mike's absolute dream to work in the Big Apple," Webb said. "Absolutely, that's where he wanted to be. New York fit him perfectly, the type of town it is."

Keenan showed up at his introductory news conference wearing a leather motorcycle jacket and a huge smile.

"New York provides the biggest opportunity and the biggest challenge," he said. "It's an opportunity that excites me. You need constant challenges in your profession."

Keenan and Smith tried to downplay the "Iron Mike" side of the new Rangers coach. Smith wanted to be everybody's friend. Being popular was important to him. He enjoyed chatting with his players around the rink. He loathed confrontation and strife. He liked to schmooze. It wasn't like him to hire a maniacal coach, so he tried to downplay Keenan's harsher tendencies.

"The reputation was he beat up on his players, that mentally and physically he beat them up," Smith said after the hiring. "I don't think that's true at all. He's a demanding person and he demands a lot of himself and his players and he won't stand for anything but the best. But he doesn't relish yelling at people. If he did all the things people said he did, it would be a crime, but he doesn't do anything like that. But where some people might let you get away with a couple of nights off, Mike won't. That's what made him successful."

The Rangers were used to taking a couple of nights off, and more. Even a player-friendly GM like Smith could see that.

"I don't think there is any secret we need more discipline. I think he's a good fit for the job," Smith said. "Mike was very hurt by the Chicago experience. And the players were hurt by what they went through here last year. You marry the two together and I think you have something very good."

As always, Keenan generated great expectations for his team after taking the helm. He was not interested in shepherding the team through a gradual rebuilding program. He didn't have time for that. Like most other New Yorkers, he was in a great big hurry.

"We're not here to avoid failure," he told reporters. "We're here to win the Stanley Cup. If we don't set that goal, the players won't know why they are here. We expect to build a program to put us in a position to win the Stanley Cup. Not in two or three or five years. This year."

Keenan picked up some style points from Riley, who, like Keenan, slicked back his hair, dressed impeccably, and carried himself like an emperor. A copy of Riley's book, *The Winner Within*, found its way to Keenan's bookshelf. In many ways, Keenan reigned over the hockey world. His stunning deal made him the envy of his peers. All of his professional dreams were coming true.

But his personal life was in disarray. Rita Keenan had been the ultimate hockey wife, soldiering on through move after move after move. She had learned to cope with her husband's professional obsessions and make the most of the limited time he gave her. But enough was enough. She had her own life in Chicago and didn't want to abandon it. Gayla was about to start high school and she didn't want to move her.

"You're not going to move with me, are you?" Keenan asked his wife.

Once again, Rita asked her husband to give up coaching. But how could he?

"You don't even know me," he told her.

Rita remained in Chicago and pursued a divorce. Keenan packed up and continued his quest.

"I rented a U-Haul," Keenan recalled a few months later. "My belongings took up only a little corner of it. My wife was playing the piano in the living room when I drove off. I began to cry as I left that house. Then I cried outside of Toronto, where I grew up. When I reached Rochester, where I had coached in the minors, I cried all the way to New York and my new house in Greenwich, Connecticut."

In the months that followed, he would regret not paying more attention to Rita and their marriage. The years had flown by, the hockey challenges had come one after another, and he had taken their relationship for granted.

"She came with me to the NHL out of loyalty, but she never came psychologically," Keenan said. "It was never the life she bargained for. God, I was selfish. You look back and wonder what you were doing."

After Keenan had returned to St. Lawrence from his academic purgatory, he had hit the career accelerator and never let up. An overwhelming fear of failure made him blindly ambitious. Rita's dreams were simpler than his: The two would teach school, Mike would coach on the side, and they would raise a nice family like the one that raised her. In Rita, Mike saw the warmth that his own dysfunctional family often lacked.

"Maybe because we didn't have as nice a family situation at home, that was one of his center focuses," Marie Garraway said. "He was trying to achieve that in his own married life."

But his dream was not the same as Rita's. He could never sit still.

"When you hit the ground, you hit the ground running and you kind of leave your family in the dust, because you have to get on with your job," he said. "I think I've moved about a dozen times over my career. My ambition was selfish in terms of my single-mindedness, even if it was with the intention of being able to provide my family with a tremendous lifestyle. But I lost the balance between the two. When I looked around at the track record of most of the coaches in the NHL, I knew the survival level was not very good. I let that fear drive me, and drive me away from my family.

"It took a toll. My wife had six miscarriages. One year I was away for two hundred days. And when I was there, well . . . a hockey coach doesn't have a day off. I was on the fast track. To reach an elite level, you have to be abnormal. Can you imagine living with that? Two hundred days gone and when he's here, he's like this! My wife couldn't comprehend it. I can't believe it. I can't blame her. She'd put up with a lot. So she asked me to give up hockey."

Keenan's split from Rita shocked people back home in Whitby. The couple had stayed together through the moves to Peterborough, Rochester, Toronto, Philadelphia, and Chicago.

"They seemed liked such a happy couple," said Ted Keenan, Mike's father. "I was in tears. I said, 'Mike, I've got to call you back.' Heartbreaking. They wanted a family so badly. Every time she'd get pregnant they'd get excited and then . . ."

During his separation from Rita and Gayla, Keenan also reflected on his hard-driving coaching tactics. He had pushed his players hard, perhaps too hard. He had found their weak points and exploited them. Now, as he stepped under the brightest spotlight of his coaching career, he was the one feeling vulnerable.

"I began wondering if the pain I was feeling was the price for the pain I'd inflicted on others," Keenan said. "You bury that old Irish-Catholic guilt, but sooner or later it bites you in the ass. I wondered, did I need people more than I thought? And if I did and I needed to change . . . could I change just a little? God, that's scary. Everything had been so all or nothing. If I changed just a little, would my career fall apart?"

Keenan always subjected his players to extreme psychological testing during the season. Now he was undergoing a similar test in his personal life. The separation from his family — who had always been waiting for him, dutifully, while he won hockey games — shook him. Who was Mike Keenan? What was his purpose in life? He had a lot to work through during the next several months.

The big, empty house in Greenwich underscored his loneliness, so he often stayed at the Rangers' practice facility in Rye, New York, watching games on the satellite dish into the wee hours and going to sleep on the couch in the exercise room. He would put the house up for sale before the season ended.

"I live alone in a house," he said. "That's the reason I don't have to be that anxious to go home. It's a really big change in my life. Change at that level brings a certain amount of pain, but it also brings a certain amount of growth and self-knowledge. I don't mind pain as long as I have learned a tremendous amount about myself, which I think has been reflected in my professional abilities. One thing I've come to realize more recently is that it is better to understand than be understood."

Marie saw a different side of her brother in the months that followed his separation from Rita and Gayla.

"This is the first time maybe in his life that he let his emotions show," she said. "He was always worried about what everybody else thought. He's showing another side of himself for the first time. The hockey people — his players especially — have always seen him one way, whether it's a fair view or not. Before, he dedicated his whole life to hockey. It was very easy to tune out what goes on in everyday life. I think he realizes he can't do that anymore."

When the Keenans separated, Gayla was fourteen, just starting her critical teenage years. Every day, her father felt the pain of not being with her. Many times, he would hang up the phone after talking to Gayla with tears rolling down his cheeks. It was a life lesson Keenan knew he had to deal with. During this period, he often urged his players to spend their downtime with their families.

"He's pounded that home quite often," defenseman Kevin Lowe reported during the season. "Coming from a hockey coach, it is a little strange. Maybe it has something to do with what he's gone through in his personal life."

Earlier in his career, Keenan routinely blew off friends and family who came to watch him coach. If the game went badly or if his team was in a slump, he had no time for even those closest to him. The guys from St. Lawrence wondered what had happened to the Nice Guy. The folks from Whitby wondered what became of the friendly boy who made so many friends.

Jarred by Rita's decision, Keenan reached out to the people he had kept at arm's length. He sent his father an airline ticket for his sixty-fifth birthday and spent six weeks with him right in the middle of the season. He called his mother every week. He checked in with his sisters. He discovered he could be the real Mike Keenan much of the time and still win.

However, the newly introspective Keenan proved to be just as mercurial as the old Iron Mike. His relationship with the Rangers was not touchy-feely. When he struggled to harness his emotions during the season, his savvy team captain, Mark Messier, would reel him in. He had seen Keenan's act during the Canada Cup tournaments and he knew the coach had to be calmed from time to time to preserve his relationship with the team.

But Messier connected with Keenan's single-mindedness and they developed one of the best player-coach relationships the game had seen.

Messier especially liked Keenan's urgency to win. "You can't be afraid of the future," Messier said. "You can't be afraid of winning the Stanley Cup. If you are, you're just floating around in the middle of the ocean."

In turn, Keenan loved Messier. He offered the commanding presence of a Yvon Lambert, Dave Poulin, or Chris Chelios from his earlier seasons, only to a greater degree. Messier was the ultimate captain, a universally respected warrior who could lead on the ice and take control of an entire dressing room with his icy stare. And when he spoke, he got a full response from his teammates. As great as Wayne Gretzky was, he never won a Cup without Messier at his side. Mark would win a couple without Wayne. Messier is as fine a leader as the NHL has ever seen.

"It's easy for me to get the other guys to do something when the best player is such a selfless leader," Keenan said as the season unfolded.

Messier's arrival ahead of Keenan had raised the bar for the Rangers. The team had spent enough time building. Now it wanted to win.

"Messier changed the philosophy of the Rangers," Smith said. "Once you get a Mark Messier, you're committed to trying to win the Stanley Cup every year he's there. You're never in a rebuilding stage. Mike was a very important — no, that isn't strong enough — an extremely important part of the building process. We felt we had the base of talent to do it. All we needed now was the leader."

Unlike Neilson, Keenan bonded with Messier immediately. "I underestimated the power a player like Mark Messier could have with his teammates," Neilson said. "Mike and Mark have a mutual admiration society for each other."

This downtrodden team needed a major lift. Keenan went down his familiar checklist to create a winning aura. He ordered framed photos of the Rangers' 1928, 1933, and 1940 Stanley Cup winners to be hung at the team's practice rink. A framed photo of the Stanley Cup was prominently displayed, too. Keenan had the standings displayed opposite the mirrors at the practice facility, giving players the chance to reflect on the playoff race before heading home from work. He asked a television producer to prepare a video of previous New York City ticker-tape parades, so that his team could see for themselves what it would be like.

"I want the players to be able to visualize it," Keenan said at the time. "If you can't see it, you'll never achieve it."

Said Messier, "When Mike showed us the image of the parade in train-ing camp, when you could see it visually, then when all the things we went through happened, that was the one thing that got us back on track. When the season got long, when it got tough, that one image stuck in my head."

Team psychologist Dr. Cal Botterill, who had worked with Keenan in Philadelphia and Chicago, was amazed by the video's impact. "Mark Messier walked out of the room crying," he said. "The Rangers won the Cup because of their sense of mission and because one-third of their team were leaders."

Keenan wasted no time turning his attention to the team's roster. He saw lots of speed and skill, but not much size, experience, and toughness along the boards and in front of the net. During a July organizational meeting, he dismissed the talent base as unworthy of a Stanley Cup run. He targeted Gartner, Turcotte, and Patrick for immediate departure. He wondered about Alexei Kovalev, a gifted but eccentric forward. He didn't believe Leetch could be his Chelios and he doubted that the charismatic Richter had Belfour's mental toughness.

He loved Graves, Tikkanen, and big defenseman Jeff Beukeboom, but he wanted to get them a lot more help. Keenan's harsh assessment of the team left Smith reeling, although he tried to maintain a brave front.

"If he doesn't like the players I've brought here already, that's fine," Smith said. "I'll get him what he says he needs to win. Mike's track record is one of winning and whatever his winning encompasses we are buying into. If that means getting more grinders, I'll get him more grinders."

But few changes were made before the season. Greg Gilbert, a favorite of Keenan's in Chicago, signed with the Rangers as a free agent. Defenseman Doug Lidster arrived in exchange for John Vanbiesbrouck in an expansion-draft move. Glenn Healy came over from the Islanders to replace the Beezer. Otherwise, Keenan had pretty much the same team that had failed the year before.

He wasn't happy about that. His public complaining escalated after a preseason game against the Islanders on September 23.

"I've suggested we need more physical players, yes," he told reporters after the game. When the scribes left, Keenan muttered to nobody in par-ticular, "I'm working for a guy who believes this team is good enough to win the Cup."

Complacency was a huge problem for the Rangers. The NHL had changed dramatically since Keenan's glory days in Philadelphia, when top players were lucky to get one million dollars total on a long-term deal and young players were always a misstep away from the low-paying American Hockey League. The Rangers team Keenan inherited featured lots of independent wealth. Players who are financially set for life are obviously harder to motivate.

"Five years ago, the top players were making $350,000," Keenan said after settling into the Rangers job. "Now that's what the bottom players are making. Half the players on our club are millionaires, very comfortable in their lifestyles. You have to appeal to their pride, their intrinsic sense of self, make them feel responsible for the whole. It's become an entrepreneurial sport in which men have bonded together, yet have the opportunity to show individual creativity."

One by one, he went after his whipping boys on the team. He wrote off Patrick as too soft and wouldn't allow him the opportunity to prove otherwise. During an early season game at Pittsburgh, he benched Patrick, then had to put him back into the game after minor injuries and penalties had depleted his bench corps. Sure enough, Patrick was on the ice when Penguins forward Martin Straka scored. It wasn't Patrick's fault, but you couldn't have guessed that by Keenan's reaction.

"You can trade that fucking Patrick or do whatever you want," Keenan told Smith. "He'll never wear the uniform again."

Leetch was also driving him crazy. He rushes the puck like Paul Coffey and likes to get in deep — and stay in deep — like a third winger. Sometimes this backfires and allows teams an odd-man rush the other way. Keenan's teams always thrived by getting the puck in deep, keeping it in deep, and sustaining pressure. His defensemen always pinched in along the boards. But his defensemen didn't freelance, like Leetch did. And Leetch wasn't exactly Spartacus when defending his own goal. He checked like a scoring winger, too, refusing to do much hitting or shot blocking. Keenan benched Leetch and berated him after the second period of a lackluster early-season game with the expansion Mighty Ducks of Anaheim.

"You're no fucking Chelios!" he screamed. "Everybody in this organization thinks you're so great. You're not that fucking good! You're not as good as anyone says you are."

Leetch's benching caught everybody's attention. He was the franchise's budding superstar and the media's golden boy.

"There is a lot of pride and ego in the locker room," one Ranger observed. "So when Mike benched Brian Leetch, he was trying to tell him a truth he hadn't heard in a while. That he wasn't untouchable, wasn't good enough. Stars find the truth difficult sometimes."

To his credit, Leetch was up to this challenge and everything else Keenan would throw at him.

"Nothing is automatic with him," Leetch said. "He doesn't want anybody to go on the ice unless you're told to. He has you just paying a lot more attention from the bench. There's no question he's a leader. When he says something, people jump. He's so sure of himself, he commands a lot of respect. And you earn it from him by producing."

As the Mighty Ducks game slipped away and the Rangers lost, 4–2, Keenan turned to another of his favorite gimmicks: He stopped managing the bench altogether. The players had to make their own line combinations and line changes.

"You guys quit on me, so why should I bother with you?" he told them. "You haven't played, so why should I coach?"

After the game, Keenan used his meeting with the media to prod his players and his ever-patient general manager.

"Let's be mindful of the fact that this team did not make the playoffs a year ago," he said. "You draw your own conclusions. It's not up to me to evaluate. My only responsibility is to play and work the bench as well as I can during the course of a game. Better that we find out what we've got here now than wait until springtime." He believed the Rangers should have learned their lesson the year before, when Smith kept waiting for his team to awaken and it remained asleep. If the team isn't good enough, it isn't good enough.

His raging performance at the Rangers' next practice was vintage Iron Mike. He broke his stick across the cross bar, prompting speculation that he had sawed through the stick to make certain it would explode dramatically. He had used that trick at his other stops.

"Everybody get the fuck off the ice!" he yelled.

In the dressing room, Keenan berated Patrick and his other favorite targets.

"You're losers!" he screamed again and again. "Losers!"

The Rangers went back on the ice for some exhausting sprints, then were sent back inside to do their usual conditioning work in the weight room. This was Keenan's updated version of the death skate.

"People in New York expect you to win, and the upper management in New York expects us to win," Keenan said. "If people prefer not to be in this type of program, it's better to find out now while there is time to address the overall make-up of the team. They had one of the nicest men in hockey as their coach last year and you saw their response. Their response to me hasn't fundamentally changed that much. Ask the players why they didn't play for a coach who was a real gentleman in Roger Neilson, and I'm sure that Ron Smith was as well."

Cal Botterill helped keep Keenan from going too far.

"Mike's temper was probably his biggest weakness," one Ranger said. "You know that team psychologist he has, that's not for the players. It's for him, to tell if his particular motivation is working with a player. That guy didn't help us one bit, but he helps Mike determine if what he's doing is working."

Botterill understood that a big part of his job was getting Keenan to back off. He and another sports psychologist, Howie Wegner, helped keep the team on track. A word here and a suggestion there kept some of the more fragile players out of major slumps.

"Mike is always looking for any kind of an edge," Lowe would later say. "In terms of impact, I'm not going to say those guys won the Cup, but you can never discount the genuine positive aura they brought to the team."

Lowe respected how much rest Keenan gave his veterans. Keenan wouldn't work the older players for the sake of working them. All he cared about was their shift-to-shift performance.

"With Mike, everything has to do with winning that hockey game," Lowe said. "Everything. But when I tell people that the Rangers went through a six-week stretch and never once had a practice, they find that pretty bizarre. He knew we were a talented, veteran team that needed the rest more than the practice."

Still, Keenan was no softy. He wasn't going to sit still until the make-up of his team changed. He relentlessly hounded Smith to acquire Steve Larmer, the diligent soldier who was refusing to play for the Blackhawks and demanding a trade. Whenever Smith called Blackhawks general manager Bob Pulford about Larmer, however, Pulford demanded Tony Amonte in return. The young, explosive scorer was just the sort of building block the Blackhawks needed. Amonte had grown up playing with Roenick and appeared to be the perfect complement to J.R. on the Blackhawks' top line.

Smith held the line on Amonte, so Keenan went over his head to force a deal. He believed Jaffe was firmly in his corner. Pat Riley had advised him to go to Jaffe whenever he really needed to get something done. Jaffe considered Keenan's plea after a disappointing tie with Montreal on October 28, then instructed Gutkowski to deal with the situation.

The plea created a stir in the Madison Square Garden offices. Keenan got his audience with Jaffe and Gutkowski and reiterated his concerns about the team. The Rangers were too small. They were too soft. Many of the players who had failed miserably the year before had to go.

"Mike, we're not going to trade everybody," Gutkowski told him. "We hired you to make these guys better, that's why you're here, that's your responsibility. That's why we're paying you the money we're paying you."

Jaffe reminded Keenan that there were some untouchables on his roster.

"We're not going to trade Brian Leetch," Jaffe said. "We're not turning the Rangers into the New York Blackhawks, because, to be honest about it, Mike, what have they ever won?"

Smith knew he had to placate his coach. The opportunity to make a three-way deal that didn't include Amonte finally emerged in early November. Turcotte and Patrick would go to Hartford, Larmer would come to New York via Hartford, and the Rangers would also get tough guy Nick Kypreos from the Whalers.

Amonte was spared, for the time being. But Keenan would never let up on him, just as he had never let up on Scott Mellanby. He believed Amonte, like Mellanby, was the product of a cushy upbringing. He questioned his work ethic. He questioned whether he belonged on the team. During one meeting with Amonte, Keenan pointed to a board that had Amonte listed second from the bottom among forwards. Amonte was listed underneath a number of players with far less skill.

"Who do you think you should play over?" Keenan asked. "Who do you think you are better than? Go up to the chalkboard. Are you better than him? No, you're not better than him. You're not better than him. And you're not better than him."

Amonte never got out of Keenan's doghouse. He had scored more than 30 goals in each of his first two seasons, but would score only 16 for Keenan. The trips to the coach's office were always unpleasant.

"I walked out of there crying sometimes," Amonte said. "He made me feel like I couldn't play in the league anymore. He said I had no heart, that I didn't compete, that I didn't want to be hit. You go out and try as hard as you can and when you come off the ice, he says you're not trying. It's demoralizing."

Later, he would come to the same conclusion that Bob Bassen had come to in Chicago: Maybe he was too respectful of his coach. Maybe he was too meek. Perhaps he should have been more confrontational in return.

"My biggest problem with Keenan was not standing up for myself," Amonte would say. "He seems to respect guys who stand up for themselves and guys who don't back down from him. He told me I was a rich kid from Boston and I didn't know how to work hard because I never had to, and that couldn't be further from the truth."

The addition of Larmer was just what the team needed. He was a quiet, self-starting veteran who commanded respect from teammates. And he knew Keenan's routine by heart. Whenever Keenan would go postal, Larmer knew how to clean up the mess left in the dressing room. He knew when the tirades were coming and he knew how the team should respond to them. Larmer had gone to the Cup finals with Keenan and knew the script. He also brought perspective, the ability to tell the Rangers that this Keenan was less insane than the one he had played for in Chicago.

"He's a lot more composed behind the bench, and I think that's rubbed off on players when we're in difficult situations," Larmer observed.

Larmer quickly saw the strength of the Keenan-Messier relationship. "In a strange way, they almost think alike," Larmer said. "They're both highly motivated, very dedicated, almost win-at-any-price guys. I think Mark had a calming effect on Mike and Mike had a lot of respect for Mark. Mike learned a lot from Mark, and vice versa. Yeah, there's always a lot of controversy, but there's controversy everywhere, not just around Mike."

The Rangers got hot and lost only once during a stretch of twenty games from late October to mid-December. The 17-1-2 run made believers out of the skeptics. The team morphed into the juggernaut it should have been the year before. They skated circles around many of their opponents.

"From early in the year, there was no question in my mind: We were the best-conditioned team in the league," utility forward Ed Olczyk said.

Keenan got them to that level without killing them. His training regimen was still difficult, but it was more refined. "He has been demanding, but very fair," Graves said. "We work hard, but get quality rest. I've never played for a coach who can get you so prepared to play a game, physically and mentally."

That preparation gave the team confidence. Winning reinforced that confidence. The same team that gave up the year before developed a persistent, resilient personality under its new coach.

"Mike's reputation as a power-hungry dictator is well known," Messier said during the turnaround. "But most of all, he's a great coach. We're starting to believe we're a good team. But we know if we let down, Mike can really make it tough on us. A huge factor in any team sport is that you believe you have the ability to go out and win games and do what it takes to get it done. Mike has helped us believe that."

Messier believed Keenan was a far more polished coach than the madman he had played against during the Oilers-Flyers series. He was more rational, more mature. He understood the value of positive reinforcement.

"That's the great thing about life and sports," Messier said. "As you go, you learn from the good things and the bad things. Mike's intelligent enough to know what works and what doesn't. He'll give somebody a kick in the rear, but he'll offer a pat on the back, too."

One guy who got no pats on the back was Mike Gartner. He had a reputation as a top-notch regular season player who tended to fall back in the playoffs. It became abundantly clear that he wouldn't get a chance to erase that rap on Keenan's watch. After a loss in Montreal, Keenan tried to humiliate him in front of his teammates. He wondered out loud if Gartner had "ever gotten the shit beat out of him by the Montreal Canadiens, and if so, is that why you're playing so scared?"

After a loss in Dallas, Gartner again took the blame.

"Mike Gartner," Keenan barked, "what have you ever done in your life?"

"Excuse me?" Gartner asked.

"You were embarrassing yourself out there," Keenan said. "You just embarrassed yourself."

"What are you talking about?" Gartner said. "Explain yourself."

"I don't have to," Keenan said. "Just ask the two million people who watched you in New York."

Gartner wasn't Keenan's type of player and never would be. He scored his goals off the rush. Keenan preferred wingers who hit hard and went to the net.

"I haven't been able to figure out what a Mike Keenan player is," an exasperated Gartner would say. "It seems to be a moving target."

Playing part-time frustrated him, but Gartner believed he was being a good soldier. "I had dealt with the situation earlier in the season," he said. "I more or less made it policy that it wasn't going to bother me because we were a first-place hockey team, and if that's what it took to have a Stanley Cup contending team that's what I was going to do."

Richter held up considerably better under such browbeatings. Unlike back-up Glenn Healy, who quickly became sour under Keenan, Richter stood up to the challenge. He had prepared himself for the worst. Keenan had a well-earned reputation for jerking goaltenders around. The netminders he loved most, Ron Hextall and Ed Belfour, were combative sorts who returned their coaches' fury. Keenan's goaltenders were the kind of guys you wanted on your side in a bar fight. Richter wasn't that sort of battler, but he refused to fold.

"We expected a difficult year, a demanding year because of his reputation as someone who was not afraid to intimidate or use any method in order to get his players to play well," Richter said. "Someone's hitting you in the head, going boink and making you go out there and play harder. It's a skill. It's a skill for a player to be able to do it to himself. It's a skill for a player to be able to hear a criticism or any kind of input from a coach and respond in a positive way."

Keenan used another trick with Alexei Kovalev during a game on February 23 against Boston. Weary of watching the gifted Russian take eternal shifts instead of coming off the ice with his linemates, Keenan left him on the ice to take shift after shift after shift in the third period. This didn't get Kovalev's attention — the spacy forward thought he was being rewarded with more playing time. But Keenan's decision to move him to center made him one of the best Rangers over the last third of the season and the playoffs.

But Keenan wasn't happy. A loss to Detroit on March 7 sent him into a rage.

"They are far bigger than we are and far more physical than we are," he told reporters. "If you are asking me, I don't know if we can compete with them in a seven-game series."

During a loss at Florida on March 14, he quit working the bench again for eight minutes. Keenan was so exasperated that he asked former New York Islanders great Denis Potvin, a Panthers broadcaster, if he wanted to come out of retirement for the stretch run. This was not the first time he had asked a legend to come out of retirement. During his first season at Philadelphia, he had asked Flyers general manager Bobby Clarke if he wanted to activate himself for the playoff push.

"Larry Robinson played when he was forty, Gordie Howe when he was fifty," Keenan explained at the time. "The great ones can."

Potvin declined. "But it was flattering," he said. "Keenan said he looked at me as one of the few people who should not have retired when they did. He said I had lots of playing time left in my career."

After a loss to Chicago on March 18 left his team in a 1-3-1 slump with the playoffs fast approaching, Keenan instructed Campbell to call Gutkowski and once again complain about the team's makeup. But Gutkowski didn't want to interfere with hockey decision making. He urged Keenan and Smith to sit down and iron out their differences. A summit was held on March 19.

"I had told Neil we weren't good enough to win with Amonte and Mike Gartner," Keenan said. "He thought we were. I know I can get up in the morning, look in the mirror, and have a clear conscience. But there's lots of people in New York who can't. It's unfortunate."

Smith felt Keenan had undermined him by going over his head once again. He feared that Keenan was making a power play for his job. That concern made working with his coach impossible.

"I can understand Neil being upset about that," Keenan would say. "But Neil felt we could win with the team we had last July and I disagreed. I even told Neil during the season not to be seduced by the fact we were first in the league, that the team you have in the regular season is not necessarily the team you want in the playoffs. I had the experience of being first in the league in Chicago and then getting beat out in the playoffs."

Somehow, Keenan and Smith were smiling when they came out of their face-to-face meeting. For a few days, they operated off the same page. The trade deadline was two days away and Smith got busy. By March 21, with the clock ticking, Smith was ready to remake his team. Gartner was sent to Toronto for Glenn Anderson, another former Oiler with a history of clutch playoff performances. Amonte finally exited, moving to Chicago for muckers Stephane Matteau and Brian Noonan. Phil Bourque was shipped to Ottawa for doughnuts. And speedy youngster Todd Marchant went to Edmonton for checking center Craig MacTavish. The message was clear: The Rangers were now Keenan's team.

"I think he is running everything," Bourque surmised. "It's his show."

"For a first-place team to make all those changes is rather dramatic," Gartner observed after getting traded. "Now the team's success or failure is squarely on the shoulders of the coaching staff and management because of the changes they've decided to make so late in the year."

Keenan likes taking chances. He seems to relish the challenges such bold moves create. And he really believed that all the moves gave him a better team. The Rangers were bigger, stronger, and more playoff tested. Having so many former Oilers and Blackhawks was good.

"They've all gone through certain wars together," Keenan said after the trading ended. "Many of these players have been down the road before. All have been to the finals."

The new-look Rangers responded with an 8-2-2 finish in the regular season and a rousing four-game sweep of the Islanders in the first round of the playoffs. Islanders coach Al Arbour predicted that the Rangers would win the Cup after getting a good look at Messier's determination in their first-round series.

"When you see that glare in his face, you know somebody is going to pay," he said. "The first time I noticed it was in 1983, when I went to shake his hand after we beat the Oilers for our fourth Stanley Cup title. He wasn't growling, but you could tell he wasn't happy about losing, and you knew somebody would pay for it. The next year, of course, the Oilers came back to beat us and Mark led the way. I saw that same glare against us through the whole series against the Rangers. That's one of the big reasons why I think the Rangers will win it all."

Next, the Rangers dispatched the Washington Capitals, a perpetual playoff disappointment, in five mostly uneventful games. This set up a showdown with their cross-river rivals, the deep, talented, and well-coached New Jersey Devils. The Devils fired the first salvo by winning Game One 4–3 in two overtimes. After the loss, Keenan showed his first sign of strain by accusing his team of being disrespectful toward the Devils. Lowe felt he had to step up and stay something positive, so he reminded his teammates how good they we really were. Botterill said Lowe hit just the right note.

"On a day-to-day basis, Kevin was probably more active in a leadership role than Mark Messier," Botterill said. "Kevin addressed the team at a critical point, got everybody to take a deep breath, and defused the pressure. 'These are the games you play for,' he said. A leader believes when others don't. And Kevin Lowe is the epitome of a leader."

The Rangers won Game Two easily and Game Three on a Matteau backhander in double overtime. A victory in Game Four would have given the Rangers a stranglehold on the series. But in the first period, Keenan benched Leetch and yanked Richter with the Rangers trailing 2–0. Later, Noonan, MacTavish, and even Messier were benched. The team was baffled. Veteran defenseman Jay Wells pleaded with assistant coach Colin Campbell to put Leetch back in, but Leetch sat for most of the rest of the game.

The Devils won, 3–1, to even the series at two games each. Again, Keenan failed to maintain his composure. Keenan's post-game rant — "What the fuck are you doing? Do we want to win? Do you care? Does anybody have anything to say?"— left the players more angry than chagrined. They wondered about his post-game comments to the media as well. Why was he ripping them now? Where was his belief?

"It was very obvious we weren't getting a very good response to start the game," Keenan said. "They came out with authority and took it to us right from the beginning of the first shift. Throughout the first period, they were by far the best team and that proved to be enough for them to win."

Keenan hinted vaguely at injuries, including Leetch's balky shoulder. Sensing that his teammates were confused and concerned, Messier decided to take control of the team atmosphere. He went into Keenan's office before practice for another meeting with the boss. But this was not another routine chat, like their regular sessions during the seasons. This time, Messier challenged his coach. In measured tones, he put the grievances on the table. The players believed Keenan hadn't given them their best chance to win. The players believed he had cooked up the injury angle to protect himself from criticism. The players needed a positive reinforcement at this point, not the sort of spanking they might have expected in November or December.

The other Rangers sat anxiously, awaiting their captain's word. Messier came out of Keenan's office and allayed their fears.

"It won't happen again," he said.

"I've always been curious about what exactly was said in there," one Ranger later said. "But it's not something you ask."

Keenan's implosion proved he may have evolved as a coach, but he hadn't changed. He had lost his composure before and hurt his team. Now his challenge was to regroup and regain his team.

With the media ready to question why so many key players were in his doghouse at such a critical point in the playoffs, Keenan used the injury angle to create a diversion. On the off day between games, he called the key newspaper beat reporters into his office and gave them "off the record" — but mostly bogus — information about the injuries. He knew the information would get into the papers. Keenan's unusual move tied up the reporters and allowed the players to escape without having to speak to the media.

Messier wouldn't let Keenan off the hook and forced him to apologize to the team before Game Five at the Garden.

"I made a mistake," Keenan told the team. "We all make mistakes. Let's turn the page."

But the team couldn't turn the page. The Rangers played lifelessly and let the Devils roll to a 4–1 victory and a three-games-to-two lead in the series.

Again, it was Messier's turn to take charge. At practice the next day, he saw a lot of resignation in the eyes of his teammates. He assured them that they would win Game Six. Then he told the media, in no uncertain terms, that the Rangers would even up the series and force Game Seven.

"We're going to go in and win Game Six," Messier said. "That was the focus this morning and it's the way we feel right now. We've done that all year, we've won all the games we've had to win. I know we're going to go in and win Game Six and bring it back here for Game Seven. We have enough talent and experience to turn the tide. That's exactly what we're going to do in Game Six."

But the Rangers fell behind 2–0, at Meadowlands Arena, and looked dead. Rangers fans began dwelling on the franchise's fifty-four-year Cup drought. Then Messier set up a Kovalev goal late in the second period, giving the Rangers life. Between periods, Keenan stayed with the team, imploring them to keep working. He knew he had pushed his team too far after Game Four and now he had to bring them back.

At 17:12 of the third period, Messier tied the game. Messier also scored the tie-breaking goal and the empty-net clincher in a 4–2 victory. His performance was one for the ages.

"That has to be the most impressive performances by any hockey player in the history of this league," Keenan gushed after the game. "People will be talking about Mark Messier for many years to come, the way they talk about Gordie Howe, Bobby Orr, Wayne Gretzky, and Mario Lemieux."

Messier's "We will win" guarantee had made headlines the morning of the game. It was a gutsy move considering the team's emotional condition.

"I remember thinking I had to do something to instill our old confidence," he explained. "I consciously said it, but I was thinking in such a narrow scope that somehow I figured only our players would get up and read the papers the next day, not all of New York and the Devils players as well. I guess I didn't care about the consequences at that point."

Game Seven at Madison Square Garden was a thriller. The Rangers edged ahead, 1–0, on a spectacular goal by Brian Leetch midway through the second period of the tight-checking game. Scoring chances were scarce. The score remained 1–0 entering the third period and the clock slowly ticked down. With less than a minute left, Rangers fans were on their feet in anticipation of the victory that would send them to the Cup finals.

But a goal by Valeri Zelepukin with 7.7 seconds remaining tied the game 1–1. Fans slumped back into their seats. The first overtime came and went. A second overtime began amid almost unbearable tension. Then Keenan's guy, Matteau, scored the game-winner on a wraparound goal from behind the net. New York City celebrated.

The Rangers entered the Cup finals as heavy favorites against the Vancouver Canucks. The Rangers dominated Game One, but lost in overtime. The Rangers won the next three games, including two in Vancouver, to set up a coronation in Game Five at Madison Square Garden. By winning that game, the Rangers would end their Cup drought.

But another Keenan stunt distracted the team at just the wrong time. During the finals, the Red Wings had fired Murray and assistant general manager Doug MacLean. Owner Mike Ilitch told coach Scotty Bowman, whom he hired in 1993 after passing on Keenan, that he might not be back behind the bench. Major changes were afoot and Keenan, as it turned out, was right in the middle.

Rob Campbell had called Red Wings counsel Jay Bielfield earlier in the playoffs to tell him that Keenan would be interested in coming aboard. The Keenan-Smith rift had become irreconcilable and the two men had stopped talking to each other. Yes, Keenan had another four years left on his contract, but Campbell suggested his client could be set free. Keenan could re-enter the marketplace. Given the Red Wings' playoff failures, it seemed logical that Ilitch would finally seal a deal with Keenan after flirting with him for many years.

The first report of Keenan's interest in the Red Wings came from Prince Edward Island, MacLean's home turf, and it sounded authentic. Campbell didn't dismiss the report categorically and neither did Keenan. They wanted to keep the pressure on Smith.

"No comment," Keenan said. "I'll talk about it after the season."

Smith was furious with Keenan and Campbell. The club was baffled and didn't understand how Keenan could be shopping for a new job while his current team was in the middle of the finals.

"There's a lot of speculation," Keenan said, refusing to refute the rumors. "But I haven't had any time to spend time thinking about it. Those things happen in this game. My focus is on winning the game."

Keenan seemed to be loading up some leverage for his post-playoff battle with Smith, one that promised to get ugly. But this was not the time for controversy. Realizing that the speculation was getting out of hand, Rob Campbell tried to quell the media frenzy.

"There is absolutely no truth to it," Campbell said with a straight face. "I handle all of Michael's business affairs and I haven't spoken to anybody. I think the whole thing is really inappropriate. It's probably wishful thinking by Detroit. I have had no discussions with the Detroit Red Wings. In fact, I haven't spoken to Mike Ilitch in about two years."

With New York City ready for a celebration, the lifeless Rangers lost 6–3 at the Garden, forcing them to fly back to Vancouver for Game Six. The Canucks won that game, too, 4–1. With the Rangers reeling, Keenan considered taking the players to Lake Placid before Game Seven to keep them away from the distractions he had created. Messier convinced him that the team should return to New York, stand tall, and not run from the situation.

Keenan eventually mustered a more energetic denial of his Red Wings dalliance.

"I am coach of the Rangers," he told reporters. "I signed a five-year contract and there is no escape clause. I came here to coach the Rangers for five years. I don't know where these things are coming from, nor do I care at this point. I will be coaching the New York Rangers next year, unless my bosses don't want me to."

Smith made his feelings clear to his friends in the media. "If we win the Cup and he leaves, it will be like winning two Cups," he told a reporter privately. To another he said, "Escape clause? No, he doesn't have an escape clause, but if he wants to go, I'll drive him to the airport."

Once again, Messier had to take charge of the team. Next year was next year. The Rangers had the Stanley Cup in their sights. Forget about Keenan, he urged his teammates, and think about the championship.

"Was he going to be here next year?" MacTavish recalled. "Well, nobody really cared. At that point, nobody really cared who'd be there next year. It's a very fleeting role we all play on different teams. Who knows who's going to be here next year? Mark really put those things into perspective very quickly, in a way we all understood."

Leetch insisted that Keenan's contact with Detroit was a non-issue among the players. They were too engrossed in their title bid.

"Didn't mean a thing to us, never got in the room," Leetch said. "Things had happened all year. We were used to Mike. It was routine."

Colin Campbell used a ruse to prepare the team for Game Seven. He wanted to go over some Xs and Os with the players about the Canucks' defensemen, who were successfully jumping into the offense. Campbell also wanted to give the team some positive reinforcement by reviewing highlights of the first four games of the Cup finals, games dominated by the Rangers.

The trouble was, Keenan wasn't big on Xs and Os and video review. So Colin had Rob Campbell, who was his agent, too, call Keenan and keep him busy for twenty minutes while he and fellow assistant coach Dick Todd made a presentation to the team.

The team was prepared tactically. Now Keenan's challenge was preparing them mentally. He, too, had to clear his head of distractions and focus. He recalled something Gayla, in New York to see the finals, had told him two days before Game Seven.

"Dad, do me a favor," she said. "Promise me you'll spend the next two days thinking only of hockey. You owe it to yourself. You've spent your whole life to get to this point. I don't want you to worry about me or Mom or the divorce."

Keenan thought back to 1987, when the Flyers had a chance to topple the Oilers but couldn't quite finish off the series. On that night, he couldn't muster the words to inspire his team to greatness. Now he had a second chance.

"I learned from that," he said. "I didn't know enough. I didn't have the experience. It was just instinctive this time. I was staring out my office window at the water, collecting my thoughts, and I didn't think it was anything striking. But it was what I felt needed to be said."

He delivered the pre-game speech of his life. At the most critical moment of his career, he rose to the occasion. Messier, a man who had heard and given some great pep talks in his life, was awed.

"I just told them they owed nothing to anyone," Keenan recalled. "Me. The city. Nobody. They had done everything I'd asked of them and they should be proud of themselves no matter the outcome of the last game. I told them to play hard and enjoy themselves. Yeah, my eyes got a little red. They saw an exposed side of me. You know, I wouldn't have been able to come up with that speech if it wasn't for my daughter."

The Rangers raced to a 3–1 lead, then had to hang on to 3–2 margin through a tense third period. The flow of the action was choppy and one mistake could have tied the game. Rather than pressing the play and going for the kill, the Rangers were clinging. Canucks winger Nathan Lafayette had a chance to tie the game with less than five minutes left, but he hit the post with a shot that could have forced overtime.

In the final ninety-one seconds, the Canucks had four faceoffs in the Rangers' zone. If they could win a draw, kick the puck back to the point, and get a shot through and a bounce in front of the net, they'd have a great chance to tie the game. But the Rangers hung on. Time expired with Larmer killing the puck along the boards. The Rangers poured onto the ice. Messier jumped up and down. A fan held up the sign "Now I Can Die in Peace." Finally, the Rangers could hoist their Cup. The curse was over. They would never hear the derisive chant of "Nineteen-forty!" again.

"The challenge was laid out to all of us to be the ones to end that run, and we all ran with it," Leetch said after the victory. "We all wanted to be the team to do it. What an amazing thing."

Messier was used to winning in Edmonton, but the victory in New York was his best yet. "I've won five Stanley Cups before this and I've never experienced anything like the last two months," he said. "I'd thought I'd seen it all and I really wasn't saying much, but in my own mind I was saying, 'This is incredible!'"

After years of working constantly to achieve his goal, Keenan finally clutched the Cup in his arms. Since 1975, he had been driving himself to this point. And here it was. With Gayla at his side, he proudly accepted the chalice from Messier. More than anybody in the Garden, Gayla knew what this meant to her father.

"It's a deep feeling of satisfaction," he said after the triumph. "You realize how much people had to go through and all the hardships and all the obstacles, how difficult it is to win the Cup, how fortunate you have to be. To have Gayla standing on the bench when Mark brought the Cup over to me was phenomenal.

"We started out as underdogs but contenders, then turned to favorites. To be favorites in New York City, people don't realize how difficult that is. It takes every ounce of energy you have, all your physical energy, your psychological energy, everything you can think of has to be put into it in order to accomplish this."

The Cup mesmerized Keenan. "The goddamn thing is unbelievable, I tell you," he said. "It has its own personality. Like it's talking to you — talking of all the broken hearts, the broken legs, the broken families that went into it. For a small period of time, all the heartache goes away. I just looked at it and cried."

The Rangers got their chance to party with the Cup. The difficult season under Keenan had paid off for those who survived it. They couldn't complain about being champions.

"Mike took a lot of criticism, but he brought the Stanley Cup," MacTavish said. "Any coach who does that is doing something right and he obviously was. Mark and Mike worked very well together because Mike would come in and he'd cause more damage than he thought he was doing. He'd be a little more vindictive, or berate the team a little more than he would have thought. That's my impression of Mike. But Mark would quickly put those things in perspective and if there was any damage control that needed to be done, he did it very quickly. They worked very well together in that aspect.

"By and large, Mike is the type of coach, when you're winning he's a great guy to play for. He treats his players very well. When you're losing, maybe he does overreact at times and can become a little irrational. But Mark put those things in perspective quickly."

If Messier hadn't been there to pick up the pieces after his various detonations, Keenan would probably still be searching for his first Cup ring. The Rangers would still have been hearing about 1940.

"Only the players in this room and the people in this organization realize how close the whole thing was to blowing up in his face," Healy said.

Said Amonte, "I think we all know who was leading the way when they won the Stanley Cup. It wasn't the guy standing behind the bench, it was the guy wearing number eleven on the ice."

In his mind, Keenan had been a cream puff with the Rangers compared to the way he had been with his other teams. "It was my most fun year of coaching," he said. "There were only a half-dozen times I had to be a sonofabitch, versus forty the year before."

But winning the Cup didn't change his dim view of Smith. Under normal circumstances, he would have simply made a him-or-me ultimatum to the team owners and have won the power struggle. Either he would have seized the general manager's job or he would have had a lackey installed.

During the playoffs, however, Viacom had purchased Paramount and indicated that the sports properties — the Rangers, the Knicks, and Madison Square Garden — would immediately be put up for sale. While the properties were on the block, Viacom ordered that no major changes be made.

Gutkowski was a lame duck at the Garden, since the new owner would doubtlessly install his own leadership team. In the meantime, Gutkowski had to carry out the wishes of Viacom CEO Frank Biondi. There would be no changes, despite Smith's plaintive pitch to have Keenan removed.

"I'll work with this guy because I don't ever really want to leave the Rangers," Smith told Gutkowski. "But I sincerely believe it's in the best interest of this franchise to let him go. He will destroy the organization. Anyway, the guy's already been talking to Detroit."

Rob Campbell asked Smith whether a mutually beneficial divorce could be worked out. Smith was eager to make that happen, but Gutkowski held up the stop sign.

Campbell and Keenan also met with Gutkowski to go over all the options. One was to fire Smith and let Keenan do both jobs, but Biondi ordered that nobody was to be fired before the sale. If Keenan agreed to stay, there was a chance Smith would quit. Thinking ahead to that possibility, Gutkowski checked with Rangers broadcaster John Davidson to gauge his interest in the job. Davidson was intrigued. Gutkowski asked Keenan if he could work for Davidson. Keenan said he could. Furthermore, he said he would promise Viacom to stick around if Gutkowski was kept in charge.

Gutkowski went to Biondi one last time and was told, again, that no changes were to be made. Smith and Keenan would have to live with each other.

"They couldn't get along this year and it worked," Gutkowski said of Smith and Keenan. "We fully expected that this year they would work together again. They were told to make it work. They're bright, intelligent men, and bright, intelligent men have to find a way."

Fat chance. Smith wasn't going anywhere, so on July 15 Keenan decided to leave. Keenan and Campbell devised a late-payment scheme. When a $620,000 bonus check from the Rangers arrived late, Campbell immediately proclaimed that Keenan's contract had been breached. Keenan rented a studio from TSN in Toronto and held a televised news conference that afternoon to proclaim his free agency. It was a flimsy claim.

"Of course it wasn't the one-day-late payment of the playoff bonus," Gary Webb said. "Mike couldn't stand Neil Smith. To him, Smith was the ultimate spineless corporate wimp and Mike was floored when the Rangers wouldn't let him run the operation after he'd delivered them their first Cup in fifty-four years. What else did he have to do?"

Campbell already had the makings of a deal with St. Louis in hand. He and Keenan took another run at the Detroit job on the Saturday. But Bowman warned Mike and Marian Ilitch that Keenan already had an offer from the Blues. The Ilitches seemed lukewarm to Keenan and insisted that Jimmy Devellano would stay in the front office.

So on Sunday, July 17, Keenan and Campbell showed up in St. Louis to sign a contract with the Blues to become their new general manager and coach. In three dizzying days, Keenan had turned the NHL on its collective ear.

Gutkowski had been furious on Friday, when Keenan made his announcement, and became angrier as the weekend progressed. Keenan's quick signing with the Blues left the Rangers wondering if he was committed to leaving all along.

"There was absolutely no interest to see Mike Keenan leave the organization," he said. "He was our coach. We'd just won the Stanley Cup. We have a responsibility to our fans and we worked long and hard to get Mike Keenan as our coach and we wanted him to remain as such."

Suits, countersuits, and a league investigation quickly followed. Somebody, perhaps an angry Rangers fan, blew up Keenan's mailbox at his home in Greenwich, Connecticut. Commissioner Gary Bettman was outraged by the situation.

Keenan claimed, at least for public consumption, that Smith withheld the bonus check on purpose to void the contract and encourage him to leave. He argued that they didn't get along from the start and Smith wanted him gone. The late check was just a vehicle to rush him out of town.

"He knew about [the deadline] for forty-five days," Keenan said during the aftermath. "He intentionally made it late to set up a course of action. He wanted me out because I got too much credit. So I became the bad guy leaving. But I didn't want to leave. Neil Smith didn't want me there.

"I'd really looked forward to the challenge of coming to New York. It was an energizing place. You can ride that energy. I love it. I prefer the pressure of being a favorite. It gives you a psychological edge. Other teams fear you. They play scared. Underdogs have an excuse to lose. Favorites don't.

"Neil Smith didn't understand what it took to win. In our first meeting in July with the coaches, after I arrived, I asked Neil the question 'Is this team good enough to win the Stanley Cup?' The answer from Neil was 'Yes.' I said, 'How can you say that? Your team just missed the playoffs.' From that day on, we were moving in opposite directions."

Neil Smith denied conspiring with Rob Campbell to void Keenan's contract with the late bonus check. According to Barry Meisel's book *Losing the Edge,* Campbell asked Smith about the possibility of sending the check late. But Smith told Campbell that he had no control over the delivery of the check. "All I do is check to make sure the bonuses are correct," Smith said. "I check them against the contracts. Then the figures go to finance. I have nothing to do with the checks now."

Gutkowski was incredulous that Keenan would pull such a stunt to get out. In his mind, the late check was a non-issue.

"He never called me," Gutkowski said. "Whenever there was a problem, he or Rob Campbell always called me. Mr. Campbell never had a problem calling me when he wanted Barbra Streisand tickets. But for some reason, they never picked up the phone this time. As a matter of fact, I think he was one day late on his payment for the Streisand tickets."

Gutkowski didn't hold back during the news conference to present the Rangers' response to Keenan's exit. There was a tawdry, World Wrestling Federation–like feel to the presentation. Big corporations normally don't conduct business in such an entertaining fashion. Big corporations don't summon reporters so executives can heap abuse on former employees. Somewhere, Vince McMahon was taking notes. It was as if Keenan had turned heel.

"Mike has baggage wherever he goes," Gutkowski said. "He's now just picked up a couple of additional suitcases. He'll have to live with his own actions. I'm very unimpressed with the way he dealt with leaving. It lacked character. He was certainly attractively compensated. I wouldn't call being coach of the New York Rangers a hardship."

Keenan's departure from the Rangers mirrored his departures from other teams. In Philadelphia, he had clashed with general manager Bobby Clarke. In Chicago, his nemesis was Bob Pulford, owner Bill Wirtz's confidant. And his bid for the Detroit job was short-circuited by Jimmy Devellano, who still had the Ilitch family's ear.

"In all three places I've been in the league, someone was either jealous of me or felt their position was being threatened and being undermined," Keenan said. "There are snakes everywhere in this jungle."

The Rangers weren't surprised by the news, given all the speculation during the Cup finals. Some were disappointed to see Keenan leave.

"I learned a lot under him," Richter said. "I think he'll be missed in a lot of ways and I hate to see him go. I liked playing for him a lot. I owe him an awful lot. He came at a great time, not only for me, but for the team. You can only go so far with talent, but the discipline he instilled is a great thing."

But other players were relieved. "When we won there was the question of how things could ever be better," Leetch said. "I have to say that when Mike left, it was better in a hurry for a lot of players."

◄ 6 ►

Suffering through the St. Louis Blues

It got to the point where I wasn't even able to go out for a shift and function. I would be sitting there thinking about him and how I wanted to kill him. I'd be on the bench and I wouldn't even be watching the game. I'd have no spit in my mouth. In my mind, I'd be cutting his eyes out with my stick. It was awful. I never felt so hopeless in my entire life.

— FORMER BLUES STAR BRETT HULL,
ON HIS UNHAPPY LIFE WITH MIKE KEENAN

MIKE KEENAN'S HIRING SHOCKED ST. LOUIS. YES, THERE HAD BEEN talk of him coming to town as far back as 1988, but he had become a mortal enemy during his run with the brawl-happy Blackhawks. Blues fans never really believed their franchise would cross over to the dark side.

Then the team embarrassed itself during the 1994 postseason. After a promising 91-point regular season, they rolled over against the Dallas Stars and were swept in the first round. The Blues had ample talent, with 50-goal scorers Brendan Shanahan and Hull up front with slippery play-maker Craig Janney and speedy utility forward Kevin Miller. The defense featured gifted puck movers like Phil Housley and Steve Duchesne. Acrobatic Curtis Joseph was in goal. The Blues also loaded up for the stretch run by signing two free-agent centers after the Olympics, future Hall of Famer Peter Stastny and the talented Petr Nedved. Veteran defenseman Alexei Kasatonov was added, too. On paper, this team appeared formidable.

But the Blues demonstrated little heart on the ice. They did pirou-
ettes in the corners to avoid checks. Their wallets might have been heavy,
but their hitting was anything but. They skated around the ice in fancy
loops, like a "Disney on Ice" troupe. Housley and Duchesne played like
Chip and Dale on the blue line. Nedved was just plain Goofy. These mer-
cenaries were an affront to those warriors who had worn the Blue Note
before them, rugged characters like Bob and Barclay Plager, Bob Gassoff,
Brian Sutter, and Rob Ramage. These Blues did everything but wear tights
on the ice and sprinkle sequins on their sweaters.

Even NHL Commissioner Gary Bettman ridiculed their playoff per-
formance during acrimonious labor negotiations with the NHL Players
Association. When Bettman mocked the Blues' egregious failure,
Shanahan stood up to confront Bettman about his bargaining table quip.
It was the most spunk a Blue had shown in some time.

The 1994 fiasco convinced team chairman of the board Mike Shanahan
and president Jack Quinn to take a tougher approach. They desperately
wanted to win a Stanley Cup for their loyal fans. They had done a brilliant job rekindling hockey interest in their town, creating teams that filled
the old St. Louis Arena to its leaking roof. This revival inspired its ownership group, a who's who of the local business community, to build a
new downtown showplace arena for the team. They had spent aggres-
sively for glitzy talent, exploiting the seldom-used free-agency mecha-
nisms in the NHL's collective bargaining agreement. By chasing after free
agents Scott Stevens, Brendan Shanahan, Housley, and Nedved, they
helped trigger runaway salary inflation in a league that prided itself on
cost control.

Blues management had become outcasts from the NHL's old boys' club.
The Blues' tactics appalled Glen Sather, Harry Sinden, Bill Wirtz, John
McMullen, and others. They snubbed and insulted Quinn and Mike
Shanahan at league meetings. Shanahan and Quinn began to relish their
renegade image, noting that their allegiance was to Blues fans, not league
decorum. The more other teams complained, the harder they worked at
poaching talent. If they won games, filled seats, increased revenue, and
gave New Jersey Devils general manager Lou Lamoriello heartburn all
at the same time, then it was all worth it.

St. Louis fans loved the Blues' moxie. They bristled at the fiscally conservative management of the St. Louis Cardinals by Anheuser-Busch.
They loathed hapless football Cardinals owner Bill Bidwill, a bumbler

who mismanaged his team before moving the franchise to Arizona. They had grown weary of the previous Blues owner, California entrepreneur Harry Ornest. Sure, he rescued the franchise from oblivion in 1983 and nursed it back to health, but he was almost comically cheap. He didn't quite recycle nacho cheese that spilled onto the Arena concourse, but the man was tight.

Now this Blues management team was doing whatever it could to win and fans rallied around the cause. So what if they had to endure staggering ticket price increases year after year. The Blues' quest for the Stanley Cup became the fans' quest, too, and they enlisted for the war. If it meant that income-challenged fans had to eat pork rinds instead of pork chops on Thursday nights, so be it. Champions had to sacrifice.

But for all their good intentions, the management team never developed and adhered to a championship program. Most of the talent it acquired had run afoul of coaches or general managers elsewhere. Agents looking to liberate their clients burned up the phone lines into the Blues' offices. Quinn, Mike Shanahan, and general manager Ron Caron operated by the seat of their pants, grabbing players whenever the opportunity presented itself, often without considering how the personnel would fit together.

Quinn had become increasingly involved in the hockey operation once Brett Hull's landmark $7.4 million deal in 1990 raised the financial stakes for the franchise. Ironically, Quinn had been stingy even by NHL standards during the Ornest era and he continued that pattern after Shanahan's group bought the team in 1986. But "Action Jackson," as the local scribes liked to call him, turned into one of the league's most notorious spendthrifts in the early 1990s. In less than a decade, the Blues payroll would explode tenfold from $3 million in 1989. Rather than ditching players who were due big raises, as Ornest had ordered him to do, Quinn began wooing players who reached that point with rival clubs.

The Blues had shocked the industry by signing Scott Stevens as a restricted free agent in 1990, on the heels of the landmark Hull re-signing. The club gave Stevens a $5-million offer sheet, then sent the Washington Capitals five number-one picks when the Caps elected not to match the offer after a week of deliberation. No team had ever gone after such a high-profile free agent in such a fashion. Salary-controlling collusion among owners (and NHLPA czar Alan Eagleson, as it turned out) had ruled the sport.

Giddy from this success, Quinn went after restricted free agent Brendan Shanahan the next summer. This time, the NHL lashed back. With a rather deliberate stroke of irony, an arbitrator awarded Scott Stevens to the New Jersey Devils as compensation for losing Shanahan. So there! The league also investigated the Blues for allegedly signing Shanahan to a longer, more lucrative offer sheet than the sheet it sent to the NHL office. The league had the Blues' offices searched for proof of the secret deal. The search proved futile, but the message was clear: The Blues were on double-secret probation.

There was a lot for Keenan to like about the Blues. The Blues were mavericks, gamblers who loved to wheel and deal. When the NHL went after the Blues, the Blues went after the NHL. Their courtship of free agent Michel Goulet cost the Blackhawks a fortune. They signed Dave Christian, even though the Boston Bruins insisted they still had him under contract. They stepped up to make Nedved an offer after the Vancouver Canucks resolved to let him sit an entire season. They exploited the tough economic conditions for Canadian teams by first bidding for Phil Housley, forcing Winnipeg to deal him to St. Louis in 1993, and then by foisting Housley on Calgary the next summer for the free-agent rights to Al MacInnis. Such talent chases built entertaining rosters and made the Blues the talk of the town, but the franchise moved no closer to the Stanley Cup.

Coaching was the missing element. Ornest had let Jacques Demers get away after he took the team to the Western Conference finals in 1986. After that, the Blues struggled to find similar leadership. Caron hired Jacques Martin after he won the Memorial Cup in Guelph, but his lack of NHL experience left some veterans grousing. One of those grousers, Brian Sutter, retired to take the helm after the Blues gave Keenan some consideration. When Sutter failed to lead the Blues past the second round in his four seasons, management turned to player-friendly Bob Plager and installed a player advisory panel to help him run the show.

Oops! Touchy-feely doesn't go in a sport where stick-wielding behemoths engage in bloody combat. The Blues didn't need a facilitator, they needed a leader. Old-schooler Bob Berry replaced the pitiable Plager and restored order, but he, like Sutter, couldn't push the Blues to the NHL's upper crust despite all the pricey player additions. The 1994 playoff flop created new urgency, as did the team's pending move to the sparkling new

Kiel Center. The owners had already undermined Michael Shanahan's power by buying his equity stake in the franchise. The investors agreed to leave him in the office as a hired hand, but he was working on borrowed time.

The time had come for the Blues to go for it. Keenan had just won the Stanley Cup in New York before declaring himself a free agent, despite having four years left on his contract. The hated Red Wings seemed ready to toss ethics aside and steal him away. Pizza maven Mike Ilitch had been after Keenan for years. Quinn and Mike Shanahan couldn't let that happen. Who were the outlaws here, anyway? They shoved Caron aside into an advisory role and gave Iron Mike a stunning six-year, $12-million contract to become general manager and coach.

"We really wanted Mike's coaching ability," Shanahan later explained. "Either it was accept those terms or pass on Mike Keenan. So we took those terms. He gave up a contract to accept a contract. Is it right or wrong? Who knows? We knew he was a high maintenance guy. He really hadn't been a GM before, except for two years in Chicago. And he had to report to Bob Pulford there."

Keenan could have landed the Red Wings job, but that would have meant pushing aside Scotty Bowman, his mentor.

"That's one of the reasons why I didn't pursue [the Red Wings job]," Keenan said. "I told Mr. Ilitch at the time that it would have been like coming to your home and throwing your father out."

Bowman clearly wasn't happy about Keenan's near-hiring in Detroit. When the topic was brought up a few years later, Bowman had a snit.

"Talk to him about it," Bowman snapped. "I have no reaction to what other people say." The Bowman-Keenan relationship chilled for a few years.

There were also serious questions about how much autonomy he would have in Motown. The Blues would be Keenan's show. He had finally realized his dream to run a franchise from top to bottom.

"I'd like to be in one place and help build an organization," he said after joining the Blues. "The goal is not to win the Stanley Cup. The goal is to win many Stanley Cups."

When the deal was done on July 17, 1994, Keenan, Shanahan, and Quinn sipped wine and celebrated the signing at a suburban St. Louis restaurant. Keenan was thrilled to be running a rebel operation. He had found the corporate suits at Madison Square Garden exasperating to deal with. His new bosses loved to wheel and deal.

"I can coach in a more palatable way now," he said. "I can surround myself with people who are willing to go the distance. I've realized I can't change people. I can only change the teams they play on."

Shanahan and Quinn rejoiced. Finally they had championship-caliber leadership for their team. The NHL would be furious, of course, but the league was always furious at the Blues. The lawyers would work everything out.

"We are not afraid," Caron said. "That's what makes us different. We've added a guy with the same bloodline. We're not afraid to take risks."

Keenan immediately raised the goals for the Blues. "We don't want to be average," he proclaimed. "Average to me is .500. It takes a huge commitment to be above average. We want to be exceptional. If you pardon me for saying so, to win a Stanley Cup you have to go through hell, both mental and physical."

He realized immediately that the Blues had lots of talent, but very little grit. He didn't mind trading the enigmatic Nedved to New York for career pest Esa Tikkanen and defenseman Doug Lidster as part of his breach-of-contract settlement with the Rangers.

"We feel the more Stanley Cup winners we have in our locker room, the better," Keenan said. "It's good for the Blues, adding the experience of these two players. Esa's a very strong player, a very important player in playoff competition." Keenan would have saved himself a lot of aggravation had he made the deal he really wanted: Hull and Nedved to the Rangers for Jeff Beukeboom and Alexei Kovalev.

But he didn't mind this deal. The self-absorbed Nedved represented everything the Blues had become and every reason they couldn't hope to win without making dramatic changes. He refused to pay the price to score tough goals, preferring to stay on the perimeter and snap off long wrist shots. Nedved should have been one of the elite players of his era; instead, he remained one of the most confounding. The Blues had provided safe haven for many such players over the years.

"They filled buildings without developing a winning culture," Keenan observed. "They produced a very selfish culture."

But this culture had produced a successful business. The marquee players filled seats. The stars helped the franchise multiply its revenues, increase its value, and solidify its future in the marketplace. The stars helped get the new arena built, complete with luxury suites and club seats where harried waiters attempted to serve junk food on the same day it was ordered.

Cup or no Cup, the Blues were commercial champions. Shanahan and Quinn had earned a wide berth from the investors.

Hull had personally taken the franchise to new heights. He captured the city's imagination with his 228-goal burst in three years, drawing a lot of first-time fans to the rink. Glib, gracious, and charismatic, he was a team marketer's dream. He strove to answer every piece of mail he received during those giddy years. He blasted the puck like his Hall of Fame father, Bobby Hull, and charmed fans the way Bobby had, too. Hull built personal equity in the St. Louis market, gaining the widespread popularity that gives an athlete plenty of latitude. If he quarreled with the coach, clashed with teammates, or popped off about the team's mismanagement, what were the Blues going to do? Trade him? Hull knew that wasn't going to happen, not with all those premium seats to fill. But Keenan and Hull were an ego clash waiting to happen.

"Mike has a different concept of work and it's not for everybody," Caron said at the time. "He asks the game be played his way. He made Jeremy Roenick a pretty good player. His work concept is a rude awakening for a lot of players and Brett will be one. But if he works, Brett will be the better player for it."

Curtis Joseph and Brendan Shanahan rivaled Hull's popularity in 1994. In the 1993 playoffs, Joseph had single-handedly sent the dreaded Blackhawks packing in a first-round sweep. He shut out the Hawks in Games Two and Three, then capped off his brilliant performance with a 4–3 overtime victory in Game Four. He carried the Blues to a seventh game against the Toronto Maple Leafs in the next round before going down in a hail of shots. Joseph had a catchy nickname, Cujo — semi-inspired by the Stephen King movie about an unpleasant dog — and a flashy style that mesmerized fans. His underdog persona was appealing, too. His natural parents had given him up for adoption at birth and he had spent much of his young life being overlooked. He never played major junior hockey and never got drafted by the NHL. He was a college kid (who, in fact, had played at the University of Wisconsin, just like Mike Richter). Yet he worked his way toward stardom and inspired spectators to stand and bow after his special saves, offering a mass "we are not worthy" gesture.

Shanahan was the team's hunk. He was combative, handsome, and humorous. He could fight the league's heavyweights, score fifty goals a season, and give some of the NHL's best quotes. He was a rough-and-tumble player the Plagers would have gladly gone to battle with. Women adored him and the working class men respected him. He was community-minded and raised money for Alzheimer's disease research through his annual softball game. Shanahan had lost his father to Alzheimer's and took the cause seriously.

To deal with the Blues' stars, Keenan brought back Bob Berry as an assistant coach to help ease the transition. He also kept Ted Sator around for another year, just as he had done under similar circumstances in Philadelphia. Berry and Sator ran the team at Keenan's first training camp with the Blues, because Keenan was serving his sixty-day NHL suspension for leaving the Rangers.

Keenan tried, unsuccessfully, to argue that his Iron Mike reputation was overblown. He wasn't Iron Mike, but Iron Mike Lite. "Hey, my reputation precedes me now, so I don't have to be that way anymore," he insisted. "Fear is a factor already. So I can be softer and be a lot more effective. Most people think I enjoy conflict. I hate it. Rita and I never argued or shouted, even at the end. I saw so much conflict when I was young, I'm sick of it. I'd walk away after doing those things to players and I'd feel awful inside."

The Blues had been one of the highest-paid teams for a couple of years. In 199–95, their $23-million payroll ranked second in the NHL. Keenan set out to make the Blues earn their money by winning something substantial for a change. He had a photograph of the Stanley Cup put on prominent display in the team's dressing room at the Kiel Center. He had the old carpeting removed from the room and ordered new carpeting in the likeness of a hockey rink. He wanted the players to focus on their on-ice responsibilities between periods of games. This was an old trick, but the Blues hadn't seen it before. Strength coach Bob Kersee, who had trained many Olympic champions, came aboard to create a more aggressive fitness program. State-of-the-art fitness centers were installed in the new Kiel Center and the team's new suburban practice facility.

Such classy touches wowed the troops. Hull threw down his welcome mat for Keenan. He had scored plenty of goals and earned tons of money in St. Louis, but now it was time to win. Finally he had a coach with real credentials.

"He is unbelievable," Hull gushed. "He's so hard to describe. He's the man. He knows exactly what's going on. He knows exactly what it takes. He's got the respect of everybody here. I don't think it's just me. You can see a change in every single person, the way they carry themselves around the room. Last year it was get off the ice and get out, who the hell wants to be around here? This year, you're here early, you're riding the bikes. It's a joy to be here. My perception was, this is a guy who is going to make my life hell and I'm not going to have fun. And it's been the exact opposite. When you meet him, it's such a pleasant surprise after all the crap that's been written about him."

The league sanctions prolonged the honeymoon, since Keenan had to monitor training camp from afar. And before he could coach a single Blues regular season game, the league locked out its players, hoping the players association would capitulate and agree to a lesser contract to restore economic order. Ultimately, the lockout accomplished little but to shorten the 1994–95 season to forty-eight games and give the Blues an extended Keenan-free vacation.

The lockout allowed Keenan the time and opportunity to reorder his life. A tall blonde named Nola McLennan had entered his life and their romance blossomed.

"I asked her if she liked short, fat, bald guys," Keenan joked.

They had met on a Florida beach earlier in the year, during his estrangement from his wife Rita. Nola, a nurse from Maine, was nine years younger than Keenan, but she was a strong-willed woman reeling from marital difficulties of her own.

"She's a lot like me," Keenan said during their courtship. "We've had some real Pier Sixes. She told me, 'I hope you don't scare off easily.'"

Keenan's move to St. Louis got him closer to Gayla, who was now just an hour's flight away in Chicago. He spoke optimistically about actually building a life for himself away from the rink.

"I didn't put the time or energy into my personal life that I put into my professional life," he said. "I want more balance. It's absolutely imperative to my health."

Keenan had spent his professional life building, refining, and occasionally complaining about his dark image. It was exhausting work. "I'm sick and tired of being sick and tired," he said. "You reach a point where you have enough security and you say, 'I'm just not doing it anymore,'" he said.

Every time he took a new job, he had to insist that he really wasn't a hothead or a madman. It became his standard stump speech. "Ask the players I coached last year who knew me from before," he said. "I'm a lot more patient, so those questions don't apply to me anymore. Look, I've come to realize I'm a decent human being and I'm a goddamned good coach and I've had enough of people running over me."

Back home in Ontario, Keenan had become closer to his family during the previous two summers. His resort property on the Georgian Bay featured five buildings. His father lived there and his mother moved to a nearby village.

"The family enjoyed wonderful evenings together," Marie, his sister, reported. "Sing-alongs . . . going over the happy family memories. Mike has a better understanding of people's feelings."

Well, sort of. Back in St. Louis, Keenan's imperious manner quickly turned off his co-workers. His high-handed behavior made even his staunchest allies wince. The trouble began early. He helped line up Nik and the Nice Guys to play a party for the construction crew and arena staff when the Kiel Center opened. Keenan was supposed to introduce his old band and say a few words to the workers. Instead, he didn't show up until late in the evening when another band was playing. He got up on stage, waved to the crowd, and left. Kiel Center officials weren't amused that he had been out with Rob Campbell instead of tending to business.

Trainer Ron Dubuque, who had been hired just before Keenan arrived, met his boss once and got fired in that meeting. Keenan wanted his own people. (Dubuque later landed with the Rams and won a Super Bowl ring.) Later, venerable equipment man Frankie Burns got the ax. Keenan hired a personal assistant to tend to his chores and had underlings do personal favors, like fetch him a Christmas tree. His bosses suspected the number one reason he hired a massage therapist was that he enjoyed rubdowns.

Keenan routinely tried to circumvent Quinn to get what he wanted from Mike Shanahan.

"You know, Mike, I work for you," Keenan would tell him.

"No," Shanahan would say. "You work for Jack and Jack works for me."

When the NHL lockout ended in January 1995, Keenan wasted no time implementing his program. Vacation was over. The Blues were about to be worked harder than they believed possible. It was time for this franchise to shed its also-ran reputation.

"The people in this locker room have had a lot of disappointments and embarrassments on a team basis, not an individual basis," he observed. "They should embrace the opportunity."

Keenan drafted the marshmallow-soft Craig Janney as his first whipping boy. Janney was almost too easy to pick on. He was the anti-Messier, a gifted playmaker with little toughness and no discernible leadership skills. His aversion to weight training was legendary. Even in peak shape, he looked like a sportswriter when he pulled off his gear. His idea of a vigorous workout was to do a dozen or so twelve-ounce curls. Despite his solid career point production and his magical chemistry with Brendan Shanahan, he wasn't a St. Louis fan favorite. The Blues had traded the beloved Adam Oates to get him, breaking up the historic Hull and Oates combination. Janney was good, but Oates was great.

The end of the lockout caught Janney off guard and he reported in dreadful shape, even by his admittedly low standards. Keenan flogged him mercilessly and banished him to the press box. Then he sent him home to await a trade. Janney lasted eight games before getting traded to San Jose for defenseman Jeff Norton. He had no chance and he knew it, so he asked Keenan to move him. His personal life was in disarray and now his professional life was going down the toilet, too. Janney was so eager to leave that he agreed to restructure his contract to make himself more palatable for the Sharks.

"It was a difficult situation when I left, but it was one other players have gone through many times," Janney said after relocating. "It's difficult for anyone to go through something like that, but Mike Keenan just didn't want me to play for him. I asked for a trade to get out of there because I was upset I was becoming a distraction to my friends on the team. I was making a lot of money and not earning it. Mike Keenan has control of that organization. He is the general manager as well as the coach and is trying to get the guys he wants on the team. That's his prerogative. He's the boss."

Brendan Shanahan, one of Janney's friends, was also having a tough time with Keenan. Sick and rundown early in the season, he got off to a sluggish start. He clashed constantly with Keenan. After a 5–0 loss to Chicago on February 9, Keenan blasted Shanahan in front of his teammates for allowing Janney to "hold his hand" for two seasons. Later, Keenan questioned Shanahan's work ethic during a media briefing. During a closed-door meeting with Shanahan, he held his index finger and thumb about an inch apart and told Shanahan he was "that close" to being traded.

"What you have to understand is that Keenan used his power to generate fear," Caron observed. "Shanahan wasn't afraid of him and Mike couldn't handle that."

Keenan also rode Curtis Joseph hard. He questioned his work ethic, citing the goaltender's late arrival for a practice session during a team retreat to Vail, Colorado. Joseph claimed he missed a team bus that left five minutes early.

"I ran about a quarter mile down the road after them in the snow, but nobody turned around," he explained. "Then I came back and called a cab, but they said it wouldn't be there until twenty minutes later. There was no other way to get to the rink. It was ten miles away. That's when Mike and Bob Berry saw me and said to come with them. So I left some money at the front desk and I rode with them. The 'fact' I don't care, that's ridiculous. Just ask anybody I ever played with if I cared about them, if I cared about every game, if I cared about every shot."

The Blues motored to a record of 28-15-5 in the shortened regular season, creating great expectations for the playoffs. The franchise had hired Keenan to win in the playoffs and the fans couldn't wait to see him work his magic.

"In this profession, we're judged on how we do in the playoffs," Sator said. "With Mike, there is not a lot of gray. There's black and white. And there's one direction he steers his team: toward getting ready for the playoffs."

Keenan had to have his type of team in place. That's why he added grinding winger Greg Gilbert in the waiver draft held before the season. Gilbert knew Keenan's routine from Chicago and New York. Another former Ranger, Glenn Anderson, signed as a free agent during the stretch run. Both players helped their new teammates interpret their coach's actions.

"It's not all psychological ploys," Gilbert said. "He sets it up as challenges and he sees how guys respond. If he has to rip out your backside, he'll do it, and I respect that. I'd rather have somebody yelling at me, telling me what I'm doing wrong, then letting things go. But people react differently."

Gilbert had a point. Joseph wilted when challenged. He entered the season expecting to get a lucrative new contract before he became a free agent, but Keenan wasn't sold on him. He didn't see a combative personality like Ron Hextall's in his makeup. He didn't see an edgy Ed Belfour or a resilient Mike Richter. He wondered aloud how Joseph could expect big money without proving himself in money games. Rise to the playoff occasion as Richter did, Keenan suggested, and perhaps the team could commit to him.

Keenan hit all the wrong buttons with Joseph, just as he had misread Scott Mellanby in Philadelphia and Tony Amonte in New York. Joseph was as competitive as anybody, but he needed reinforcement. He was fretful. The contract impasse hung over his head all season. Fearing the worst, he put his suburban St. Louis home up for sale. He felt singled out after having done so much for the franchise.

"I had had it," Joseph said. "I even cleared his desk one day when our conversation got a little heated."

Keenan kept turning the screws and, sure enough, Joseph cracked in the playoffs. He won the series opener against Vancouver 2–1, but then all hell broke loose. The Blues lost Games Two and Three by a combined score of 11–4. The Blues won two of the next three games to force a Game Seven. The onus was on Joseph in the deciding game.

"The one thing you need to win [in] the playoffs is goaltending," Keenan said during the series. "I feel badly for Curt. He's not playing very well. He knows it, we know it, and everyone else knows it. He is fighting the puck. He has played much, much better throughout most of his career."

Indeed. Joseph was a spastic mess in this series. Had Shanahan not suffered a broken ankle in Game Five, the Blues might have been able to dominate the Canucks and win despite their shaken goaltender. But they couldn't. Joseph was bombed in Game Seven, 5–3, and the Blues finished a distant thirteen playoff victories short of their goal. Joseph was done in St. Louis and he knew it. After the game, he choked back tears while discussing his spectacular failure.

"At the time, it was hard," Joseph said. "I let him get to me. He could say I didn't play well in the playoffs that year. I'm mad at myself for letting him get to me."

Keenan also lashed out at Hull during the Canucks fiasco, even though Hull scored six goals in seven games. He compared him unfavorably to Vancouver captain Trevor Linden, who enjoyed a strong series.

"You can see Trevor's physical attributes and you can see Brett Hull's physical attributes," Keenan said. "But you can't see the intrinsic attributes unless they do something extraordinary. That's why Mark Messier is a winner and a leader. Mark Messier's physical attributes don't change. But his determination, drive, passion, and commitment change and become deeper and richer as playoff competition progresses."

The first-round disaster triggered a predictable overhaul. The turnover started at the top, with the ouster of chairman Mike Shanahan. On June

15, 1995, Shanahan was called in for a lunch meeting with the ownership group, investors who called themselves the Kiel Center Partners. Shanahan was shown an organizational chart that didn't include his name.

"I'm out?" he asked.

"No, you're not out," a partner said.

"Then I'm in?" Shanahan asked.

"No, you're out," the partner said.

So it went with the Blues. After nine-and-a-half years on the job, including five as general partner, Shanahan was told he was being reduced to a member of the board. Rather than accept the demotion, he decided to leave the franchise he loved dearly.

Thanks to a handy escape clause in his original deal, Shanahan's removal gave Keenan a thirty-day window of opportunity to seek work elsewhere. He chose to stay when the Blues added another guaranteed year to his contract and guaranteed that a drastic payroll reduction wasn't in the works.

Keenan celebrated the extension by going wild on the free-agent market. He signed center Dale Hawerchuk, his former Junior B star at Oshawa, to a three-year, $7.5-million deal on July 8. The fact that Hawerchuk, thirty-two, was over the hill didn't concern Keenan at all.

"There were a few teams interested in signing me and they were all offering $2 million a year, then St. Louis came in offering $2.5 million a year and, basically, when that happens you feel the team really wants you," Hawerchuk explained.

Aging, injury-prone goaltender Grant Fuhr, who had won four Stanley Cups with the Oilers in the mid-1980s, came aboard as a free agent on July 14. Feisty left winger Geoff Courtnall rejoined the franchise the same day, also as an unrestricted free agent. On July 28, Keenan's old friend, Brian Noonan, signed as an unrestricted free agent and restricted free agent Shayne Corson of the Oilers got an offer sheet. In all, Keenan spent a whopping $25 million on free agents.

Players were leaving, too. Brendan Shanahan was traded to Hartford for defenseman Chris Pronger on July 27. Steve Duchense was sent to Ottawa for a draft pick.

"At the end," Shanahan said, "I wondered if he would have preferred to see me break down, if he wanted to see me lose it."

Shanahan was in New York City doing a fashion shoot for *Mademoiselle* magazine when he found out about the trade. He was in a

restaurant with some other NHL players, Bettman, and NHL public relations operatives when he was called to the phone.

"Who is it?" Shanahan asked.

Told it was Keenan, Shanahan thought, *Oh, God, here I go.*

The conversation was short and sweet. Keenan said, "I've traded you
to Hartford for Chris Pronger. Mr. Shanahan and Jack Quinn would like
to thank you for all you've done for St. Louis. Good luck."

Shanahan was shocked. "I went back to the table and told them I was
traded and left," he said. "I went back to the hotel." He had hoped to sit
down with his coach and clear the air about their first season together.
He believed their relationship could have been salvaged.

"There was some friction between Mike Keenan and me, but I felt
the way I came on in the second half of the season and the playoffs, that
Mike and I had a professional understanding of each other. It took a matter of time before I was healthy, physically. I did everything he asked of
me. Although I wasn't happy with some of Mike's moves, I never challenged him in front of the team and I never gave him the impression I
was more important than the coach."

Keenan cited a variety of reasons for trading him. Since Shanahan
couldn't play on the top line, how could the club justify paying him top-
line money? The franchise needed to trade for a big defenseman like
Pronger. Privately, Keenan cited issues in Shanahan's private life that made
trading him imperative. For one, Shanahan was close friends with Craig
and Cathy Janney and tried to help them through their marital troubles.
Years later, though, the Janneys divorced.

Keenan claimed he was acting on an ownership edict when he moved
Shanahan. He was told to trim costs to keep the payroll from soaring
completely out of control. Keenan claimed he was ordered to trade either
Shanahan, due to make $3.2 million that season, Hull, due $3.8 million,
or MacInnis, due $3.5 million.

"I had to shoot one of them," Keenan insisted. But trading Shanahan
didn't provide tremendous economic relief. The Blues would have to continue paying Shanahan's deferred salary and agreed to pay $500,000 of
Shanahan's 1995-96 salary as well. Then the club extended and upgraded
Pronger's contract into a $14-million deal. Then Keenan acquired Noonan
and Corson, adding another $2 million a year to the payroll. The eco-
nomic excuse just didn't add up.

A week later, Keenan shipped Joseph's free-agent rights to Edmonton with prospect Mike Grier to regain the draft picks spent on Corson. Joseph would spend half the following season in exile playing in Las Vegas of the International Hockey League before finally signing with the cash-strapped Oilers. Considering Joseph's playoff failure, nobody was surprised by his departure. Keenan justified the move by continuing to question Cujo's dedication.

"He had the lowest fitness rating of any professional athlete we ever tested," Keenan sniffed. "But that didn't bother me as much as the fact he didn't improve by the end of the year."

Joseph didn't dispute the latter point. He had been awful in the play-offs. But questions about his commitment riled him.

"Keenan was very outspoken about me," Joseph said. "Even when I was in Las Vegas in the IHL before I signed with the Oilers, I had people coming up to me and saying, 'I saw Keenan on TV and he gave you a shot.' Every chance he got, he took a shot at me. I had a lot of great years in St. Louis before he came there. Maybe he was doing it to justify trading me. He didn't think I was capable as a player. And one thing he said was that I wasn't in shape. More than anything, that baffled me. Before Keenan came, the press was writing that they were perplexed that I got better for the playoffs and that I didn't burn out playing sixty games and facing forty shots a game."

Joseph was astonished by the abuse Keenan heaped on him. "I couldn't imagine treating human beings that way," Joseph said. "The trade to Edmonton was the best thing that ever happened to me. I couldn't take it anymore."

In order to build a championship team, Keenan believed he first had to tear it down. In his mind, almost every team came with the label "Some disassembly required." If the established leadership base wasn't strong enough, it had to be reconstructed. Players who gained great popularity and wealth without winning the ultimate prize tended to get compla-cent. He saw this with Denis Savard, Doug Wilson, and Mike Gartner. To win, he had to destroy comfort zones and any player unwilling to put down the Chee•tos and get his ass off the recliner. He had won with edgy teams in Philadelphia, Chicago, and New York.

Keenan's critics suggested he ran off stars so that he himself could be the star. By eliminating players with power bases, he gained more power himself. The Blues would become his show and his show alone.

"Give me some credit for having some brains," he snapped. "First of all, I wouldn't set myself up like that. Second of all, that's not remotely close to my motivation. The motivation is to make my team better. We got rid of some very popular players. But it's not like we brought in five guys off the minor league club."

The public relations fallout from this shocking summer was huge. The franchise had made itself viable by marketing top players. That strategy worked because St. Louisans are more starstruck than fans in larger markets. They embrace players who perform well, show a little personality, and give back to the community. Years later, St. Louis would go ga-ga over Mark McGwire of the Cardinals and Kurt Warner of the Rams. In the early 1990s, they loved Hullie, Cujo, and Shan the Man.

"There's a special relationship between the players and the fans that Mike didn't understand, but I think he resented [it] because it existed before he was there," Brendan Shanahan said.

Said Hull, "It doesn't matter if we win or lose. The fans still want to see their favorite guy, the one player they've embraced. I'm not questioning the moves Mike made, but I think the organization underestimated the fans' loyalty to their favorite players. They're pissed off because they took Shanny and Cujo in. They were part of the St. Louis family."

The Missouri Athletic Club named Shanahan the city's Sportsman of the Year in balloting that took place after he was traded. He flew to St. Louis on a day off to accept the award.

Keenan later owned up to his miscalculation. His only goal was to win it all, while the ownership group's top goals were to fill seats and pay off the arena debt. These trades compromised those goals.

"I was totally unaware of how much those sports heroes — as opposed to having a winning team — meant to this city," he said as the backlash washed over the franchise. "But this team has gone past the second round of the playoffs once in the last twenty-four seasons. So we could do what some people wanted and have five or six very popular players and give them 60 percent of the payroll. But there's one problem with that. We're not going to win. Now if that's what the town wants, then I don't know why ownership brought me in."

The gulf between Keenan and the public became enormous. He had come to town as a conquering hero, landing his own television segment on KSDK and his own radio show on KMOX before he had won anything in the city. Fans viewed him as a sure thing. For decades, diehards had poured their hearts into supporting the franchise and had nothing to show for it except some old Perry Turnbull replica sweaters. Keenan seemed certain to change all that. But as he exiled their heroes to distant outposts, fans started turning against him.

His style was a problem too. The public never saw Mike's fun side, the charming side, the music-loving, motorcycle-riding, pool-playing side. Cameras never caught his self-deprecating side. Instead, fans saw Keenan droning on with manage-babble sentences like this one: "We found out professionally that we weren't prepared to play the game. That comes from the group's intrinsic values of the athlete." A simple "We sucked tonight" would have sufficed. He should have saved his big words for corporate speaking engagements.

Keenan carried himself regally. He used hand gestures to spur his charges into action, like a rich guy motioning to servants. He looked past support personnel when he talked to them, as if to underscore their insignificance. After watching a player take one shift, he announced the guy would never play for the Blues again. When pressed to explain a particular trade, Keenan said he made the deal because he was bored.

"The money got to Mike a little bit, with how he treated people," one of his most-trusted Blues aides admitted.

He enjoyed spending the franchise's money, too. He booked lavish team retreats to Fort Lauderdale, Florida, and Vail, Colorado. Was he trying to build a winner or give himself a vacation? Some of his "scouting trips" to desirable locales raised eyebrows in the front office. Staying in four-star hotels became customary for the team. He was big-timing it, and that act didn't sell well in St. Louis.

"Certainly, a lot happened here that probably Mike would do differently now if he was coming in," Blues assistant coach Jimmy Roberts said. "I know Mike pretty good and Mike is one great guy. I just wish people here had got to know him, that he had let the people get to know a little more of what he really was. It hit the Midwest pretty hard."

Keenan would feed statements like this one to writers who came to town to profile him: "I was a visionary, even as a kid. I just wasn't as preoccupied until I got older. One of the problems with being a visionary is that I could see things in people that they couldn't see in themselves. I'd picture the whole and break it into all the little parts. People have this image of me as a knee-jerk decision maker. But there's almost nothing I do I haven't thought about for months, down to the smallest detail. You can't compromise the details, because details are what lead to the whole."

Then there was this gem: "I coach hockey because I'm an artist. It's like a chess match. You read the situation and maximize it. To be great, you have to be creative. That's the art of it."

With Keenan carrying on like a caricature of himself, his relationship with the local media got ugly. In Philadelphia, Chicago, and New York, Keenan had won over some key reporters. By feeding information to supportive scribes and stonewalling his antagonists, he made certain he had some allies on the beat. Since Keenan consistently won in those markets, he had no trouble building a support base. But St. Louis has just one major newspaper, the *Post-Dispatch*, and its beat writers had grown skeptical of his tactics. They fueled the fires of discontent in the Blues dressing rooms by running Keenan's comments to the players, then running the players' responses back to Keenan.

"When I took this job, people said, 'Oh, St. Louis, the media is going to be so much easier to deal with,'" he said. "Well, it's been twice as difficult. Believe me, one newspaper is tougher to deal with than five or six."

Keenan had no appreciation for public relations. By moving most of the Blues' practices and game-day skates to a facility on the outskirts of town, he limited television coverage of his team. He complained when players made public appearances during the season. He wanted them to focus solely on hockey. He skipped booster club dinners and sent representatives instead. He gave key reporters his home number and encouraged them to call for his reaction to developing stories, then largely ignored the calls he received. He never understood how important media relations were in a mid-sized market like St. Louis.

When members of the *Post-Dispatch* sports staff attempted to make this point during a truce meeting arranged by Blues vice president Tom Maurer, Keenan stood up, removed his very expensive suit coat, and said some very blunt, angry things about the media's take on his PR problem. He saw no need to change his style to reach St. Louisans and resented the input. If St. Louis could have seen more of that Keenan, the one who cut through the bull and spoke his mind, it might have liked him more.

All of the changes made the Blues a much worse team to start the 1995–96 season. Forty-six players would play for the Blues that season. Players would be recalled from the minors for the day-of-game skate, then would be returned to the minors without playing. Or they would play only a shift or two. There was no time to fall in love with Fred Knipscheer. There was no chance to pose for a photograph with Alexander Vasilevskii.

By the time all the number-33 Ken Sutton replica sweaters came in, he was gone.

Training camp started with the usual bang. Fuhr reported in pathetic shape, prompting a furious Keenan to suspend him. Keenan had gone to great lengths to mock Joseph's fitness in order to take the heat off himself for dumping him. Fuhr's jiggling gut dismayed Keenan, who unleashed a withering personal attack on the goaltender.

"He's thirty-two years old," Keenan said. "He's a fellow who's had a lot of personal problems and doesn't have a great deal of strength or backup. You think he'd make more out of it than he did. Grant was basically thirty pounds overweight. He played in Buffalo at 192. He weighed 220 pounds. His comments were, 'I've done this for ten years.' Well, maybe it's time he took the responsibility."

Fuhr eventually whipped himself into shape and played spectacularly for the first few months of the season. Hawerchuk, however, immediately encountered problems with Keenan. He knew he really wasn't a Keenan-type player, but he came to the Blues because they had offered the most money. He had never been a productive playoff player. It wouldn't take Keenan long to hold this reputation over his head.

"My father said I was crazy for coming here, but I wanted the challenge," Hawerchuk said. "I know a lot of people are down on Mike, but I also know he's the one coach who can get the most out of me."

This relationship was playing out like the Keenan-Savard scenario, except Keenan had brought this mess on himself by signing a veteran so firmly entrenched in his ways.

"I went out on a limb for him," Keenan said. "I'm disappointed. His attitude for the last ten years has been to pace himself and he's forgotten how to work."

Slowed by hip troubles and accustomed to playing a trapping defensive system, Hawerchuk never got in step with Keenan's high-tempo program.

"He started sitting me right away for certain little plays that I would make," Hawerchuk said. "I did adjust, but I don't think it was best for my game. That type of game is suited for a different player. After playing for so long a certain way, and being successful at that way, to go the way he wanted to go, more of a grinding game, chip it in, chip it out, along the boards . . . I need the looseness in my game. If it's there, I can go for it and not worry if I make a mistake I'm going to sit the rest of the night."

When the Blues traveled to Buffalo to face the Sabres on October 22, Hawerchuk knew Keenan might have something up his sleeve. He had been in the coach's doghouse since the start of the season. Hawerchuk's family and friends would be coming down from Ontario to watch him play his old team. Keenan knew this, too, so Hawerchuk figured he could be in for some pine time.

"I said to my wife before I went to the airport, 'I wouldn't be surprised if he scratched me in Buffalo,'" Hawerchuk said. "That's the kind of thing he does."

Sure enough, Hawerchuk was in street clothes as the Sabres blasted the Blues, 5–2. During that game, Keenan also benched Hull for long stretches and later suggested that Brett "took the night off." The tension between the two had been building for weeks. Keenan had blown up after overhearing Hull grouse at Fuhr during an earlier game for mishandling the puck. Keenan criticized Hull for what he perceived as disloyalty toward a teammate.

"Mike misinterpreted what I said," Hull said at the time. "He wouldn't listen and I just lost it."

There was no misinterpreting Hull after the game in Buffalo. He was sour about getting benched and he was really upset over Hawerchuk being scratched.

"His folks were there, he played there," Hull said. "That's not something I would consider very respectful for a Hall of Fame player. If you want to win, you have to play your best players. He's a Hall of Famer. He should at least be given a chance."

Hull figured he was just doing his job by sticking up for a teammate and pointing this out. "I'm the captain, it's my responsibility," he said. "But it's almost like [Keenan] wants to be confrontational."

Hull's insubordination brought swift retribution. Keenan stripped Hull of his captaincy the next day and gave the "C" to Corson.

"The Hawerchuk thing was just icing on the cake," Keenan said. "Hull's verbalizing his thoughts on Hawerchuk had nothing to do with the decision. The decision is already made. We knew we would take some flak for it, but it was worth it. We had to make the change."

Hull was definitely not a classic captain. He tends to be a disruptive force instead of a unifying presence in the dressing room, but his demotion made him something of a martyr in St. Louis.

"The positive thing is, I had the 'C' taken away because I stood up for my teammates," he said. "I could have gotten in trouble for something off the ice, something that would bring disrespect for the team and my family, but I didn't do anything like that. I didn't do anything bad. If that was the case, it would be different. But this is kind of an honorable way to lose the 'C.' I stood up for my teammates and I'm proud of the fact. The coaches didn't like that, but there's nothing wrong with questioning them, is there?"

There was to Keenan. He enjoyed being challenged by captains he admired, like Messier or Chelios, but the smirking Hull was another matter. Brett knew nothing about winning at that point in his career. Nonetheless, Hull kept chirping like a magpie when reporters stopped by his locker for a comment.

"Why is the coach immune to making mistakes?" he wondered out loud. "Just because you're the coach, whatever you do is right? If you put the wrong guys on the ice, why should I sit there and let you say that the players didn't play good? Put the right guys on the ice. Why is your mistake not a mistake and ours is? We make a mistake and get chastised. Why shouldn't he get chastised?"

The media rallied around the noisy Hull, making his coach's life more difficult. Keenan started to slip off the deep end. He blasted *Post-Dispatch* beat writer Dave Luecking during television and radio interviews. Such outbursts, nearly unprecedented for a professional sports coach, only made Keenan appear childish and insecure. So did his installation of a back door to his office, which allowed him to sneak out and escape media scrutiny. St. Louis reporters ran Iron Mike ragged. Privately, the players found the spectacle rich.

Keenan's life would have been easier had Chris Pronger, twenty-one years old and a former second overall draft pick, shown up prepared to become the next Larry Robinson. Instead, he appeared to be the next Charlie Bourgeois. He was awkward and mistake-prone. His game had fallen in Hartford, and now he couldn't get it back. He reported to camp in poor shape, finishing forty-fourth out of forty-six players in fitness testing to earn a tongue-lashing from Keenan. Fans booed him because he wasn't Brendan Shanahan and they booed him because he didn't appear to care. Keenan's response was to join the cacophony against him. Pronger, by his own admission to *Sports Illustrated* magazine, had been too much of a party animal during that stage of his life.

"Obviously, he wasn't easy on me," Pronger said. "That's kind of the way he is, the way he goes about handling those types of situations. It's more reinforcing the negatives with negatives and riding you. At the same time, I think he realizes how much certain players can handle."

After the Blues lost to Buffalo 2–0 on November 27, a furious Keenan threatened to resign as coach. The Blues responded with a six-game unbeaten streak.

"He does whatever it takes to win," Fuhr observed.

On December 30, the Blues fell to the Maple Leafs 4–3 at home, on a goal six seconds into overtime. Keenan was predictably upset. He described the team's play as "disappointing and troubling" and "extremely inconsistent." A pair of his favorites, Peter Zezel and Shayne Corson, had been beaten on Toronto's game-winning play. But while discussing the general failings of the team, he noted that the Blues' mistakes weren't entirely of his making.

"It's very frustrating . . . [but] two of the critical pieces of the puzzle I had nothing to do with, Brett Hull and Al MacInnis. I had nothing to do with them in terms of them being here. Ultimately, it is my responsibility. But I'm pointing out that it's not entirely my team."

MacInnis blanched at those remarks, but declined to comment. Hull, of course, was only too willing to respond.

"He's blaming everybody else again," Hull said. "That's two guys. There are eighteen other ones. That's like saying you're not responsible for your stepkids if you get remarried."

On December 31, Keenan offered Hull to the Rangers again. He didn't bother calling general manger Neil Smith, preferring instead to go through coach Colin Campbell. Hull found about the proposed trade and rallied Blues fans around him again.

"If I get shipped out, it's because Mike Keenan and Jack Quinn have done it," he said. "It has nothing to do with me. I'm not leaving unless they throw me out. Why would I want to leave? This is the greatest place in the league to play. The fans are great. This is my team."

One of the many spectacles of the season was Keenan's first trip back to New York since his acrimonious departure from the Rangers. During the game on January 14, fans at Madison Square Garden serenaded him with the chant "Keenan sucks!" and greeted him with signs like "Welcome back, Judas," "The Garden Rat Returns," "Keenan, You're a Weasel," "You Lied to Every One of Us," and "Keenan, You Traitor!" It was an unpleasant experience for the former hero.

"We won the Stanley Cup and to me that's the bottom line," Keenan said after the Blues played the Rangers to a 3–3 tie. "It's to be expected, I guess. It really wasn't that bad. I can understand the fans' reaction, but it doesn't mean I have to enjoy it, accept it, or embrace it. I was prepared for whatever. It's fine with me. It's an unforgiving business, I guess. We'll leave it at that."

During the All-Star break, Hull shrugged off rumors that he could be traded. He figured Blues fans wouldn't let that happen. Cujo was gone. Shan the Man was gone. The newcomers, except for the heroic Fuhr, had been disappointing. The fans would not stand for a Hull trade. Keenan's popularity was evaporating.

"There's not a lot of like for him," Hull pointed out. "That's pure blatant honesty. He's moved a lot of people, but without sounding egotistical, he can't move me because they'd kill him, the fans. They've basically had enough already. They're tired of having their players shipped out."

With the Blues scuffling around .500 and empty seats becoming the norm at the Kiel Center, Keenan needed to make a big score. He went for the biggest score of all: Wayne Gretzky.

In Los Angeles, the Kings were in disarray and The Great One wanted out. His contract was expiring after the season and he made it quite clear he wasn't coming back. The Kings had to get something for him while they could, or lose him for nothing to free agency. Keenan and Quinn made their first inquiry in December, then kept after the Kings until they closed a deal for Gretzky on February 27, 1996. The Blues sent youngsters Roman Vopat, Craig Johnson, and Patrice Tardif, plus first- and fifth-round draft picks, to the King for the greatest player in hockey history.

Giddiness replaced exasperation in the Blues camp. Keenan began rounding up Gretzky's buddies, former Oilers like Anderson (again!), Charlie Huddy, and Craig MacTavish. Keenan was back on track and Blues fans cheered up. For the moment, the media got off his back. The Great One was actually a Blue and St. Louis couldn't have been happier.

"You may not have faith in me, but I'll tell you what," Keenan told a reporter. "You'd better fasten your seat belt. You're in for one hell of a ride."

Before Gretzky's debut with the Blues in Vancouver, Keenan canceled the morning skate and instead summoned sports psychologist Sol Miller.

Miller advised the troops to stay focused despite this great player's arrival. Gretzky's mere presence wasn't going to win this team anything. Hard work and dedication would be necessary for the Blues to have any success.

Still, the Blues couldn't wipe the grins off their faces. Canucks fans flocked to the Blues' first practice session with Gretzky. North America's hockey press assembled to chronicle the start of a new era. Gretzky spoke optimistically about finishing his career in St. Louis as the team cracked open its vault and offered him a contract worth $23 million over three years. When the Blues returned home, Gretzky and his wife, Janet, a native St. Louisan, began looking for homes and evaluating schools. Meanwhile, Blues fans gobbled up tickets and all the number 99 merchandise they could find. It all seemed too good to be true. Perhaps Keenan was a genius after all.

And then again, maybe he wasn't. Gretzky and Hull, as it turned out, couldn't click on the top line, which drove Keenan crazy.

"He hasn't played with near the intensity that he played with prior to Wayne arriving," Keenan said of Hull. "If he says he can't play with Wayne Gretzky, then I don't know who in the hell he can play with."

Keenan questioned Gretzky's fitness level. Gretzky is a pretty sensitive superstar and Hull warned him that more salvos would be coming from the coach. On the business front, Gretzky's agent, Mike Barnett, haggled with Blues management about the structure of the contract offer and kept his client from signing.

The club had to fit Gretzky's salary into the budget, so Keenan traded Hawerchuk to Philadelphia for MacTavish on March 15. "I just wish I had a better opportunity," Hawerchuk said. "There's a lot of things I like about Mike and there's a lot of things that piss you off. I felt that, after fifteen years, I wasn't ready to go through that again."

MacTavish did little for the Blues. Ditto for Anderson and Huddy. Midseason acquisition Stephane Matteau, a heroic Keenanite in New York, proved useless after his midseason arrival. Winger Steve Leach was similarly ineffective. Newcomers Courtnall, Corson, and Noonan were pretty unremarkable all season. Winger Yuri Khmylev, a trade-deadline acquisition from Buffalo, might have been the least motivated player who ever took to the ice for the Blues.

The Khmylev deal was a classic Keenan blunder, the sort of move that created long-term problems for the franchise. The guy was done in Buffalo, yet Keenan decided to deal defensive prospect Jean Luc Grand-Pierre and a second- and third-round draft pick at the trading deadline to acquire a used-up player. In his nine-game Blues career, Khmylev scored exactly one goal before the team bought him out at great expense. That Yuri had scored just 16 goals in his previous 114 games in Buffalo might have been a warning sign worth heeding.

The Blues backed into the playoffs despite winning only one of their last twelve games. They managed to get past a bad Toronto team in the first round, but not before losing Fuhr to a knee injury when Maple Leafs goon Nick Kypreos fell on top of him. Kypreos insisted the collision was a complete accident, of course, but the Blues viewed the incident as criminal. Fuhr needed knee surgery and was done for the playoffs.

Keenan was at his frantic best in the second-round series against Detroit, doing anything and everything to distract the more talented Red Wings. He pointed out the discrepancy in the lengths of the team benches at Joe Louis Arena. He accused Red Wings center Sergei Fedorov of taking dives to draw penalties. He ripped referee Terry Gregson and accused Detroit toughman Darren McCarty of trying to cripple goaltender Jon Casey, who took over for Fuhr. But then Gretzky was on the ice for four goals against in his first six shifts of an ugly 8–3 Blues loss in Game Two.

"I stink," Gretzky moped after the game. "It's my responsibility to lead this team and I consider myself responsible for these two losses."

Gretzky was looking for some support from his coach. What he heard instead was criticism.

"Wayne let his man go twice," Keenan said, "and that's pretty much the hockey game."

Reporters wondered if an injury could explain Gretzky's poor play. Red Wings coach Scotty Bowman speculated that Gretzky had to be hurt.

"He's in real pain," Bowman said. "He's really hurt. He played only nineteen minutes and that's unusual for him."

Keenan would hear none of this talk. "I know Scotty thinks he's hurt," he said. "If he's hurt, he's not telling me and he's not telling the trainers." He even suggested that Gretzky might not have prepared himself for the grueling playoff grind.

"Maybe he's forgotten how much abuse he's taken in the past," said Keenan, who later apologized to Gretzky for singling him out. Gretzky was unmoved. He didn't need to put up with such crap from anybody.

The Blues rallied to win the next three games, then lost Game Six 4–2. A memorable Game Seven showdown went into overtime scoreless and lasted until Steve Yzerman surprised Casey with a blast from the blue line.

Gretzky would never play for the Blues again. After Game Two, Quinn had pulled his $23-million offer off the table. Quinn claimed that Barnett's request for an additional $2.4 million in interest on the $10-million deferred signing bonus ultimately broke the deal.

"There will be offers for Wayne, but in my opinion, the offers are not going to come close to the offers the Blues gave him," Quinn said. "They'll never see anything like it again."

Barnett suggested the Blues got cold feet when Gretzky struggled against the Red Wings. That $23-million offer could have been the basis for a deal if the Blues had left it on the table.

"To have those two games against Detroit to be the cause of concern at the senior level of Blues ownership, it was very troubling," Barnett said. "When they won Game Three, they said, 'We'll get it done.' Wayne chose not to put himself in the position to have the second-guess take place based on the quality of his last shift or his last game."

The Blues later offered $12 million over two years and $15 million over three years, but these were hollow gestures. Instead, Gretzky signed with the Rangers for a few million dollars less than the Blues' original offer. Gretzky had lasted only thirty-one regular season and play-off games for the Blues, and his departure essentially ended Keenan's regime.

"It's unfortunate it didn't work out from a business point of view, from Wayne's perspective and our ownership's perspective," Keenan said. "The whole thing was dealt with at the ownership level. It was way beyond my level, that's for sure. One thing I've learned in this industry is that things are way beyond your control. Owners own, managers manage, coaches coach, and players play. There was nothing I could do about it. It was probably the only time I've seen the whole board assembled to make a decision regarding a contract. Again, it was a decision based more on economics than anything else. If it hadn't come to that, I guess that he'd still be playing here."

Gretzky had developed grave reservations about the Iron Mike experience. Keenan will never admit his culpability in the Gretzky affair, but he clearly turned Wayne off. The adversity started upon Gretzky's arrival, when Keenan cited his lack of conditioning. Then Keenan criticized the lack of production from Hull and Gretzky.

"I didn't have a problem with Michael," Gretzky would later say. "Yeah, it's not easy to play for him. It's tough. It's difficult. I don't think he treated me badly, but I had a choice whether I wanted that or didn't want that and I chose to move on."

From the sideline, deposed chairman Michael Shanahan couldn't help but smirk. The franchise he once fought for was now in upheaval. The big shooters had shot themselves in the foot. Shanahan looked back over the previous year and shook his head.

"I thought Cujo was good for St. Louis," he said. "I thought Shanny was good for St. Louis. I thought Brett Hull for good for St. Louis. Al MacInnis. A lot of players. I thought it was a good team. I thought with a few minor tweaks it could have been a great team. I didn't think they needed a major overhaul, but that's why I'm out of sports and the geniuses are in sports. I read that the current management felt we had marquee players and were in the entertainment business with fans. The new GM said he was going to do it differently and bring a Stanley Cup here. My personal opinion is the team at the end of the 1994–95 season, my last season, is a better team from any standpoint than the team they have today."

He also wondered about the sanity of the Gretzky pursuit. "How a team can trade away a number of young players and draft choices for a talent like Gretzky, pay a high salary, then bring him in and criticize him unmercifully, put all the pressure on his shoulders, and expect him to perform?" Shanahan said. "You can't bring in one player and say, 'Win a Stanley Cup.' I don't think it's realistic. That was somewhat unfair to Wayne Gretzky, the way the whole thing played out. It's putting too much responsibility on one player at this stage in his career."

Keenan had to retool. He dove back into the free agent market and signed free agents Joe Murphy and Trent Yawney. Why would he risk $10 million on the famously erratic Murphy? Why would he take another shot on Yawney after running him off the Blackhawks during his Chicago regime? And why did Yawney choose to relive his earlier struggles with Keenan? He made his decision for the same reason Hawerchuk had: money and opportunity. He figured the best offer brought him the best chance to play.

"What happened in the past, I put that behind me," Yawney said. "I just wanted an opportunity to win. One thing about Mike, you can't argue against his record. His record speaks for itself. He's got his way and some people don't like it. I've played for a lot of different coaches throughout my career and definitely he was the most demanding."

Keenan loved bringing back his alumni, even if they had failed him. These players could always help him educate the fresh recruits. They tended not to need much prodding the second or third time around.

"When I came here and when he was still here, Mike was Mike, but I had seen all that," Yawney said. "So it wasn't that big of a deal. All I was trying to do was convey to the rest of the players, this was the way he is."

Not everything Keenan did during the summer of 1996 was stupid. Free agent defenseman Marc Bergevin proved to be a solid signing. Keenan had quickly run him off in Chicago, but Bergevin became an enduring commodity this time around. Having squandered decent young players like Mike Grier, Grand-Pierre, Ian Laperriere, Craig Johnson, and Igor Korolev (needlessly discarded in the 1995 waiver draft), Keenan had his scouts round up useful minor league retreads like Scott Pellerin, Harry York, Jim Campbell, and Jamie McLennan. Each paid dividends. With St. Louis hosting the NHL Entry Draft in 1996, Keenan held on to his first-round pick and let scouting director Ted Hampson pick center Marty Reasoner.

The draft set the stage for another Keenan outburst against the St. Louis media. He became furious when this writer wrote a column mocking some of Keenan's deals, like the Khymlev trade. All of his colleagues were in town and the *Post-Dispatch* had made him look bad again. Keenan had his minions attempt to track down me and my sports editor. I was out of town after the draft, but the sports editor was reached at a convention. Keenan came on the line and yelled at him.

The 1996 training camp became a land of opportunity. The standouts included York, a former roller-hockey player who had worked his way up from the East Coast Hockey League to get this chance. Keenan tested him and he passed.

"I guess Tony Twist was telling me he always picked one game to test a rookie that he thought had a chance to make the team," York recalled. "There was an exhibition game in Buffalo and he was pretty much all over the whole game. He sat down beside me on the bench and said a couple of choice words here and there. It actually got to the point where he actually kicked me over the boards, almost, when I was waiting for a change. He definitely tested me."

As the season unfolded, however, the Blues obviously weren't going far with their patchwork roster. They had banked on Gretzky and now The Great One — and most of his buddies — were long gone. Losing got to Keenan. One night, the Blues were losing to Gretzky's Rangers, 2–1, in New York. The Madison Square Garden timekeeper let 2.3 seconds tick off the clock after a penalty was called on New York defenseman Brian Leetch with 19.3 seconds remaining in the game. The 2.3 seconds hardly mattered. The Blues probably weren't going to win the game, but Keenan snapped anyway.

"The timekeeper cheated in the game, there's no question about it," Keenan charged. "If the NHL is going to allow people in this building to cheat, there should be an examination made by Gary Bettman. There were at least two seconds. We keep the time on the ice. We have it recorded. The man in the penalty box synchronized his watch with the time clock so they both cheated at the same time for the same amount of time."

Keenan made a blockbuster deal, sending the used-up Corson and soft, mistake-prone defenseman Murray Baron to Montreal for slick center Pierre Turgeon, speedy checking forward Craig Conroy, and spare defenseman Rory Fitzpatrick on October 29. Canadiens general manager Rejean Houle should not only have been fired for making this deal, he should have been jailed. It was that criminal. The sensitive Turgeon couldn't have lasted long under Keenan's withering glare, but, as it turned out, he wouldn't have to.

After a 6–3 loss at Toronto left the Blues 6–9 for the young season, Keenan skated the team hard the next day at Maple Leaf Gardens. When the team continued lagging through the drills, he left the ice in disgust without speaking to his players.

"It's a funny group," he told reporters without a trace of a smile. "I don't know how far they have to go before they want to start paying attention. We're in the basement of our conference, but there's not a sense of urgency. It's pretty casual. Guys aren't taking charge out there. No one wants to be the leader. Somebody has to take charge, whoever that is. It doesn't have to be one particular person. I can only talk about people I've had before and what they do. They make sure the group is out there and alert, either by talking or yapping or instructing or saying nothing and leading by example. Leading one way or another."

Joe Murphy was a miserable flop, although he lightened the mood around the dressing room with his odd behavior. He called himself "Joe-

Joe" and referred to himself in the third person. Once, Keenan tapped him on the shoulder to take a shift and Murphy declined.

"Joe-Joe's tired," he announced.

He also created a small stir in the Blues dressing room by piling his equipment in the shape of a pyramid in front of his locker.

"Don't touch it," he instructed the equipment men. "See how I got myself set up? The mother ship is coming and I want to make sure I'm ready to get on board."

The St. Louis lineup featured too many fading veterans, like Peter Zezel, Craig MacTavish, and Steve Leach. Fuhr lost the edge he had demonstrated during his first Blues season as age and injuries took their toll. The constant turnover of players had taken its toll, too. In Year Three of Keenan's regime, the Blues had no cohesiveness, no team chemistry. Turgeon helped, for sure, but the Blues' other in-season acquisitions included over-the-hill hit men Sergio Momesso and Mike Peluso. Keenan was just grabbing bodies.

"I firmly believe you have to have stability as an organization," Al MacInnis said. "It's got to start at the top and work itself down to the dressing room. We just didn't have any of that. You can't have changes every day and expect to be successful. It's tough for the players. You look at any successful organization, one that won the Cup, and the most commonly used word is stability."

Jim Campbell was a pleasant surprise, coming out of nowhere to produce a 20-goal season, but young Czech defenseman Libor Zabransky faded after a promising start and Craig Conroy couldn't connect with Keenan after arriving from the Canadiens. Harry York, on the other hand, took to Keenan right away.

"You've got some guys who didn't deal with it very well, like Craig Conroy," York said. "It's tough. The weird thing to me is that some players thrive under certain hockey coaches and some people don't."

Tactics were also an issue. Keenan's system — aggressive puck chasing and heavy body checking — seemed obsolete in the increasingly passive NHL. The league had changed dramatically after the New Jersey Devils won the 1995 Stanley Cup with a neutral-zone trap strategy and Detroit won two Cups with its left-wing lock. Keenan refused to follow the trend toward NFL-style zone defenses.

"We probably have the least amount of structure in our game plan of any team in the league," he admitted during his third season.

But these Blues lacked the speed or commitment to break down opponents with their search-and-destroy approach. Instead, they appeared tentative and confused as they skated willy-nilly against more disciplined teams. To buck the trend, Keenan needed a big, fast, and tremendously motivated team. The Blues were slow and indifferent.

"The league was getting faster, it was getting younger," Roberts said.

The Blues lacked the ability or willingness to improvise as much as Keenan hoped they would. "As far as the hockey goes, it was definitely an experience for me," MacInnis said. "In Calgary, we always knew what we were going to do. We all knew our jobs when we don't have the puck, when we do have the puck. To come here, not work on special teams, to come here and almost just go out there and work hard, that was a hell of an adjustment. You need more of a coach who has a system and everybody works at that system, rather than just a motivator. There are times, no question, when you need motivation in the room. But my belief is, you shouldn't have to come into a professional dressing room, whether it's basketball, hockey, or baseball, and have to motivate your team to play."

Keenan's career-long aversion to special teams practice caught up to the Blues, who couldn't steal many games with their power play. Keenan noted that his teams never practiced the power play and usually won.

"We never practiced the power play in New York at all, except for breakouts, which we've done here, and we ended up in first place," he said. "There's no need whatsoever. You get better results than when you chart everything for them and tell them where to go. Practicing the skills — one-time passing and one-time shooting — that's practicing the power play."

On November 27, Keenan made another huge move that wouldn't pay dividends until after he was gone. He acquired the rights to free-agent forward Pavol Demitra from Ottawa for spare defenseman Christer Olsson. This would prove to be one the worst decisions in Ottawa Senators history, rivaling the $12.25-million contract the team gave ice dancer Alexandre Daigle. Demitra was playing in the International Hockey League at the time as an unsigned restricted free agent.

Demitra, Turgeon, Pronger, and Pellerin would become the foundation of an impressive rebuilding effort. Pronger would prove to be especially valuable, blossoming into a Norris and Hart Trophy winner a few years later and validating the Shanahan deal in spades. But Keenan would not last long enough to benefit from these moves. His never-ending feud with Hull was a tiresome distraction that was wearing down the team, driving down attendance, and aggravating the ownership group. As the walls closed in, Keenan singled out Hull during a typically contentious team meeting.

"Whether it's me coaching or someone else, he's still going to have to deal with that guy over there," Keenan said. Hull responded by suggesting that his coach could stuff himself.

MacInnis and MacTavish tried to play the role of peacemakers, but not even the United Nations could have straightened out this mess.

"There were a number of times we tried to talk to Hullie, tried to talk to Mike, tried to soften things up here and do it, hopefully, so everybody would get along," MacInnis said. "We tried. Myself, MacTavish, and a couple of guys. It just got to the point where no matter what the players did, it was out of control, out of our hands."

Jimmy Roberts, who joined Keenan's staff after serving as coach of the Blues' farm team in Worcester, admitted that the feud hurt the team.

"Nothing usually got to Mike," Roberts said. "If you wrote something about him, he'd look you in the eye and say that you're wrong or you're right the next day. But I think he let Brett get under his skin a little too much. He couldn't shake it when that happened. That's the only time I've seen him let something get a hold of him too much. It became a personal battle between the two of them. It certainly didn't help the team, because it put all the players on edge. Players certainly didn't want to take sides. They didn't want to be on the coach's side, Brett's side, or anything else. It certainly created a lot of friction on the team."

The battle came to a head December 6, when Keenan scratched a healthy Hull for a game at Colorado. The team was stunned, but it managed to win 4–3. The Oilers, their next opponent, were stunned, too.

"I don't think it was right to sit him out," observed Jeff Norton, a former Blues defenseman playing for Edmonton. "He's a star, a talent you can't have out of your lineup. It's embarrassing. Brett's been pretty good to his word this year, too. He's been very quiet, no confrontations."

Zezel, a Keenanite brought to the Blues as a buffer, stepped in to play peacemaker. He calmed down the two men and helped ensure Hull's return for a victory at Edmonton. "He's the type of player we need," Zezel said. "He understands he has to be the leader of this hockey team. We look to him. If he's scoring like he's capable of scoring, he's a force for us."

When the Blues followed those two victories with a sloppy 5–5 tie in Dallas, Keenan sounded like a coach on his last legs. There had been a lot of media speculation about his impending demise and Keenan seemed resigned to his fate.

"If that's all the pride we have," he moped, "it doesn't matter who we have coaching the club. It has nothing to do with it."

Fans were staying away from Blues home games in droves. Those who came booed when Keenan's face was displayed on the overhead scoreboard screen. The scoreboard operators were told to stop putting up his visage. Though the Turgeon trade gave the team a glimmer of hope and the Demitra deal would help later, Keenan knew he needed to score another major trade to revive the Blues. He believed the Washington Capitals would take Hull in return for bright young talents like Sergei Gonchar and Jason Allison. But Jerry Ritter, installed as the owners' pointman after Michael Shanahan's demise, nixed the deal after consulting with the key investors. Keenan was done.

The final straw was an 8–0 loss to the Canucks. Reprising a trick he had used in New York, Keenan stood impassively behind the bench and did nothing. His players were forced to make their own line changes.

"They don't want to hear me all the time," he reasoned. "Sometimes, the players have to learn from each other. They've got to go get it on their own. It's like a parent with their child. When your child is a teenager and ready to drive, the parent can't go along and say turn this way, turn that way, stop, slow down. The youngster has to do it on his own."

This tactic may have worked with the Rangers, who were spurred to play better. But the Blues took this tactic to mean their general manager and coach had simply given up. Keenan made a handsome living inspiring teams to play with passion, but now he seemed to have no passion left for this job.

On December 19, 1996, the Blues fired Keenan and Quinn. The owners hired hard-nosed sports executive Mark Sauer, late of the Pittsburgh Pirates, as the new president. Caron was returned to the general manager's office on an interim basis. The Blues were 15-17-1 when the changes were made. For the record, Keenan expressed surprise at his dismissal.

"It hits you like a thunderbolt," he said.

The decision was costly for St. Louis. Keenan claimed he had about $11 million left on his contract when the Blues cashiered him. Ritter offered him a $1.2-million lump sum settlement to quit and gave him a half hour to think about it. Otherwise, the Blues were going to fire him. Keenan wisely took the firing and asked to be paid in full. Ritter argued that Keenan was fired "with cause" and the club refused to pay him another dime. They built a case against him with the help of Quinn, who was retained as a consultant after losing the president's chair. The club initially pointed to its concerns about Keenan's free-spending habits.

However, the matter was headed toward a hearing with Bettman seven weeks later when the two sides settled on a buyout of roughly $5 million, the cash equivalent of Keenan's remaining contract. He would use some of that money to have a blue note tattoo removed from his shoulder.

The firing was expensive, just like the rest of Keenan's regime. At the time of Keenan's dismissal, the franchise owed nearly $10 million in contract buyouts, deferred compensation, and salaries assumed in trades to thirteen former players. It killed them to send checks to Janney, Casey, Yawney, Norton, Hudson, Wells, Gilbert, Peluso, Shanahan, Creighton, Basil McRae, and the immortal Khmylev. The new management team often referred to the mess left by Quinn and Keenan as "Chernobyl." Hockey salary overruns and the onerous debt service on the Kiel Center had the arena / hockey operation running at a major loss. The ownership group had to pump $52 million into the Blues and Kiel Center operation with three separate cash calls.

The Blues had dressed eighty-two different players in Keenan's two-plus seasons. Paul Broten passed through. Keenanite Mike Hudson made his inevitable appearance. Rob Pearson got a look. Jay Wells put off retirement to pull a regular defensive shift for a season. All these guys had grit. And all these guys were finished as effective NHL players. They lumbered about the rink on their last legs. About fifty of the eighty-two players who toiled for Keenan should have kicked back half of their salaries to their benefactor. Keenan's "plan" as general manager was to replace his old guys with more old guys. The downward talent spiral continued until most of the players quit caring.

"When I signed with St. Louis, we came down and they had some great core guys," Al MacInnis said. "I thought I was going to be one of the pieces of the puzzle that was going to help take the next step. That's where I wanted to be. Hull, Shanny, C.J. [Janney], Cujo, all those guys, that was a hell of a group of core players. I just wanted to be one piece of the puzzle."

Roberts figures Keenan's ultra-aggressive style caught up to him, quickly, once the team slipped. "I think he thought if he kept pushing, the same situation could happen here that happened in New York," Roberts said. "If he had, he probably would have come off as some kind of genius here. It had never been done. But it didn't happen and, you know, it went the other way on him.

"He doesn't really care about risk. He loves it. I think he thrives on controversy and risk. But I don't know if that goes around here and the Midwest. It goes in New York. They write one thing, forget about it, write the opposite the next day, and keep going. Around here, it kind of sticks with you. Once you get the bad reputation, it's hard to shake."

That Keenan fled St. Louis without addressing the media was no surprise. He despised the reporters and didn't like being held accountable for his failings. He told less inquisitive reporters elsewhere that the Blues organization just wasn't ready to pay the price to win.

"We were trying to develop a team-oriented concept and a team that would adhere basically to the same principles for everyone," he said. "It didn't work out that way. Basically, you try to do what's right. You might not always like my style, but I think I do have a handle on what it takes to be a winner and the implementation of a good program. At this point, I guess, they weren't ready for it."

A big problem, Keenan insisted, was the negative media coverage he got in St. Louis. The constant fueling of the Hull-Keenan clash kept controversy roaring. The analysis of his personnel moves, in his eyes, were biased and turned fans against them.

"The public certainly didn't get an honest view of my situation there," he said. "There was really biased and irresponsible reporting for the most part, and no accountability for sure. It bothers me because they should step back and look at the team and what happened. It bothers me that there's this perception that I'm a bad guy.

"I'm not unhappy with what I accomplished in less than two seasons. First of all, our team in the first year was in the top three in the league and, secondly, we acquired a number of great players there, including Grant Fuhr and Chris Pronger."

Years later, the Pronger trade looked like a gem. Back then, though, it was a dog. Shanahan for Pronger is not the sort of deal a quick-results guy like Keenan should make.

"At the time, it was difficult for people to understand," he said. "I guess that's why I was run out of town, but people have to realize that Chris was seven years younger than Brendan. That's a huge difference in terms of their development. At the time, I can recall making some comparisons between Chris and Larry Robinson and saying that Chris has even a little more offense than Larry.

"I tracked Chris, not only in Hartford, I tracked him in Peterborough. I had coached and managed in Peterborough where he played junior hockey, so I had a real inside track on him from the time he was a real young kid and then followed him through Hartford. We were watching him — at least I was, and some of the people that worked for me — for years, so we knew him. I talked to his coach at the time, Dick Todd, and Dick and I are very close. Dick had worked with Roger Neilson and the whole Peterborough connection. He was going to be one of the best kids to come out of there, and that included the Yzermans and Murphys and everybody we had coached there, the Bob Gaineys of the world."

If Keenan had traded Hull early on and won over Shanahan, he might still be coaching in St. Louis.

"Brett Hull is one of the four most talented players I've ever coached," Keenan said, "but I was unable to convince him that he had to be a complete team player to win a Stanley Cup. I was disappointed in the fact I was unable to convince Brett Hull to be a complete team player. That was the most difficult challenge I had. I feel one day he'll understand that he hurt a lot of people and not just me."

What if Mike Shanahan hadn't been run off as team chairman? He believes he could have kept Keenan on track and averted some of the conflict that occurred after his departure.

"I'm not sure anything went wrong with Mike," Shanahan said. "The initial plan had a little different operating strategy. And that did not unfold. The idea was that he would get some help from Jack Quinn and Ron Caron. That's the situation we were setting up here, for better or worse. And it didn't work out that way.

"What I guess I regret is that Mike, just like any other person with a certain talent in sports or show business, is somewhat high-strung. Had we stayed together and worked together, I could have helped him in the areas that I perceive him to need work."

Nobody was able to reel in Keenan during his St. Louis run. "This business can turn on you pretty quick," Roberts said. "If something you've tried doesn't work, then you're on that line. It happened pretty quick for Mike. I don't know if Mike, through his excitement, handled it very well. You sometimes have to regroup and get at it again in a different way.

"I think it just worked on him a little too much and his emotions got a little bit carried away."

◄7►

What a Mess in Vancouver

Who knows if madness isn't a characteristic of genius? Mike makes no apologies to anyone. He hasn't got the time, and he doesn't care to give apologies. The people close to him have to be hard, too. He backs people into a corner and challenges them. He has no room for the weak. There are great expectations wherever he goes and I don't expect him to waste any time changing the chemistry there.

— NEW YORK RANGERS COACH COLIN CAMPBELL
AFTER THE CANUCKS HIRED KEENAN

PERHAPS IT WAS ONLY FITTING THAT MIKE KEENAN WOULD effectively replace Pat Quinn in Vancouver. Just as Keenan turned the league on its ear by jumping from the Rangers to the Blues while under contract, Quinn drew league sanctions for signing with Vancouver while still coaching the Kings. In December 1986, Quinn was feeling restless. Canucks executive Arthur Griffiths caught wind of his restlessness and made his move, while Quinn was still coaching the Kings. He hired him to be president and general manager of his club, beginning the following season. Quinn's landmark five-year, $1.2-million deal included a company Mercedes, a $100,000 signing bonus, and handsome incentives — like $200,000 for simply making the playoffs. Coaches and managers simply didn't get such lucrative deals in those days. Quinn would stay ahead of the earnings curve, with salaries and bonuses pushing his annual compensation above $1 million later in his run.

The NHL was outraged by Quinn's original Canucks deal. How could a man coach one team after agreeing to run its fiercest rival? The league removed Quinn as coach of the Kings. The Canucks' front office was found guilty of tampering. Quinn was allowed to join the Canucks as general manager, but he was barred from coaching until 1990. Undeterred by the sanctions — he had no immediate plans to coach the team anyway — Quinn set out to make the Canucks a winner.

He traded for goaltender Kirk McLean and power forward Greg Adams in 1987. He drafted franchise cornerstones Trevor Linden in 1988 and Pavel Bure in 1989. In his famous 1989 deal, he traded dour playmaker Dan Quinn and aptly named defenseman Garth Butcher to the Blues for productive forwards Geoff Courtnall, Cliff Ronning, and Sergio Momesso. The nucleus of his team matured and Quinn began elevating the team during the 1990–91 season, when he replaced Bob McCammon as coach.

After 96- and 101-point seasons in 1991–92 and 1992–93 earned the franchise Smythe Division titles, the Canucks stormed to the Stanley Cup finals in 1994 and came within inches of beating Keenan's Rangers to win it all. But the Canucks failed to sustain that success after Quinn stepped away as coach to concentrate on his duties as GM. His first decision backfired, naming acolyte Rick Ley as his successor. Ley was a good hockey man, but as a head coach he couldn't lead mice to cheese.

The Griffiths family also faltered. After extending themselves financially to build the new General Motors Place (at a cost of more than $160 million, about 60 percent over budget) and bring a National Basketball Association expansion team to town (for another $125 million, another 60 percent more than budgeted), the Griffiths needed help. Frank Griffiths Sr., the patriarch of the sports family, died in 1994 as the cost overruns and the NHL lockout were threatening the empire. The debt accrued by the sports operation reached $350 million. Family friend John McCaw, a reclusive Seattle telecommunications mogul with assets approaching $1 billion, bought into the sports operation in 1995, via Arthur Griffiths' Orca Bay company. The family store would never be the same. A year later, McCaw bought control of the Canucks, Grizzlies, and GM Place.

"This was a game where millionaires used to play, now it's billionaires," Griffiths said after the takeover. "You should have a billion dollars if you want to get into professional sports. It got to the point where I wondered if I wanted to blow my brains out in this business."

The downward spiral continued for the Canucks. A 32-35-15 season in 1995–96 left McCaw and his minions restless. Ignoring Quinn, McCaw made a pitch for Wayne Gretzky, who had decided to leave St. Louis after clashing with Keenan and seeing a $23-million contract offer evaporate. Gretzky seemed ready to join the Canucks, but he turned away after the franchise gave him a sign-it-immediately-or-leave-it contract ultimatum. The Canucks were concerned that Gretzky would merely use their offer as leverage to go elsewhere. Insulted, Gretzky left without signing and went to the Rangers instead.

The Canucks continued to stumble. McCaw's people forced Quinn to fire his buddy Ley. Quinn held off the corporate heads as long as he could, then made the change several weeks after Ley was supposed to get canned.

"That was when it dawned on me that I didn't run this anymore," Quinn said. "It shoved a stake in all our hearts. It happened not only to Rick, but I was undermined, too. I knew I would be going out the door, too. And I did. When I first came here, I was given total control. When the ownership amalgamation happened, that was no longer the case. I saw mom and pop become a big corporation. There were changes necessary to try to figure out the financial burden. But some of it became a challenge to be involved with. Some of it started to affect parts of the hockey club that I felt shouldn't be affected. I had to fight battles to do the things I needed.

"The money people come in and they don't mess around. They're not hockey people, they're money people. And along with them came a lot of other people with opinions on how the business should be run. There was a lot of conflict there."

Tom Renney proved to be a feckless replacement for the hapless Ley. Renney had a fine track record for teaching young players, but he was well over his head with stubborn NHL veterans. For instance, he placed this sign along the runway to the ice at GM Place: "The Vancouver Canucks Possess Tradition. Every Person Who Walks This Hallway Has an Obligation to Maintain This Tradition. With That in Mind, We Must Pursue Only One Objective, with Little Regard for Pain, Fatigue, or Personal Ego. The Objective . . . Don't Even Ask!" If that wasn't enough to numb the mind of any Canadian farm boy, the capper was this sign: "Master Technique. But Let the Spirit Prevail."

Yikes! A simple "Skate Boys, Skate" might have sufficed. Renney was trying to turn hockey into some sort of spiritual and intellectual adventure. In reality, it is a medieval test of will. The boys don't get to wield pole axes, but they do joust with sharpened sticks. They don't need wordy slogans to spur them on. They need testosterone, and lots of it.

Vancouver plodded to a 35-40-7 record in 1996–97 and McCaw got the sportsman's itch, again, to make a major score. This time he got his man. Ignoring Quinn's input again, he barged into the marketplace and wooed free agent Mark Messier. Quinn was ordered to make a deal happen, so Messier got a contract worth $20 million over three years, with an option for two more. With Keenan long gone in New York, Rangers general manager Neil Smith balked at giving this balding warrior a massive long-term deal. McCaw, who possesses near-boundless wealth, had no such reservations about Messier. The deal was finalized on McCaw's yacht in the San Francisco Bay. From a distance, Keenan applauded the move.

"Mark has a mystique about him," Keenan said. "I think the Canucks made a wonderful move for their franchise. He won't just change the culture of the team, but the culture of the whole organization. There's a presence about Mark that others feel. He's like the Joe Montanas and Michael Jordans of the world, a special individual."

In the summer of 1997, the mysterious-yet-generous McCaw was the talk of hockey. But all was not well with his franchise. Renney was still overwhelmed by the challenge of coaching in the NHL. The team's two Russian stars, Pavel Bure and Alexander Mogilny, had been through nasty contract disputes with the team. Neither would ever again play with much enthusiasm for the Canucks. After winning a fistful of Stanley Cup rings in Edmonton and in New York, Messier was appalled at the state of the Canucks. The team had a $32-million payroll, but that outlay hadn't bought the club a heart. In their twenty-seven years of existence, the Canucks had posted only five winning seasons. Their uniforms got appreciably better over the years, but the team itself continued to underachieve. Maybe all that rainfall in the Pacific Northwest got to the players.

"When I got there, this was anything but a team," Messier said shortly after his arrival. "Team, in my dictionary, stands for together. That certainly wasn't the case in Vancouver. I think everybody was pretty comfortable here. They had a close-knit bunch. But, obviously, they were failing in the most important part of the business, and that's winning. I don't have anything against the players who were here. But there were obviously a lot of problems before I came to the Canucks."

Renney had no hope of turning things around. He turned off his key veterans by banning beer on team flights, as if it were a junior team, and refusing to seek their counsel on team matters. The NHL is a man's world and Renney treated his players like kids. Messier quickly became fed up. McCaw's right-hand man, Stan McCammon, decided to step in. He never got along with Quinn, and with the team cast adrift with a 3-10-2 record, he fired him as president and general manager. With a $887,500 buyout in hand, Quinn left quietly.

Orca Bay president John Chapple was recalled to Seattle to tend to other business. He was replaced by Stephen Bellringer, who arrived from BC Gas. He knew as much about the ins and outs of the NHL as a common woodchuck, yet he wanted to maintain control of the hockey operation. Instead of hiring a replacement for Quinn, he formed a doomed management committee that included himself, vice president of hockey operations Steve Tambellini, and assistant general manager Mike Penny.

The scenario was chaotic. McCaw phoned Quinn three days after McCammon fired him and asked if he wanted to coach the team again. A flabbergasted Quinn said no. McCaw asked him to recommend possible replacements for Renney, who had been fired shortly after Quinn's departure. Again, Quinn said he just wanted to move along.

Arthur Griffiths was appalled at what happened to Quinn. He had big dreams for the sports empire that his late father had entrusted to him. The Griffiths had controlled the franchise since 1974. He heard the news of Quinn's firing on the radio while driving to work. A week later, his office was removed from GM Place, the building he had worked so hard to build. He left his post as vice chairman of the sports empire sooner than planned.

"As someone who has gone through a lot of changes in my life in the past year, I'm actually happy for Pat," Griffiths said. "He won't be, for a while. But I am happy for him. The way things are going, it was not a good working environment. It's a different way of running a business now. Very, very different."

Keenan was on the job market after getting fired in St. Louis less than three months into the 1996-97 season. He had talked to several teams in the summer of 1997, but the Flyers, Phoenix Coyotes, and Canadiens didn't make an offer. He believed the Bostons Bruins were ready to hire him, but at the last moment the club passed.

"A lot of general managers are fearful of him coming in and dominating them," agent Rob Campbell said. "It's been a sobering experience."

When the Canucks whacked Renney, Keenan immediately began campaigning for the job, even though a combined GM–coach role wasn't immediately available. For the time being, the Canucks intended to stick with their management by committee.

"I would like to get back into the NHL with coaching as part of my duties," he said while openly flirting with the Canucks. "I think my track record as a coach stands pretty good. The same person can coach and GM if the organization is structured right. Pat Riley [then with the Miami Heat of the NBA] is doing it, but he was allowed to bring in his own people."

When the Canucks offered him a coaching-only role, he grabbed it. He knew the team was horrendous, but he'd been on the bottom with Chicago and nearly made it all the way to the top. The Canucks had endured a ten-game losing streak shortly before Keenan's arrival on November 13, 1997, but at least they had had Messier in the dressing room. Perhaps they would ride high again.

Besides, unemployment was starting to drive Keenan nuts. He was accustomed to constant challenge. He was used to being in the spotlight. He missed the adrenaline rush of working the bench in tense games. Few things in life could match the thrill of victory. Besides, coaching paid well; the Canucks gave Keenan a three-year deal worth more than $2.5 million.

"It's a humbling experience," Keenan said after coming in from the cold. "There's a level of uncertainty. There's no question it makes you feel uneasy. You feel strongly to be involved in the game and you feel you can contribute at different levels, but it doesn't seem to fit and that's frustrating. I feel confident about my ability. Will an opportunity come? I'm not positive or sure. It's disturbing because those fears arise from time to time."

Keenan had used his down time to travel, spend time with Nola and Gayla at his various residences, and reflect on his career. Despite all his success, he seemed perilously close to becoming an NHL outcast. Why? How should he change? Or should he change? His career had been motivated by an acute fear of failure. And his Blues tenure, in the eyes of most

NHL experts, was a catastrophe. He was eager to erase this smudge on his otherwise sterling resume.

"I've gone through some very difficult, very challenging, very troubling times," Keenan said. "You don't realize when you're in it for a long time just how emotionally beat up you are. This is a tough business in that regard. I look into the faces of some of the coaches I see and they look worn out. It's the pressure of the job. It's called burnout.

"But I've had the good fortune to be in the right place at the right time. If I didn't have the flexibility, I wouldn't have lasted as long as I have in this business, because it is very unforgiving. In retrospect, there are some good things that I've done, some things that I would have changed. It was a great opportunity to sit back and learn to be realistic, be patient, and learn to deal with myself. The experience will make me a better coach, because I've had the chance to learn more about myself. Being unemployed, you learn to be patient. I took the opportunity to be more introspective, to learn more about myself, to learn what makes coaches successful by adapting to the athletes of the '90s and the new millennium."

One adaptation Keenan had to make was relearning how to deal with the media. In Vancouver, he worked to develop some allies, something he didn't have in St. Louis. With two Vancouver newspapers engaged in fairly spirited competition, he could play reporters and columnists against each other and spin some stories his way. He loved to motivate his players through well-placed barbs in the newspapers, but he needed some cooperation to make his points.

"I know that's one area Mike's thought about, cultivating the media," observed Flyers coach Roger Neilson, who had joined Keenan's Blues staff as an assistant coach after Sator left in 1995. "You can bet he's had time to think about his St. Louis experience. One thing he probably learned there is that you've gotta stay cooperative with the media."

Keenan assumed control of a team that was 4-13-2 on November 13. Turning these losers around was not a task for the faint of heart, but Keenan was as confident as ever. He was convinced he wasn't to blame for the St. Louis failure. He was convinced the Canucks would respond to his standard program.

"I'm still very young and I feel I can contribute a great deal to help our players master the ability of being a winner," he said, still refusing to talk like a normal person. "We'll position ourselves and work diligently toward the ultimate objective. And that is to win the Stanley Cup."

At the beginning, he didn't mind not being general manager. The dual coach–GM role had worn him down in St. Louis and Chicago. And when guys like Joe Murphy, Dale Hawerchuk, Brian Noonan, and Yuri Khmylev failed spectacularly, there was nobody to blame but the coach–GM. He preferred distancing himself from disaster, but that was difficult when he enjoyed near-total control of the hockey operation.

"I look back and I can't believe the workload," he said. "Now I don't want it. I talked a lot with Scotty [Bowman] this summer and he kept saying, 'Be a coach, you don't need the rest of it.' It becomes all-consuming. You have no personal life whatsoever. I made a lot of sacrifices and it ruined my marriage."

The Canucks hired him to kick some butt on the ice. But, once again, Keenan insisted that he was a kinder, gentler man after some time away from the game. His forced sabbatical afforded him more time for introspection. As for his bad guy image, he said, "My reputation as a taskmaster is good copy. But I don't think, in particular, it is a reflection of my ability. I think Mark Messier said it best. Of the five hundred fifty players I've coached in the league, probably five hundred would play for me again. And those fifty who wouldn't probably don't want to do what it takes to win."

Once again, he was starting from scratch. The Canucks had little going for them, save for the leadership potential Messier and Keenan possessed. Messier had sold McCaw on Keenan and now he was ready to help Keenan do in Vancouver what he had done in New York. The new coach immediately deputized the grizzled captain as his most trusted aide. He was virtually a player–assistant coach.

"Mark is one of the finest leaders in pro sports," Keenan said. "His presence alone means a lot to me. When you have a great star in the locker room like Mark, he knows the ingredients of winning and that's hard to find."

Messier had only fond memories of his time with Keenan, because he had done nothing but win with him. Both in the Canada Cups and with the Rangers, they had hit it off smashingly. Mike gave Mark much latitude, allowing him to police the dressing room and be his standard bearer. Mark, in turn, saved Mike from being flogged by the troops.

"Coaches in one room, players in the other — that went out with the hula hoop," said Messier, making no apologies for his tight bond with his coach.

Messier tried to sell the Canucks on Keenan. He worked the dressing room, trying to convince players that the ends would justify Keenan's meanness. He insisted Iron Mike had a caring side to offer players. He pointed out how Keenan, unlike Renney, treated the players as men. He assured the players that their input would be considered.

"I think the unfortunate thing is that nobody wants to publicize the good things, only the negative things about him," Messier said. "Look at his record, it's unbelievable. He's a proven winner and that's what this club needs."

The Canucks needed a good spanking. Quinn had gotten their attention, but Ley had none of Quinn's aura and Renney was hopelessly overmatched. Messier believed he could still lead players to glory, but not when his coach lacked credibility. He needed a general, a commander like Keenan or former Edmonton Oilers coach Glen Sather.

"Mental toughness is something most teams that aren't successful lack and I think that's one area our team has to improve dramatically," Messier said. "Winning demands that. Winning sometimes can be very brutal. Winning is not all flowers and fun and games. Winning, sometimes, is sheer hell."

Losing is sheer hell too, as Keenan would find out. He tried his usual tricks, like posting a photograph of the Stanley Cup over the dressing room chalkboard and ordering carpeting with the likeness of a hockey rink on the dressing room floor. Mug shots of each player were placed over each locker, giving players a sense of belonging — at least until they were abruptly shipped out. A first-rate stereo system was installed in the dressing room to pump up the men at work.

On December 8, the Canucks made their first trip to St. Louis with Keenan as coach. The prospect of facing the Blues, who had dumped him so unceremoniously, had him on edge. The day before the game, the Canucks practiced at the Blues' suburban practice facility, the one he had helped design and refine. Keenan had an NHL security officer keep reporters away from him. The St. Louis media was kept out of the team's practices and cardboard-covered windows kept people from looking into the rink. It was as if nuclear scientists were at work, not a second-rate hockey team.

But Keenan was willing to share his feelings with the out-of-town media. His firing by the Blues still had him smoldering. He still felt wronged. He didn't like to have this failure, the first in his hockey career, rubbed in his face.

"How in the hell do you build a franchise in less than two seasons?" he asked reporters. "I didn't even have 164 games here. In the first year, we were third overall and in the playoffs, [Shanahan] breaks his leg and [Joseph] plays very poorly. The next year we went to Game Seven overtime against Detroit, which went to the Cup [semi] finals.

"There were new rules and new directives. Trade this guy and trade that guy for draft picks, drive the salaries down, the team is no good. We got Wayne Gretzky and filled the building up. Now it's too much to sign him. It was nuts. The Brendan Shanahan trade was a corporate payroll decision. We could have had a really good player for Steve Duchesne, but we couldn't take any salary back. Every other week the directives were being changed. There was no mention of that. We left them with stars like Grant Fuhr, who never gets any acknowledgment. I don't care what anybody says. He's a better goaltender than Curtis Joseph. And Chris Pronger is a Norris Trophy candidate. They've got a pretty good team now, and I was there less than two years."

Besides blaming his downfall on slanted sportswriting by the *St. Louis Post-Dispatch* and the demise of Mike Shanahan as team chairman, Keenan expressed regret for turning his differences with Brett Hull into a needlessly entertaining public feud.

"The thing that is disappointing in myself is that, if you can't change a situation that you feel is not tenable or correct, then your responsibility as a leader is to manage the situation better than what I did," he said. "I didn't handle the Brett Hull situation properly either from the management perspective or a coaching perspective. I let it frustrate me and I could be criticized for that. Brett was the most influential player on the team at the time. Brett was the only leader I couldn't connect with. It just didn't work out."

That's an understatement. In the NBA, when Golden State Warriors guard Latrell Sprewell tried to strangle his coach, P.J. Carlesimo, it stirred up some old emotions for Hull. "I was thinking something must have been said to him to make him act like that," Hull said. "Many times I thought about strangling Mike, but of course that was far from reality." Of course.

Before the Canucks-Blues game, Hull asked to meet with Keenan so they could put their conflict behind them. Hull is emotional, noisy, and disruptive, but he tries not to hold grudges. He usually forgets whatever insult he utters within a few minutes of saying it. In retrospect, he realized that his skirmishes with Keenan made him appear every bit as childish as Keenan. The estranged couple chatted amiably and Keenan even autographed a stick for Hull, writing this message: "To Brett, all the best to you and your family, Mike Keenan."

"I just wanted to tell him there were no hard feelings," Hull said. "I like him as a guy. It just didn't work out in hockey. I had no problems with Mike, personally. It was just that we had opposite philosophies on the game of hockey. He's so intense about winning. That's the bottom line and every player wants it too, but the way he wanted to go about it was completely different from me. I told him I learned a lot from it, and he said that he did too. I didn't handle it well, either, but those days are gone. It's time to move on. He loves the game a lot and it's good that he's back. Only Wayne Gretzky loves the game more than this guy."

Knowing he was in for a hostile crowd reaction when he went behind the bench for the Canucks, Keenan wondered aloud about staging an altercation. Could an off-duty cop run down to the bench and dump a beer on him early in the game, to get the acrimony over with and relieve the tension in the Kiel Center? Keenan was talked out of this scheme. He had to stand there and take the fan abuse. He deflected some of the fans' anger with a sarcastic wave, but the night wasn't pleasant.

His reappearance in St. Louis drew the Blues' first sellout of the season. The crowd of 19,295 chanted "Keenan sucks! Keenan sucks!" all night. The alternative chant was a derisive "Keeeee-nan, Keeeee-nan." A radio station issued signs with Keenan's face circled and a slash running through it, as if it were the international anti-Keenan symbol. Among the banners displayed by fans were "All I Want For Christmas Are Keenan's Two Front Teeth," "The Rat Is Back," and "Keenan's a Canuck, That's Their Tough Luck."

Said Blues fan Mary Beth Shipley, "Even my mother called — she's eighty-six — and said to boo Keenan for me." It was a humiliating scene for a coach who was accustomed to winning games and earning plaudits.

"Hopefully, the St. Louis fans can bring closure to it now," Keenan said a few days after the ordeal. "They were a lot more abusive than New York Rangers fans were. In St. Louis, they gave me a standing ovation when I arrived in town and kicked me out at the end. When it was happening, I thought about Scotty. The fans booed him in Detroit and then they went out and won the Stanley Cup. It's painful when you're booed. I am human. When you get kicked around, it's painful."

Keenan didn't enjoy being embarrassed on a big stage. His team's dreadful showing in a 5–1 loss left him raging against his indifferent players. His primary target was Trevor Linden, a favorite of Canucks fans and an established leader in the dressing room. Linden, like Shanahan in St. Louis, was tremendously popular in Vancouver. Like Shanahan, he was a media darling and a fan favorite. He was handsome and articulate. He was generous with his time, aiding various charities in the community. He was a beloved figure in Vancouver and around the league. Keenan believed Linden's status had made him complacent and uncoachable.

Keenan strove to keep his players guessing. He worked to create desperation in their games. He wanted them playing pissed off. He wanted his best players to be his most tenacious players. Linden, in his mind, was loafing. He urged him to play with more grit and determination. He challenged him the way he had challenged Shanahan. He asked him to live up to his lofty image on a nightly basis. Keenan was determined to drive Linden from his comfort zone, but Linden, like Shanahan in St. Louis, refused to budge.

The Blues game was Linden's first in the lineup after missing eight games with a strained groin. Angered by the ineffective play of Linden's line, Keenan benched him and instead used the mucking line of Gino Odjick, Mike Sillinger, and Steve Staois. Linden was encouraging those guys in the locker room after the second period when Keenan walked in and started screaming at him. According to Gary Mason of the *Vancouver Sun*, the tirade went like this:

"Sit down, you fucking idiot!" Keenan yelled. "Shut the fuck up! Just shut the fuck up! Who are you? What have you ever done?"

This outburst mortified Canucks fans, as did his subsequent dig at Linden: Keenan suggested he wasn't worthy of playing for Team Canada at the upcoming Winter Olympics.

"Trevor has the ability to be a front-line player," Keenan said, "but he has to demonstrate to his teammates that he's a lot more committed than he is. Trevor can step up his game, unless he is not the player everybody in the country, including Team Canada, thinks he is. He's probably playing at a 50-percent level. These are desperate times. Trevor has to make up his mind if he wants to be part of this or not. Right now, he hasn't made up his mind. I can only base that by his conduct on the ice. I think he is capable of making those changes, but it's entirely up to him."

Later, Keenan did some backpedaling from his Linden tirade to save public face. Canucks fans, like Blues fans, embraced their favorites. When Keenan made Linden uncomfortable, he made Vancouver uncomfortable, too.

"By criticizing him publicly, there was a huge risk involved for me that I undertook and understood," he said. "I exposed myself to criticism. I didn't have to, but I did it because I care about Trevor. I wanted him to be part of the program. If I hadn't cared, I wouldn't have taken the extraordinary measure to call his attention and try to draw him into the program. I would have let him go by the wayside."

Canucks enforcer Gino Odjick had the courage to stand up to Keenan and defend Linden. "There is no use slandering Trevor or embarrassing a guy who has devoted his heart and soul to the team," said Odjick, making his own departure inevitable. "I know for a fact that Trevor goes all out every time he laces on his skates. In the eight years I've been here, there's no player I respect more than Trevor Linden."

Later, Keenan admitted that the outburst in St. Louis served no useful purpose. The nature of the defeat and the embarrassment of the night had gotten the best of him. "I'd never handle it that way if I had a chance to do it over again," he said. "I was emotional with him. I should have said nothing, gone about my business, gone to ownership and said you should trade Trevor and let them decide. It wasn't right, but I'm not perfect."

This outburst finished Linden in Vancouver, but it did nothing to spur the team. Other whipping boys emerged, like grinding winger Martin Gelinas. Keenan noted how he – like Shanahan in St. Louis — failed to measure up to Rangers winger Adam Graves. Gelinas' first six NHL seasons had been a disappointment as he bounced from Edmonton to Quebec to Vancouver. With the Canucks, he finally found his niche as a hard worker willing to crash the net and score tough goals. In the previous two seasons, Gelinas had scored 30 and 35 goals. From a distance, he would have appeared to be a good candidate to flourish under Keenan. But once Keenan started shuffling him from line to line and moving him in and out of the lineup, he lost confidence. His coach pushed all the wrong buttons.

"Last year, I knew my turn would be coming no matter what, even when I made mistakes," Gelinas said after getting benched during a 5–2 loss to Colorado on December 13. "This year, obviously, everybody makes mistakes, but if you make too many, you might be sitting on the bench."

Gelinas exasperated Keenan, who couldn't understand Gelinas' reaction to the benching. His demands on Gelinas, in his mind, were hardly extreme. He wanted his wingers, Gelinas included, to dump the puck deep into the offensive zone. Then they were to go after the puck hard. Keenan did not want his wingers trying to carry the puck around a defenseman, risking a turnover at the blue line. He did not want them making lateral passes or, heaven forbid, drop passes as they gained the zone. He wanted the puck deep every single time.

Dump and chase. Dump and chase. *Is this a complex concept?* Keenan wondered. *Is this tactic too complicated to understand?* Dump and chase. Perhaps he could speak more deliberately while making this request. Dump . . . and . . . chase. The Canucks coaching staff had gone over this with Gelinas during a video session. What did they have to do next? Pull out flash cards and hand puppets?

"Martin Gelinas was told about a certain thing we want him to do, in previous games first of all," Keenan said, explaining his actions to the team's beat reporters. "We told him we'd like him to work on that part of his game. In this instance, he did it three times before I benched him. I talked to him about it the first time. I said, 'Martin, we don't want you to do that.' Second shift, he did the same thing. Third shift he did the same thing again. So I said, 'Martin, time to take a rest.'"

Sensing that Gelinas was tensing up under scrutiny, Keenan had tried to loosen him up during a game in Detroit earlier in the season. He tried to elicit a smile with some mid-game banter.

"Martin, your tie is too tight," Keenan said.

"What?" a puzzled Martin Gelinas asked, wondering what neckwear had to do with hockey.

"You're wearing a tie. I've never seen a [player] wear a tie before and it's way too tight."

Eventually, Gelinas got the joke. But he never got any better.

The Canucks continued to piddle and lose. The Canucks didn't forecheck well. They didn't backcheck well. Their defense was mediocre and their goaltending was horrid. Keenan couldn't take this. He tried to push the players, but the team's veterans were apathetic beyond redemption.

"If John McCaw is going to pay players an average of $1 million a year, then they'd better step up to the plate every single day," Keenan said. "And I will not compromise that and I don't think any top coach will."

The players seemed to have no idea where their coach was coming from or what they were supposed to do on the ice. "There is no system," one player complained to the *Vancouver Sun*. "It's complete chaos out there."

From a distance, Dallas Stars goaltender Ed Belfour knew what the Canucks were going through. He had been through the turmoil in Chicago, where Keenan had transformed the lethargic Blackhawks into a tenacious Cup contender.

"He's an intense competitor," Belfour said. "He wants to win the Stanley Cup. And if there's a barrier, he'll find a way to go around it. Anyone who is in it for the ultimate will put up with all that extra stuff going on."

Keenan eventually muscled into the leadership void at the top of the Canucks' hockey operation. He termed this management structure, or lack of one, the "Scotty Bowman model" after the no-GM hockey operation Detroit used for a while. McCaw's lieutenants seriously negotiated with former Buffalo Sabres general manager John Muckler, but, ultimately, Muckler was not hired as the GM. Nobody was. And since management by committee absolutely never works, somebody had to take charge of the hockey operation. On January 23, 1998, the management team gave Keenan the right to negotiate trades.

"It's going to be interesting to see how the team responds now," Keenan announced. "They know where the ship's going. It's a matter of whether they want to be on it."

Players started coming and going as soon as their flights could be booked. Keenan would bid farewell to the dispirited Gelinas, as well as Linden, Odjick, McLean, defenseman Grant Ledyard, winger Lonny Bohonos, forward Mike Sillinger, and defenseman Dave Babych. He would welcome winger Brad May, Peter Zezel (of course!), defenseman Bryan McCabe, winger Todd Bertuzzi, goaltender Garth Snow, forward Brandon Convery, defenseman Jamie Huscroft, and defenseman Jason Strudwick. And he would say hello and goodbye to winger Geoff Sanderson, tough guy Enrico Ciccone, and goaltender Sean Burke, acquiring and trading them within the same season. Whew!

"It's just a matter of time," Keenan said. "You go through a process and sometimes people want to be part of it, and sometimes they don't. Other times, adjustment takes more time than what we'd like in this sporting lifestyle. It's not normal compared to the average citizen and the way we live on a daily basis, because in sports, there is a timeline, and that timeline is very restricted."

Keenan blamed the team's mediocrity on the indifferent atmosphere he inherited, an atmosphere that was proving difficult to change. That the Canucks players blew him off wasn't his fault, at least not in his eyes.

"It has nothing to do with me or my program," he said. "The culture here has been unacceptable. This is a very, very untrained team. I don't know if there has ever been a standard here. To me, that responsibility goes right to the top. Whether it was Tom Renney or Pat Quinn, I don't know. It was never reinforced here."

Each week brought another flare-up and a new round of headlines. Gelinas and McLean were the first to go in a January 2 trade with Carolina for Burke, Sanderson, and Ciccone. Keenan had coaxed the management team into making this deal after his efforts to move Linden were blocked. At the time, he was still three weeks away from officially gaining the power to make trades, but his influence was growing. McLean was both sad and happy to leave after eleven seasons.

"Mentally, it's been draining playing for this team," he said after departing. "It eats away at you. I don't know what the hell's going on with this team. The right mix isn't there."

Even after January 23, Bellringer told reporters that the club was still looking to hire a general manager. But Keenan wasn't waiting for that to happen. He made deal after deal, looking to give his moribund team a spark. On February 4, Keenan sent Sillinger to the Flyers for a draft pick and got May from Buffalo for Sanderson.

"I don't think he liked my size," Sillinger said. "I wasn't his kind of player. Mike wants bigger players. There are a lot of excellent players who are under six foot, but he believes we all have to be big, strong guys."

The next day, Zezel came from New Jersey for a draft pick. The day after that, Keenan dropped his big bomb: Linden was shipped to the New York Islanders for McCabe and Bertuzzi. Linden refrained from blasting Keenan after learning about the deal, but described it as a relief.

"I have to say things weren't really going well here, the team was struggling, and I was as well," Linden said. "I was given a lot of opportunity here and things weren't happening for me. So I think it became a situation that was going to happen and it wasn't the biggest surprise. It's a chance for me to start again and move forward."

He never came close to resolving his problems with his coach. "I thought I would be his type of player," Linden said. "I never envisioned leaving. It was something I never thought about."

He and Keenan didn't chat long after the deal went down. "I was working on my knee in the [training] room and the trainer poked his head in and told me I'd been traded," Linden said. "I can't say that I was surprised. Mike basically told me he thought the change would do me good. I didn't have much to say. It was pretty short."

The only surprise about the Linden deal was that it took so long to happen. It was destined to occur, even if Keenan wouldn't admit as much. "I don't know if the word 'inevitable' is correct," he said. "There was certainly a little bit of controversy that was expounded on to make it a great deal of controversy in the media. The expectation was developed more by the course of events that took place recently."

Islanders general manager Mike Milbury was thrilled to land Linden. He dismissed Keenan's criticisms of Linden as "irrelevant." Quipped Milbury about Keenan, "He's pretty critical of his own mother."

In March, Keenan shipped Ledyard to Boston for a draft pick, swapped Burke to Philadelphia for Snow, got Convery from Toronto for Bohonos, and moved Babych to Philadelphia for a draft pick. He also moved Ciccone, who had had the audacity to stand up to him, to Tampa Bay for Jamie Huscroft.

Ciccone had complained to the French Canadian reporters about being scratched from a game on March 11 in Montreal, his hometown. He also told the scribes that all the horror stories they had heard about Keenan were true. The next night, he was scratched again as the Canucks blew a 2–1 lead at Philadelphia and lost 3–2. Ciccone walked into the dressing room as Keenan was dressing down the troops. Keenan asked him if there was something he wanted to say to the team. Enrico said no. Keenan went off on him, telling him he was through as a Canuck. When Ciccone asked for an explanation, Keenan demanded an apology for the comments he had made in Montreal. Ciccone refused to apologize and was told to get out and go back to Vancouver.

"One guy [May] stood up and defended me," he recalled after getting dealt to the Lightning. "I'll remember that the rest of my life, the courage that took. He's a guy who should have the 'C.'"

Ciccone saw no need to lower himself and apologize to Keenan. "He's got a God complex," Ciccone said. "He wanted me to get down on my knees and apologize. I didn't want to spend the rest of my life thinking I'd apologize to that man when I didn't do anything. Some guys do it. I won't. He's got a big ego. He's on an ego trip. I still respect the man as a hockey coach, but I can't say I respect the man as a human being. Maybe he doesn't like strong people. He's losing all the time and maybe he's trying to take the focus off him and blame somebody else."

Keenan denied having traded Ciccone simply because he wouldn't acquiesce. By complaining about not playing, Keenan suggested Ciccone was taking a shot at those who played ahead of him, like Adrian Aucoin.

"I love strong people," Keenan said. "But what Chico did was wrong. He should have apologized, not to me, but to the team. You don't go putting out complaints about not playing."

Misery enveloped the team. During a game in Ottawa on March 20, Keenan and Bure argued on the ice. Mike called Bure a "selfish little suck." Bure told his coach to screw himself, a comment he repeated after scoring the only Canucks goal in the 1–1 tie. Keenan couldn't trade Bure, a superstar, but he could trade Odjick, his best friend on the team.

"I'm really disappointed," said Bure, who would demand a trade in the off-season and never again play for the Canucks.

Odjick was sent to the Islanders for Strudwick. He was reunited with Linden and celebrated by blasting Messier for his complicity in the team's drastic overhaul. Given Messier's close ties to both McCaw and Keenan — and his unwillingness to defuse the Keenan-Linden incident when it occurred — Odjick raised some valid concerns.

"Messier was brought here to help lead us and everybody was on board waiting to go along with him," Odjick said. "We were all looking forward to the season positively. It was going to be great. But right from the start it was clear he wanted to have all the power and wanted his own people around him. He didn't break a sweat for ten games and just waited for Tom Renney and Pat Quinn to get fired. He talks to ownership all the time and he's responsible for Keenan being here and he's part of most of the trades. He sits in for four hours with management every time there's a trade. He's responsible for a lot of the changes. Look at what happened with Trevor in St. Louis when Keenan gave him shit. Did he come over to him and say, 'Look, Trev, we're with you'? He didn't say a word. How can you be captain like that? How can the team be together that way? He's not with the players. He's the one who controls everything.

"I don't blame Keenan for what's happened. Everything he does, he does in the name of winning. That's all he wants. But everything that Messier does is for more power. They signed him to help us, but all he wanted was most of us out of there so he could bring in his own people. The organization has always been great, but he just wanted to tear it apart and do it his way. But you'll never see Keenan bench Messier, no matter how bad he plays."

Keenan knew exactly how Odjick felt about things. The two had had a rather heated confrontation in Keenan's office, when Keenan referred to Gino as "one of Pat Quinn's boys."

"Mike, you can call me stupid," Odjick retorted. "You can call me a stupid Indian. But don't talk like that about people I respect." The massive Odjick reminded Keenan that they were alone in the room. If only one was to come out, Gino was ready to bet on himself. The phone rang and Keenan reached for it.

"Don't pick up that phone," Odjick ordered. "We're not finished talking."

Keenan didn't deny the gist of his confrontations with players. The acrimony wasn't unexpected, given the team's struggles. But he lamented the fact that Canucks players leaked the details to the media.

"That's always the case when you're losing," he said. "It's symptomatic of some of the things that must be changed. Any championship team has had a bond and keeps any interaction or issues that are part of the team in the team."

Given the sad state of affairs in his dressing room, Keenan had little choice but to clean house. Renney, who had been used as a welcome mat by the Canucks veterans, applauded from the sidelines as Keenan sent players packing.

"The dressing room had to change and that's what Mike has done," Renney said. "I think they're in a better position because of it. For the hockey club, not only was it necessary for Trevor to go, but others, too. Change is painful, but it can be a good thing."

May, who arrived as Keenan was changing the team, was one Canuck willing to embrace change. "It's all about winning, the whole process of winning," he said. "You can't have a comfortable attitude when you win one, then lose one. The thing is, if you're at all mentally or physically weak . . ."

Then there's going to be trouble. "What he does, I think, is not unlike [former NFL coach] Bill Parcells," May said. "Maybe there are always some little controversies around him, but the end result is what matters."

The end result of the 1997–98 season for the Canucks was a record of 25-43-14. They missed the playoffs for the second straight year and for the first time in Keenan's NHL career.

The early exit gave Keenan some extra time on Georgian Bay. When he returned from the cottage, Keenan felt better about the strides the remade Canucks had made during his first season. He believed the team was bigger, stronger, and a lot better on the blue line.

"The summer was far too long, but I won't take the entire responsibility," he said. "It was a long shot for the team to make the playoffs because when I was hired they were too far behind. Psychologically, that's how I dealt with it so it wasn't a full blow to me. I'm not skirting the responsibility, but I'm not going to be accountable for all of it either."

Although his trades and tirades seemed to have had little affect on the Canucks, Keenan didn't plan on taking a different tack in 1998–99. He had no reason to doubt his program. He believed results would come in time.

"I don't think I have to reinvent myself," he said. "I not only have the same ability I had in the past, but I have fourteen years' experience as well. I don't think I have to prove I can handle a younger group because I think my experience shows I've handled a number of different teams with various age groups and the results have been good."

But Keenan had a new boss to contend with. McCaw had grown weary of the staggering Canucks' losses and hired Brian Burke, the NHL senior vice president, as his new president and general manager. According to figures released by Northwest Sports Enterprises, the Canucks had lost more than $21 million in 1996–97 and $36 million in 1997–98. McCaw had money to burn, but his hockey franchise was turning into a cash-consuming bonfire. The franchise blamed the losses on the weak Canadian dollar and the high level of taxes in British Columbia, but the real problem was its egregiously bad management.

Because Burke is every bit as stubborn and autocratic as Keenan, hockey observers figured the rest of Iron Mike's regime could be measured on an egg timer. There was no way on earth these two men could ever work together. Burke's contract, worth more than $1 million a year, ensured he would win the battle with Keenan. When Keenan noted that his contract gave him the authority to make trades, Burke reminded Mike that, as general manager, he had the authority to fire the coach. Also, Burke was a hell of a lot bigger than Keenan and had made his professional hockey living with his fists. Keenan wasn't dealing with mild-mannered Neil Smith anymore.

Early on, both men attempted to appear outwardly civil. "Mike and I are on the same page with regards to style of play and we've been in agreement on just about every player we've discussed," Burke said with a straight face. "I don't view this as a problem — me a GM inheriting a new coach. I view this as an asset."

Nobody really believed that. As *Vancouver Sun* columnist Gary Mason wrote, "Brian Burke was as 'thrilled' to have Mike Keenan as coach as a bride is about having a cold sore appear on her wedding day." In reality, Keenan was doomed the minute Burke was hired. The question wasn't if Keenan would get canned, but when.

The 1998–99 season was a fiasco from the get-go. Keenan urged Burke to land free-agent goaltender Mike Richter from the Rangers, but Burke and his bosses took a pass. Bure, still smarting over a number of long-standing grievances with the Griffiths, decided to sit out the season to force a trade. About the only person Bure didn't hold a bitter grudge against was Keenan.

"I can tell you honestly I had no problem with Mike whatsoever and I loved to play for him," Bure later said. "He was the coach and general manager and I had 39 goals and a big bonus for 50. He called me in the office and said, 'Listen, don't worry about the 50 goals. I'll get you 50. I'll help you do it.' And he was the general manager. I really like Mike."

What about that "selfish little suck" barb that Keenan stuck him with the previous season? "That didn't bother me," Bure said. "I played for [Viktor] Tikhonov, so that was nothing." Tikhonov was from the Soviet Union's old school, where a lazy defenseman on the Red Army team could be sent out to drive tanks in Siberia if he didn't get his act together. Tikhonov was no diplomat.

The aging Messier was plagued by a variety of injuries. Keenan pleaded with Burke to deal Bure quickly and acquire some reinforcements, but his boss continued holding out for a better trade as the losses mounted.

"We have nothing beyond the first line until we make a Pavel Bure move," Keenan complained a few weeks into the season. "We have no depth."

Burke responded by suggesting that the Canucks simply had to get the most out of all their players, as they had when Quinn coached.

"Pat does it by consistent use of four lines," Burke said. "He's not a juggler. If you have a bad shift with Pat you got right back out there." Also, Burke noted, Quinn never ripped his players in front of reporters. In his mind, this approach was the best way to get teams to play better. "Pat gets players to feel that they personally owe it to him and he takes the heat for them," Burke said. "He doesn't single guys out in the media. They're loyal to him because they believe in him. He never hangs his players out to dry."

With the losses mounting and Keenan's dismissal becoming more imminent, he found a unique way to throw a tantrum. During a 5–1 loss to Toronto on November 25, Keenan pulled his goaltender during a power play early in the third period. He did it again later in the period, allowing the Maple Leafs to score a 130-foot shorthanded goal into the empty net. Toronto fans, realizing what was up, chanted "Keeee-nan, Keeee-nan" as the Canucks went down to defeat. When asked about his gambit, Keenan noted his lineup was shorthanded due to injuries and the absence of Bure.

"We don't have a great deal of offense in the lineup," he explained. Clearly, Keenan was showing up Burke, who had watched the game from the press box.

As the team's slump deepened, Keenan seemed ready to concede his fate. As in St. Louis, he was out of moves. He couldn't turn over the roster with Burke in his way and the Canucks weren't responding to him. Messier, who had been such a force for him with the Rangers, could do nothing with this group. After a 2–1 loss to Colorado on December 17, Keenan pretty much admitted he had to go.

"I find it very disappointing when players won't listen to the coach's suggestions, particularly when they're not successful," he said. "Either they are going to accept what we're asking them to do or they won't and they'll have to fire the coach. That's how it works. They get tired of listening to you. They need a kick start, a fresh start, or a new coach. That's how you ignite a team for a while, keep them going. It's disconcerting for a coach when they stop listening to you. Then you know you're in trouble. That's the way I am with this group."

Burke finally got around to trading Bure on January 17, sending him and finesse defenseman Bret Hedican to Florida for defenseman Ed Jovanovski, center Dave Gagner, goaltender Kevin Weekes, enforcer prospect Mike Brown, and a first-round draft pick. But just when Jovanovski and Gagner might have brought some relief, Burke fired Keenan.

The final straw for Burke was a 4–1 loss at Nashville two nights later. The Canucks weren't competitive. At that point, Vancouver had gone 36-54-18 in parts of two seasons under Keenan.

"I have issues with the way our hockey club has been coached," Burke said. "What accelerated my thinking on this change was the way Mike has coached since Christmas. His heart just did not appear to be in coaching our hockey club. I felt I couldn't wait any longer. Since Christmas, it has been an unmitigated disaster for our club."

When the league broke for the All-Star Game, Burke made his move on former Colorado Avalanche coach Marc Crawford. Keenan learned of his pending dismissal from a Canucks public relations staffer, who told him the story was about to hit the newspapers.

"I'm assuming it's a fait accompli. I just wish that someone would have the courtesy of making a phone call," Keenan said when reporters reached him. "My wife and I are sitting here all day wondering if somebody is going to call us. It's quite disturbing to say the least."

Once Burke had Crawford locked up, he made Keenan's firing official. Keenan wasn't shocked, but he was a bit indignant. He didn't see where he had done such a poor job of coaching. Had Burke traded Bure sooner, and gotten more for him, perhaps the season would have been very different.

"None of us are happy with the record," Keenan said. "We had three of our top four forwards out for most of the season. We stayed competitive. I think the players have worked extremely hard. I've been very proud of what they've been able to do. The team was finally getting settled after being shorthanded all season after Bure skipped out on his contract."

Keenan argued that the season could still have been salvaged.

"Todd Bertuzzi had returned from a broken leg, Alexander Mogilny's sore knee was much improved, and Mark Messier had shaken off his concussion," he said. "With those players back, the Canucks had played .500 hockey while playing the likes of Dallas and Detroit."

Messier was obviously upset by Keenan's firing, but he had to bite his tongue. The team was paying him $7 million to play some pretty unremarkable hockey. He owed ownership some loyalty, even on this issue.

"I'd be lying if I said I wasn't disappointed, but I've been disappointed before," he said. "It's always disappointing to see people you like, trust, and admire for what they've done leave any organization."

Most of the Canucks took the coaching change in stride. They couldn't exactly throw a full-scale "Keenan's Dead!" party, not with Messier still captaining the team. They had to be judicious with their remarks, at least on the record.

"Guys tried to listen, but we didn't know what he wanted," goaltender Arturs Irbe said. "I did everything he wanted and it still wasn't good enough. I think a lot of guys felt the same way."

Tony Amonte, playing for the Chicago Blackhawks, feigned devastation when informed of Keenan's firing.

"Oh, no, that's really too bad," he said. "I'd better get on the phone right now and call him."

Keenan's tenure had been acrimonious from start to finish. One of his loyalists, Brian Noonan, had once told Keenan to leave the dressing room after Keenan broke a stick during a rant and nearly clipped Dave Scatchard with the flying stick blade. Odjick had been ready to fight him in the coach's office and Donald Brashear reportedly threatened him on the bench. Another report had Keenan telling the Canucks that Ledyard had quit on the team when, in fact, he had left to visit his ailing wife. Keenan was a coach who thrived on conflict, but things got out of hand in Vancouver.

"Maybe I should have been a football coach," he surmised amid the controversy.

After getting fired, Keenan insisted his heart had still been in coaching. He slammed Burke for asserting otherwise and openly questioned Burke's credentials for his job.

"I don't think Brian has coached at any level and he certainly hasn't coached in the NHL," Keenan said. "If he's going to judge my demeanor on the bench, in terms of my performance level, then I think it's unfair and unprofessional. There's so much more that goes into coaching, starting with depth of preparation for yourself and for your team. If conduct on the bench is being evaluated as one of the primary reasons for performance levels, it shows inexperience. And for someone who has never coached to say I had lost my enthusiasm I think is unfair. I think he was a general manager for one or two years in Hartford and basically had an administrative job with the league. This isn't the same as working in the trenches or living with a team day in and day out, making decisions on a daily basis."

Keenan revealed that he had refused to fire assistant coach Stan Smyl, as Burke had suggested after coming on board as general manager.

"He did ask me about the possibility of replacing Stan, but I told him I wasn't going to do that because he had worked extremely hard and done a good job," Keenan said. Keenan also predicted that Messier wouldn't finish his career in Vancouver on Burke's watch. He was right.

Burke was willing to fire back and rebut Keenan's criticisms. "He's got something against me and Orca Bay and he shouldn't worry about that," Burke said. "So far, Mike Keenan has attempted to involve three people — Stan Smyl, Marc Crawford, and now Mark Messier — in this little fantasy he has that he was unjustly fired here. I think it's really lame that he would drag Mark Messier into this. Right now, Mike Keenan should worry about finding another job and not about the Vancouver Canucks."

Messier managed to stay out of the controversy as it raged on for weeks. He was loyal to Keenan but he still had to work for Burke. "I'm not going to get into what Mike said and what Brian said," he said. "The change has been made. It's not for me to question. I've never played politics in twenty years of professional hockey and I'm not going to start playing politics because I've moved to Vancouver."

He defended the special status Keenan had given him. Sure, he had spent a lot of time in Keenan's office discussing team matters. But he had done the same as a leader in New York, and the Rangers went all the way.

"In order for a team to be successful, not everybody is treated the same," Messier said. "That's a basic part of life in professional sports. It's understood amongst players in the dressing room that certain players need certain things to perform at their best."

After Keenan's exit, the Canucks made the same sort of observations that the Blues had made when Keenan was fired in St. Louis. "Before, it was more of a free-wheeling atmosphere," winger Markus Naslund said. "I still think you need some kind of system to be successful. We're a young team and when you don't have a lot of experience, you need guidelines to know where to be and what to do out there."

Garth Snow appreciated the guidelines that Crawford, a Cup winner in Colorado, gave this struggling team. Structure replaced chaos. "He is a little more detailed in special teams and defensive zones," Snow said. "Mike was probably more just flow drills and stuff like that. This is a club that under Mike was a high-energy club that forechecked a great deal and really tried to create havoc and take advantage of other teams. We've tried to add a bit more structure to our play and play with a little bit more purpose offensively and defensively."

Keenan is quick to point out that his unique approach had worked with other teams that were willing to bear down and make it work. "A system is just what you do defensively and there are different ways to go out about it," he said. "But if you play without any emotion or passion for the game, then no system is going to be effective. I prefer to focus on that part of the game."

The Canucks also welcomed Crawford's less confrontational style. Keenan had succeeded in getting them on edge, but the result wasn't creative tension. It was destructive tension that ate away at the players' psyches. The team didn't have any confidence when Keenan arrived and never really got rolling on his watch. Crawford's arrival brought a breath of fresh air into the dressing room.

"It's a different feeling," Naslund said. "Guys were a little more scared with Mike around. You never knew what was going to happen. Marc has shown more confidence in me than Mike ever did."

In the weekly column he wrote for *The Sporting News,* Keenan addressed his firing at length.

"Every coach is hired to be fired, but I just can't understand why the Canucks decided to fire me at this time, two games after making a huge trade that should settle their lineup," Keenan wrote. "Naturally I'm disappointed about getting fired, but I'm not going to let it get me down.

"The Nashville game finished a two-game, two-night trip that started in Dallas. It was the last of four games in six nights, came before the All-Star break and on the heels of the Pavel Bure trade. To make an evaluation at that time was unexpected and unfortunate. This was a team that was beginning to realize what it needed to be successful and had played some big games. And then it was over.

"If my dismissal was based on one or two games, that doesn't add up. If it's based on the season, there were numerous mitigating circumstances. It's hard to say where GM Brian Burke was coming from. He was unhappy with the results after Christmas, but this was a team maimed by injuries and playing a difficult schedule with many young players.

"There was also criticism that I was not developing young players. But look at how Bill Muckalt has played; he's a top candidate for rookie of the year. Mattias Ohlund was a rookie-of-the-year candidate last year, and he was an All-Star. Donald Brashear is coming into his own with his toughness and all-around rugged play. Dave Scatchard, who didn't play much under his previous coach, was taking a regular turn and rounding into a useful player. And Markus Naslund, another All-Star, is the team scoring leader and a terrific talent on the rise.

"I also can't figure out why I keep getting criticized for not working on the power play. Look at the results. The Canucks were eighth over-all on the power play and sixth on the road. What more could the team do? People might not understand, but my players do practice special teams, but in different ways. Someone's talking, but they don't know what they're talking about."

Odjick thought Keenan's post-dismissal whimpering was pathetic. Keenan, he felt, should have known that was goes around comes around.

"He felt he couldn't work unless it was his own people that he brought in," Odjick said. "He didn't want anybody who was here before him. And when he traded us, he told us that life wasn't fair. But then he got fired because another GM wanted to choose and now he's pissed off. It's like, 'Mike, you're the one who always needed your own people to work with.'

"Now that Burkie's there and Crawford's there, you hope that things are going in the right direction. I thought I might be happy when Mike got fired, but it gave me no satisfaction. I never wanted to leave there. I look at it like I spent eight years in Vancouver and of those eight years there were two bad months. After you've been in a place that long, it just seems like the place becomes part of you. And it will be a part of me."

After the backstabbing and backbiting ended, Keenan vowed, MacArthur-like, to return to the rink. The Canucks experience could not sour him on his profession. A coach was who he was. Coaching is what he did. In his mind, the sunset was a long way off.

"I have renewed vigor for coaching after my experience in Vancouver," he insisted. "I'm definitely not finished coaching."

But would the rest of the NHL agree?

◄ 8 ►

Wasting Away

He's good for the NHL. He's good for ratings, he's good
for publicity, he's good for a lot of things the NHL repre-
sents. You have to work with him and you have to let him
do his thing. He's a winner and he's always won where he
has been. That's important.

— PHOENIX COYOTES CENTER JEREMY ROENICK,
PULLING FOR KEENAN TO GET ANOTHER CRACK AT COACHING

THE NATIONAL HOCKEY LEAGUE SENT MIKE KEENAN PACKING
in 1999. Vancouver Canucks general manager Brian Burke fired him
at the All-Star break and that was that. No teams called on him to
revive them for the stretch run. A half-dozen teams hired new coaches
in the off-season, but none granted him an interview. NHL head coaching rookies Curt Fraser, Steve Ludzig, Andy Murray, Bob Francis, and
Kevin Lowe received opportunities instead of Keenan.

The 1999–2000 season came and went without him, too, so Keenan
had to find new ways to stay busy. He spent his idle season shuttling
from his home in Florida to various cities on broadcast assignments
for CTV. He did color commentary on Ottawa Senators games, allowing him to critique the work of old friend Jacques Martin, the Senators'
coach. He also did studio work, monitoring multiple games at once
and providing analysis. Ironically, he replaced former NHL goaltender
Greg Millen on this gig; Millen had been one of his torture victims
with the Blackhawks.

"It's a new experience, certainly," Keenan said. "I'm not in the hockey world now, I'm in the television world or the media world. It's a change of pace, but an interesting look from the other side."

He had dabbled in the media before, handling television work and writing a column for *The Sporting News.* "It gives me an opportunity to work with a game that I love and a game that I have quite a passion for," he said. "I'll also learn a lot about the media side of the business. And it will make me stay diligent about knowing the league and the personnel around the league."

He and his second wife, Nola, whom he married during his Canucks tenure, had the freedom to pursue whatever interested them. They fished in the Florida Keys and traveled to Europe to visit Gayla, who spent the 1999–2000 school year studying abroad. Keenan went through a lot of sunscreen. Life could've been worse: He could have been scrubbing floors or repairing railroad lines, two of the many jobs he had worked before graduating to his productive career in coaching.

During his time away from coaching, Keenan found some solace in the fact that his mentor, Scotty Bowman, also once had to bide his time doing television work after getting fired from Buffalo in 1986. Eventually, Bowman worked his way back into the mix, even though many considered him past his prime. He took a personnel job with the Pittsburgh Penguins and got pressed into duty in 1991 when coach Bob Johnson became gravely ill.

"I've talked with Scotty about it," Keenan said. "The only reason he ended up coaching again is because Bob Johnson died. I asked him what went on and why. Obviously, he persevered. But the guy with more skills than anybody who has ever coached the game couldn't get a job because the industry disliked his personality for some reason. Maybe they disliked the fact that he had a great deal of success."

More likely, general managers were afraid of Bowman's autocratic style and owners couldn't connect with his inscrutable demeanor. As the hockey business changed rapidly, the captains of this industry doubted Bowman's relevance. Now the same thing may be happening to Keenan, and the NHL is a lot less interesting as a result.

"Certainly the game needs personalities," says Blues assistant coach Jimmy Roberts, who served as the team's interim coach after Keenan was fired in St. Louis. "It needs high profile people. Mike certainly is that. You're either going to boo him or love him. Sports has always needed those types of people."

The contradictions in Keenan's style — and the contradictions between his style and his real self — make him one of the most intriguing sports figures of his time. He loves being Iron Mike, and he hates being Iron Mike. He revels in his edgy persona, yet he complains about the disagreeable image he projects.

"No one writes about the good things I've done for players," he moped during his Blues regime. "I'm not going to go around telling people that. I'm not a PR guy. And so 10 percent of my personality is always written about, never the hundred percent. I won't take responsibility for that. A monster's been created and now everyone wants to come see the monster."

He orchestrates confrontations to keep his teams on edge, yet he insists that it is not his nature to create conflict. He relishes showdowns, then expresses remorse about his psychological terrorism. He tells players to expect the unexpected, then follows an identical coaching script at each coaching stop.

Keenan prefers quick, brisk practices that don't waste players' time, but he has also ordered some of the most notorious death skates in league history. He demotes or trades players at the drop of a hat, yet they are treated like kings while they are still on the team. He insists on only the best accommodations and travel arrangements for his men — as long as they last with him.

"He's a very complicated man," Gino Odjick said after Keenan shipped him out of Vancouver. "He could be a nice person when you talked to him one on one, and then other times it seemed like he had six different personalities. Some days he was Mike Keenan, some days he was Scotty Bowman, some days he was worse. There was never a dull moment the whole time he was there."

He knows not to push players too far, then pushes them anyway. Some players respond, some rebel, and wholesale turnover ensues. He preaches accountability, but tends to blame everybody from billionaire owners to minimally paid clock operators when things go bad.

"We could get together and swap stories about Mike for hours," former Rangers goaltender Glenn Healy said after clashing with Keenan in New York. "The job of any coach is to find the best way to tweak a player to perform at his best level. I think you motivate different players in different ways, but Mike obviously doesn't. Typically, if an athlete doesn't like Mike's methods, he finds himself someplace else."

Time away from the bench has not extinguished Keenan's fire. He anxiously awaits his next opportunity to compete. He believes he is still in his coaching prime and there are still championships out there to be won.

"I'd like to get back involved in hockey," he says. "I've got a great passion for it. I think I have a talent for it. I've had some good success both as manager and coach in the NHL and I feel I'm young enough to contribute, maybe help somebody. I definitely miss coaching and I miss being a GM involved in the day-to-day activities. My heart is still in it and I still have a passion for the game. I think I've proven myself in both of those areas and I think I've shown that I can have success in building programs."

A new round of jobs opened up in the summer of 2000 and still no team came calling. He campaigned openly for the Rangers job, and ordered agent Rob Campbell to make Madison Square Garden czar Dave Checketts aware of his acute interest. The Rangers had fired general manager Neil Smith and were also looking for a coach after canning John Muckler.

"When I left there in 1994, after we won the Cup, I left because I felt I was in a no-win situation with Neil Smith and I had to leave, because if I stayed, I was going to get fired anyway," Keenan says. "That was too bad, because I felt if I was really given the opportunity, that we had the chance to win two or three more Cups there. I had a good relationship with the players, especially Mark Messier. I really enjoyed the fans and I loved the city. The whole experience was exciting for me. I didn't want to leave.

"I know people thought I was the bad guy at the time. But I wasn't left with much choice, and I think over the last few years people have come to realize — including the fans in New York — exactly what happened there. Neil just used that [bonus] non-payment as an excuse. He had no intention of bringing me back whatsoever. I'd love the opportunity to coach there again. The fans deserve to have a successful team."

Alas, Glen Sather got the New York Rangers job instead of Keenan ally Colin Campbell, who might well have brought Keenan back to New York. Sather went looking for a coach he could dominate and settled on one of his former servants, Ron Low. Keenan got only a cursory interview, despite the support of Mark Messier, who did return to the Rangers.

Keenan couldn't dream of finding work with the Columbus Blue Jackets. He had no bridge to Blue Jackets president Doug MacLean, who had lost his job as assistant general manager in Detroit after Keenan made a play for employment with the Red Wings in 1994. The other expansion team, Minnesota, went with trap-master Jacques Lemaire.

Could the famously impatient Keenan coach an expansion team over the long haul? He insists he could. Earlier in his career, the Devils, the Panthers, and the Mighty Ducks expressed interest in having him do just that. Because the Blues added a number of good young players on his watch, he believes he is qualified to fill such a role.

"That's what we did in Chicago," he says. "I went there in '88 and we went to the final four three years and the finals, but it took four years for us get to the finals. That started with the Chris Chelios trade for Denis Savard and the development of Roenick and Eddie Belfour in the net.

"I don't think it would be my preference now. I'm a little older and I would prefer to coach a team that has a possibility of being successful. It doesn't have to be the top team, but you never know what that means, either. In New York, the team I inherited was a non-playoff team and we made a 33-point improvement that season to win the President's Trophy and win the Cup from a non-playoff team. So it's hard to say. I guess they had the resources to sign some players and did. But that was a quick change and quick turnaround all within one season. I don't know how often that happens in the history of the NHL. Not that often.

"There are other franchises that would push the emphasis on winning. I don't think I would be too interested in going to a team that says we don't really care if we win for five years. Believe me, some teams are saying that. There are teams that are thinking that way."

Times were changing in the NHL and the most accomplished coach of his generation couldn't find work behind the bench. Never mind that he had taken two overachieving Flyers teams to the Stanley Cup finals. Never mind that he took the Blackhawks to the finals, too, or led the jinxed Rangers to their first Cup since 1940. Never mind that he narrowly missed taking the Blues to the Western Conference finals for just the second time since 1970. Never mind his three NHL All-Star Games as head coach, his two Canada Cup triumphs at the helm of Team Canada, his Calder Cup at Rochester of the AHL, or that national Canadian college title with the University of Toronto. Never mind that that he took Peterborough to the Memorial Cup during his one season coaching major junior hockey. Never mind the Junior B titles he won in Oshawa or the Senior A title he won as a player-coach for Whitby.

"That's all you can ask for from a coach, the opportunity to win a championship, to be successful," says Calgary Flames assistant coach Greg Gilbert, who played for Keenan in Chicago, New York, and St. Louis.

General managers went out of their way to avoid Keenan. They didn't want to see his resume unless they needed something absorbent with which to soak up a coffee spill in the front office. A few of the more nervous GMs might have gone a step farther and posted his photograph at security checkpoints, with instructions to keep him out of their buildings. All hell can break loose once Keenan gets his foot in the door.

"It's discouraging," Keenan says. "I would understand it if I hadn't accomplished anything in the league, but I've coached 160 playoff games and almost a thousand regular season games. I certainly think there is a groundswell amongst the leaders, and that would involve a lot of general managers and maybe even the people who run the league."

He wondered why so many rookie NHL head coaches were getting their chances and his phone hadn't rung. Francis? Ludzig? Fraser? Weren't general managers aware of Keenan's many successes?

"I find it a little unusual," Keenan says. "That's not being disrespectful of the people who are being hired. I'm sure they are hard-working young coaches who qualified themselves to a certain extent. But it's unusual, and I don't know where the pressure points are coming from. Usually you'll see one or two rookie coaches and a couple of veterans. To me it makes a statement that somebody in the league is pressuring ownership to make some kind of financial correction. It's too obvious."

Keenan wonders if his big-ticket contracts in New York, St. Louis, and Vancouver scared owners looking to cut payroll. "The way things have been going with the players, coaches' salaries are one of the things they could control," he says. "And when there were six openings last summer, it became a little too peculiar that all the hirings were rookie coaches who came in at very modest salaries. That, to me, is so obvious that there's influence and direction given by someone at the upper level of the league."

This theory smacks of paranoia. Coaches' salaries are the least of the NHL's concerns. Hiring an elite coach costs about one-third the price of signing a halfway decent free agent. NHL executives might conspire on other matters — like punishing model Carol Alt's boy toy, Alexei Yashin, and chilling the market for unrestricted free agents — but there was no need to send out an "Iron Mike" memo.

His fifteen-year NHL journey had been as controversial as it was successful. General managers became concerned about his harsh coaching tactics, his alarming failures in St. Louis and Vancouver, and his insatiable desire for power. Who wants to hire a coach known for alienating popular players and purposely creating unrest to keep a team on edge? Who wants to hire a coach with an extensive track record of trying to circumvent, undermine, and replace his superiors?

Bowman scoffs at such talk and dismisses the rap on his former protégé. He doesn't understand why Keenan has such an ugly reputation.

"I think it's been unfair," Bowman says. "I think a lot of it has been stretched out. I think a lot of it has been the figment of somebody's imagination. It makes good copy. . . . I think it has detracted from him because only six people have won five hundred [NHL] games."

The hockey media has dwelled on the more controversial aspects of his career because conflict sells. But they were only reporting the truth. Turmoil followed Keenan at every turn and team executives have clearly grown wary of his volatility. In their minds, conflict stinks.

"I really don't think he's necessarily a bad person," Neil Smith says. "I wouldn't say he is a good person. He always has to have chaos around him, therefore he's always drawing attention to himself. It's like a child."

Notre Dame University coach Dave Poulin prospered under Keenan's hard-driving tenure with the Flyers. He was Keenan's captain and he helped his coach drive the young Flyers within arm's reach of two Stanley Cups. He saw Keenan's style work, then he saw it drain every last ounce of enthusiasm from the troops.

"You're trying to instill in them that desire and that will to succeed," Poulin says. "You have to have that ultimate work ethic to do it. Mike worked. You can't confuse that with anything. Mike worked. The fact that he wanted to win, everybody will say that. The manner in which he did it was so difficult and human nature just gets tired of that. They just do."

Though he stuck with his hockey career, Poulin continued to study business after graduating from Notre Dame. He compares Keenan to a turnaround artist, a slasher who comes to a company, trims the waste, puffs up the profit margin, drives up the stock price and then leaves. Those types of managers aren't going to last long, but they don't have to. They don't last long in hockey, either, but then who does? Few coaches ever get the time to install a long-range program. Perhaps Keenan has the right idea.

"His primary style is to create tension and create controversy," Poulin says. "That's the point he thinks everybody is going to rally around. And while it's effective on a defined term, it's very, very difficult, very wearing. I think it could still be effective on a tailored basis now."

General managers tend to take a longer view of team success. Their goal is to remain gainfully employed while giving their franchise a reasonable chance to succeed. That can get pretty tricky around Keenan.

"I think, in all truth, Mike Keenan would always want to be coach and general manager of any team — coach and general manager and president and vice president and anything else he can handle, especially treasurer," Madison Square Garden president Bob Gutkowski said after Keenan bailed out on the franchise. "Mike Keenan moves in strange and different ways."

Unless an owner orders a GM to hire Keenan — or unless that GM has immediate retirement plans — he'd have to think twice before hiring him.

"That doesn't make a lot of sense to me," Keenan says. "If you have somebody who's qualified for the job, and you're so insecure about it as a general manager, what kind of job are you doing? Your job is to give your franchise the best chance to succeed."

Other issues have dogged Keenan, of course. The winning percentages in his last four NHL seasons were .488, .470, .429, and .400. When he got control of the Blues' and Canucks' hockey operations, he didn't wow anybody with his personnel moves. He made some great trades, like getting Chris Pronger and Pavol Demitra for the Blues, but he made some costly blunders, too. His earlier work with the Chicago Blackhawks was better, but there he had an owner, Bill Wirtz, who refused to give him carte blanche.

As he reflects on his career, Keenan blames the instability of his last three stops on ownership shifts that occurred after he came on board.

"I've had a lot of bad luck in this way," Keenan says. "In New York, for instance, I was hired by Stan Jaffe, who was fired and replaced by Neil Smith. In St. Louis, I was hired by Mike Shanahan's management team, and Shanahan was replaced by the St. Louis ownership group after the first year. When Michael Shanahan was fired, or rather when he lost his position as chairman of the board, I guess, I really didn't have an opportunity because there was nobody involved at the ownership level who had the experience Michael had to see the thing through.

"Then, I was hired by the Canucks ownership and replaced by the GM it hired. I put myself in a real vulnerable situation in Vancouver by accepting a job as coach when there was no general manager. I completely understand Brian Burke's intentions. He deserved the right to have his own coach in there. Ownership hasn't been stable on teams I've coached since my days in Philly and Chicago. In Philly, the Snider family has been in power for some time. In Chicago, the Wirtz family has owned the Blackkhawks forever."

Keenan would have been an interesting choice to coach the Flyers in 2000–2001, but general manager Bobby Clarke elected to stick with Craig Ramsey. After Keenan's friend, Roger Neilson, was sidelined by cancer treatments, Ramsey did an admirable job as interim coach and earned the job full time.

Would Clarke ever hire Keenan again? Well . . . maybe.

"I'm probably one of the few guys left who still really likes Mike and is comfortable sitting down with him and having a drink and shooting the breeze with him," Clarke says. "In so many ways, Mike's a really good guy, but somewhere along the way you don't work with Mike. Everybody works for him, whether you are the manager or the owner or the trainer or the players. And in this business, if you try to operate that way, you really alienate people."

Keenan speaks assuredly about his ability to adapt to changes in the players, the sport, and the industry, but his coaching program has changed little. He came to the Flyers in 1984 and was well ahead of his peers on many fronts. His state-of-the-art fitness program had his players skating laps around their rivals. He mastered the use of visualization as a motivational tool and consulted with a sports psychologist to better read his players. By the time the Canucks fired him in 1999, though, he seemed at least a step or two behind the more multi-dimensional coaches.

The NHL has become a very different place in the last sixteen years. Players had few rights back in 1984, due to a variety of factors. The death of the World Hockey Association had eliminated the only alternative market for players to sell themselves. Rather than looking to grow, the NHL, under president John Ziegler, merely tried to protect its share of the sports market and control costs. The too-cozy relationship between NHL Players Association czar Alan Eagleson and the league kept players in line. Stars were lucky to see $250,000 salaries and average players had to settle for two-way contracts, with a far lower salary for minor league play. Good seasons often earned $10,000 or $15,000 raises. Coaches could rule with an iron fist because players had reason to be afraid.

Fifteen years later, the league is a far different place. All-Star veterans expect $5 million salaries and superstars command $10 million. Players live in the same gated communities as their owners. The average NHL salary has soared past $1.3 million, so even journeymen obtain lifetime security unless they habitually overtip at the tavern. Backsliding veterans can still be sent to the minors, of course, but they often go with seven-figure salaries. If riding the bus gets too difficult, these millionaires can buy the farm team a more comfortable bus or charter a jet.

E.J. McGuire, a Keenan aide in Rochester, Philadelphia, and Chicago, figures Keenan would definitely have to tone down his approach to work again, given the economic realities of the game today. Coaches can't simply run off players who don't respond.

"In today's day and age, it's easier said than done with contracts or whatever," he says. "It's easy to trade the bodies, it's not easy to trade the contracts."

Keenan believes his tough regimen could still work, despite all the changes the NHL has undergone. He notes that higher salaries have created higher stakes and owner patience is at an all-time low.

"I think my program is tough in terms of its demands," he says. "But in terms of pro sports today — where the movement of coaches and players seems to be increasing because of the economic structure and demands of the industry, and at the same time the expectations of ownership are increasing because people are putting out extraordinary amounts of money to own hockey clubs — I don't think it's a matter of the program not lasting. As a matter of fact, it lasts a great deal longer than most programs in the industry."

The crash of the Iron Curtain turned the trickle of Eastern Europeans into the NHL into a flood. The flow of Swedes and Finns increased, too, as emerging players in those countries learned to play the North American game and chase lofty North American salaries. Once the bastion of hardworking Canadian farm boys, the NHL became a truly multi-national workplace in the 1990s. Coaching diverse, variously motivated players is far more difficult than whipping earnest lads from Guelph, Moose Jaw, and Val-d'Or into shape.

"The yellers and screamers aren't entirely extinct, but it's getting close," Blackhawks general manager Mike Smith says. "Today's players don't want to hear that. They don't want to be humiliated in front of other players in the room. The days of intimidation are over. Screaming and berating doesn't have long-term effectiveness, anyway."

The economics of the sport created new priorities. Extremely wealthy owners operate their teams as investments. Smaller cities like Quebec, Winnipeg, and Hartford lost their teams and cities like Phoenix, Atlanta, and Nashville came into the league. The Sun Belt has become the league's money belt. Franchises are building lavish new arenas with luxury suites and premium seats to sell. With average ticket prices pushing forty-five dollars, the stakes became much higher. Teams exist not to chase the Stanley Cup, but to fill seats, retire building debt, and build the value of their franchise in case a dot-com billionaire wants to buy a team to play with.

Superstars are asked to do a lot more than win games. They must cut commercials, pose for billboard photographers, and spur suite leases. They slap sponsors' backs and become partners with their owners. They have an equity stake in the franchise, figuratively and sometimes literally. The game's last two megastars, Mario Lemieux and Wayne Gretzky, run their own teams now. It's a players' league.

"The change in the industry is going to make it difficult for Mike," Poulin says. "Mike is at a transition stage of hockey. It's gone from being another sport to being a big-time money sport. We haven't sorted out all those things yet."

In this New World Order, coaches must be nimble. Rather than simply make demands of their players, they have to sell their programs. Rather than force key players to make the necessary sacrifices for team success, they must convince them to follow the prescribed course.

"A lot of Mike's team-building things were us against him," Poulin says. "He thrived on that. Now, because of the financial outlay of it, it doesn't have to be us against them. Guys can wander off and do their own thing. Guys can charter a plane and go off for two days during the All-Star break. Whereas we had to do things together."

Coaches can still crack the whip, of course, but they must nurture player confidence as well. Top athletes are major assets these days and smart owners refuse to squander them. Suite-holders pay five- and six-figure leases to watch the players play, not to watch the coach behind the bench. If you coach the Mighty Ducks of Anaheim, you know Paul Kariya is the show. As deposed Penguins coach Kevin Constantine discovered the hard way, Jaromir Jagr runs the deal in Pittsburgh.

"Obviously there has to be fine line between being a hard-line guy and being able to get along with your players," says Blues defenseman Chris Pronger, whom Keenan slapped into shape in St. Louis. "Obviously, you have to command respect from your players and likewise."

Keenan has softened a bit over the years, but player psyches may have softened even more. "When I broke in, young kids wouldn't say boo in the dressing room," long-time Keenanite Peter Zezel says. "Those things have changed, with players going to their agents about playing time. The respect has changed."

Jimmy Roberts believes coaches can no longer operate with tunnel vision.

"A coach has to be on his toes and keep up with what's happening to have a team that wins and satisfies the people you've got to be playing for," he says. "There's a lot of little strings you have to pull as a coach today. Looking at [current Blues Coach] Joel Quenneville, he is certainly pulling all the right strings. Mike wasn't. As far as his ability of a coach, he is certainly capable of doing it. From then to now, there is a lot of change. But he is capable of that change."

Minnesota Wild scout Rich Sutter was one of the players Keenan ran off in Philadelphia. In retrospect, though, he believes Mike was good for his career. And he believes Keenan could be good for a lot of today's players who lack the old-school work ethic.

"The problem with the players today — it's not all players but quite a few players — they have gotten spoiled over time," Sutter says. "It starts with what goes on in the minor hockey systems in the world. Some of these kids get pampered and babied and brought along. But by the time they come [to the NHL], so many of the kids are so disrespectful. They leave their equipment lying in the middle of the floor. They don't pick up after themselves. If you can't come to the rink respectful of what your job is all about, the people you work with and are around, you're not going to be respectful of your own game.

"I think, to a degree, a coach is going to have to have more power. He's got to be able to decide who's playing or not playing. There are teams in this league where the coaches are told who to play. They shouldn't have allowed that kind of money to be thrown around to begin with. It's not the coach throwing that money around. He's given a deck of cards to deal with. He's given a puzzle that he must make into something."

One puzzle Keenan could solve is Canada's failure in recent international events, such as the 1996 World Cup and the 1998 Winter Olympics.

As a two-time Canada Cup winner who has also coached in the World Junior Championships and the World Championships, Iron Mike would make an intriguing coach for Team Canada. His coaching style may create burnout over the long haul, but nobody would be better at whipping an all-star team into shape in a few short weeks. His manic intensity is appropriate when national pride is at stake and players don't really have time to get sick of him.

"You could argue that's why he's so successful in short tournaments like the Canada Cup," E.J. McGuire says. "Get on the boat or get out of the way, 'cause we've got to win by training camp. Maybe a guy would say, 'This guy is nuts, but in three weeks I'll be back in St. Louis or I'll be back in Toronto. I can put up with this maniac for three weeks, play hard and win a Canada Cup.'"

But politics cost Keenan a chance to assist Canada's effort in the Canada Cup and the Olympics. When Glen Sather selected goaltender Curtis Joseph for Team Canada in '96, Keenan ripped Joseph in the media. That angered Sather and removed him from consideration for Team Canada coaching assignments.

On one hand, Keenan's story is an inspiration. He scrambled to resurrect his collegiate hockey career, then worked relentlessly to make himself a championship-caliber coach. He is a phenomenal self-made success. He studied, he learned, and he conquered. He had no connections in the NHL's old-boy network, so he earned his shot by winning quickly and winning big at every level of hockey.

"I don't know anybody who has coached high school, Junior B, major junior, university, minor leagues, the NHL, and won at every level," says former Maple Leafs coach Tom Watt, who coached Keenan in college and with him in international tournaments. "There is nobody who has ever come close to that."

Anybody in the sports industry would do well to muster the high-octane drive that propelled Keenan from St. Lawrence University to pro hockey prominence. Yet, Keenan's story is a cautionary tale of how easily a great coach can fall. There is no way such a proven winner should be fishing in February. Keenan stubbornly threw a brilliant career into an avoidable tailspin. Whether he can revive it, as Bowman did in Pittsburgh and Detroit, remains to be seen.

"He's had a couple of bad raps in a row now," says Jeremy Roenick, who starred for Keenan in Chicago. "Two bad raps in a row. You have that, it's going to be tough to get back in the league. But Mike is such a good hockey guy that it would not surprise me if he got back in the league. But if he didn't get back in the league, that wouldn't surprise me, either."

Blues defenseman Marc Bergevin played for Keenan early and late in his career. He got the full Iron Mike experience and believes the approach could still work, with a few modifications.

"It's a little different than it was fifteen years ago, but it's the same game, you know?" Bergevin says. "Younger guys are a little changed, the game changed. The basics are still there. Hard work is the bottom line and he makes his guys work hard. So hard work could cover a lot of things. I think he is smart enough to adjust. He's a smart guy. He's very emotional. That's why he gets carried away sometimes. You have to make some adjustments. He knows the game. He gets carried away sometimes, and when he reacts, it's too late, you lose the game. These days you can't afford to bench your top line after two shifts, which happened all the time."

Gary Webb, Keenan's former collegiate teammate and band-mate, sees no reason Keenan couldn't flourish again. But he would have to be more attentive to owner relations, public relations, and organizational politics. "In the right opportunity, with an owner who would put the trust in him, he could," Webb says. "Maybe he could put together a management team to come in and try to do it right."

Roberts suspects that Keenan learned from his recent difficulties, especially in St. Louis. If he could apply those lessons in his next assignment, there is no reason why he couldn't win again.

"He knows everything that would have to be done coaching the team," Roberts says. "It would be a matter of him getting his own emotions under control where he did a great job at coaching or management in a workmanlike way. He is certainly capable of managing a team and he can coach a team. Certainly since he's been out, things have changed. I'm sure Mike's been gathering more knowledge of the changes sitting in the broadcast booth or whatever he's been doing. I think he's very capable."

Could Keenan's high-pressure, puck-chasing scheme work in today's game? Perhaps with some modifications. NHL teams have become adept at counterattacking.

Could Keenan tailor his style to succeed in the twenty-first century? Poulin knows Keenan is smart enough to make some changes. "He can clearly alter that if he chooses to," he says. "And he's going to get hired. I don't think there is a question he's going to get hired."

As a scout for the Wild, Rich Sutter saw his share of bad hockey as he toured the NHL during the 1999–2000 season. There were nights he wondered how coaches kept from going crazy.

"When these guys don't want to play, it becomes a babysitting club for the rest of the night," Sutter says. "I think that's where coaches get fed up. People can say Mike is a control freak and, well, you know to a point everyone has to be some sort of control freak. There are a lot of egos in the way. The thing for him now is it can't just be any team. It has to be the right situation. It's not how long will he not last in the situation, but how long will he be happy in that situation. Mike has won. Look at Mike's record. Mike's won. His record speaks for itself. Given an opportunity and a length of time to do a job, I think Mike can do it.

"Mike has sat back for the last year and a half now. I'm sure Mike has rationalized. If Mike can't learn from what's gone on the last two or three times he's gone around, then he's never going to learn. But I think he can learn and I think he has learned. I think he has a lot of great hockey left in him. I think the league needs Mike."

Bowman knows more about coaching hockey than any man alive. He also knows Keenan very well. Could Iron Mike change? Well, sort of. "I think coaches change from team to team and job to job and time to time," he says. "But I don't think their manner changes."

Pat Croce, Keenan's old strength coach with the Flyers, built a fitness empire, sold it for big money, and bought control of the 76ers. He doesn't own a hockey team, but if he did, he said he wouldn't mind hiring Keenan to coach it. He has no doubt Keenan has one more big run left in him. But he doesn't believe Keenan, or any other coach for that matter, can reinvent himself to get a job.

"We don't change," Croce says. "We may mold. We may adapt. We can be like chameleons. But we don't change the core of who we are."

Keenan is who he is. As the walls closed in on him in Vancouver, Keenan sensed that his time as a NHL coach could be up. There was a chance he would never again do what he most loved to do. He might never coach hockey at the highest level in the world.

"It's interesting leaving a legacy of being a winner," he says. "And if I extinguish my own career doing it, then at least I went out and I can say I did it my way and was successful at it."

◄ APPENDIX I ►

Whatever Happened to . . .

SO WHATEVER HAPPENED TO MIKE KEENAN'S MOST NOTABLE whipping boys? How did life go for the men who helped mold Keenan as a head coach? What fate befell the thoughtless fellows who fired him? Here is what became of some of the key characters in the Keenan story:

Tony Amonte

Had the Rangers not won the Stanley Cup after trading Amonte for Brian Noonan and Stephane Matteau, this deal might have gone down as one of the worst in NHL history. Neither Matteau nor Noonan lasted in New York. Meanwhile, Amonte blossomed into one of hockey's most exciting goal scorers in Chicago. Could Amonte prove to be the clutch player Keenan doubted he would become? Sure, if the hapless Blackhawks ever get him a halfway decent supporting cast to play with. At the very least, he has refuted this characterization made by Rangers general Neil Smith after the trade: "Tony is a player who has flash and dash to him, but you can snuff him out."

Smith is the one who got snuffed out.

Todd Bergen

He got so stressed out with the Flyers under Keenan that he quit hockey in 1985 to try his hand at professional golf. He didn't become the next Fred Couples, so he returned for part of one minor league hockey season in the Minnesota organization before hanging up his skates for good. Keenan saved the Flyers a lot of grief by weeding him out early.

Dr. Cal Botterill

Keenan's team psychologist didn't work regularly with Keenan after the Rangers' Cup run, but he stayed busy. This University of Winnipeg professor worked with Team Canada's hockey team and Canada's national basketball, speed skating team, and volleyball teams. His son, Jason, starred at the University of Michigan, got drafted by the Dallas Stars, and later played for Atlanta and Calgary. Cal, a former hockey player, remains a big Keenan fan.

"Motivation by mission separates the best from the rest and Keenan has a phenomenal sense of mission," Botterill said.

Scotty Bowman

After nearly getting aced out of his Red Wings job by Keenan in 1994, Bowman got Detroit on the fast track and added two more Stanley Cups to his unmatched resume. He, vice president Jimmy Devellano, and new general manager Ken Holland pulled together and created the sort of juggernaut that owner Mike Ilitch always dreamed of. In 1996, the mentor beat the pupil as the Red Wings edged the Blues in the seventh game of a memorable second-round series. Steve Yzerman, a man twice rejected by Keenan for Canada Cup duty, scored the decisive overtime goal that denied the Blues a berth in the Western Conference championships.

Brian Burke

Firing Keenan didn't change much in Vancouver. The outmanned Canucks continued losing under new coach Marc Crawford. The franchise continued losing money in eight-digit lumps and the fan base continued to shrink. Burke's Pavel Bure trade proved to be a fiasco, since Dave Gagner had nothing left and Kevin Weekes couldn't take charge in goal. Young defenseman Ed Jovanovski, the key to that deal, became the object of trade rumors at the end of his first full season with the Canucks. Burke put the future of the franchise in the hands of twin Swedish prospects, Daniel and Henrik Sedin, who consistently disappointed with their indifferent play in international competition. Essentially, everything the Canucks did after Keenan got cashiered validated the points Keenan had made after getting fired.

Lindsay Carson

After demanding a trade from the Flyers to escape Keenan, Carson's career went pfffffffffftttt. Apparently, he needed Keenan to keep him motivated.

216

He scored just five goals in twenty-seven games after getting dealt to the Whalers and he never played in the NHL again. He spent the 1988–89 season with the Binghamton Whalers and then retired.

"He didn't like Mike when he played," Rick Tocchet said. "But he said to me he understood now what Mike was trying to do. He wished he had been with him a few years longer."

Bobby Clarke

Firing Keenan didn't make the Flyers better. In fact, Keenan was right about most of the young players who came aboard during Clarke's time. They really couldn't play. After getting fired by Philadelphia, Clarke rehabilitated his career with the Minnesota North Stars and the Florida Panthers, then returned to Philadelphia for a second stint with the Flyers. He has earned a reputation as a meddlesome general manager with a penchant for making knee-jerk trades. He came to loggerheads with franchise cornerstone Eric Lindros and refused to let head coach Roger Neilson return to his post during the 2000 playoffs after he underwent cancer treatments. Clarke quit talking to Lindros, even after he suffered another career-threatening concussion in the playoffs. And people think Keenan is a hard act.

Adam Creighton

In Chicago, Keenan got great mileage out of the massive Creighton. He tried again in St. Louis, bringing the big fella aboard and re-signing him to a hefty free agent deal, but Creighton continued skating as if his feet were in cement. He became the living, breathing symbol of failure for this franchise. The odd thing was, this lumbering center really enjoyed playing for Keenan.

"He wants results," Creighton said. "He lets you hold your own fate. If you don't perform, you don't play. After playing on other teams and playing for other coaches, I missed Mike. I don't know why. He just has that edge, that intensity." With Keenan out of the NHL, Creighton went overseas and finished his career in Europe.

Doug Crossman

This talented offensive defenseman gave up on Keenan in Philadelphia and the Flyers gave up on him, even after Keenan got fired. Crossman was traded to Los Angeles and then bounced around the league, only sporadically showing his old form. His NHL career ended in St. Louis in

1994 after Keenan took over the Blues. He later tried his hand at coaching in the United Hockey League before leaving the hockey business.

Tommy Eriksson

He got tired of Keenan, leaving after lasting two seasons. He was just twenty-six when he departed and was still in his athletic prime. This top-notch offensive defenseman played nine more seasons in Sweden, once representing his country in the Olympics and twice playing for Sweden in the World Championships.

Bob Froese

He put up some incredible numbers after Pelle Lindbergh's fatal car wreck forced him into the starter's role. He won thirty-one games and led the NHL with five shutouts and a 2.55 goals-against average in 1985–86. But Keenan never liked him and he never liked Keenan. Once Ron Hextall emerged as Philadelphia's new number one man, Froese moved on to the Rangers and finished his career as a backup. He retired in 1990.

Grant Fuhr

After a terrific first season in St. Louis, Fuhr predictably caught the injury bug and saw his performance slide. His agreeable personality helped him eke one more contract out of the Blues before they shipped him to Calgary in 1999. There, he suffered still another knee injury and finished his career as a seldom-used sub. In retrospect, the Blues would have been much better off keeping Curtis Joseph than going with this destined Hall of Famer in the twilight of his career.

"I enjoyed playing for Mike," Fuhr said. "It was fun. You never knew what was going to happen. He kept you on your toes."

Mike Gartner

Keenan noted his label as a poor playoff performer and wanted him gone from New York. Had Keenan gotten his way, Gartner wouldn't have played a minute for him. Though he continued to score goals, both in Toronto and Phoenix, Gartner never got to the Stanley Cup finals. He did, however, help lead the Maple Leafs to the Western Conference finals in 1994, the year Keenan traded him.

Martin Gelinas

Some players re-energize after escaping Keenan. Gelinas did not. After those back-to-back seasons of 30 goals for Vancouver, he drifted back to mediocrity with the Carolina Hurricanes. Whatever shortcomings Keenan saw in his makeup didn't go away. He was right: Gelinas was no Adam Graves.

Greg Gilbert

He played for Keenan in Chicago. He played for him in New York. He played for him in St. Louis. And he probably would have played for him in Vancouver, too, if he hadn't run out of gas. Instead, Gilbert turned to coaching and demonstrated great promise running the Worcester IceCats of the AHL. He figures to become still another Keenan pupil who ends up behind an NHL bench.

"Mike is a demanding coach, there no question," Gilbert said. "He wouldn't demand anything that he didn't think you could give."

Dale Hawerchuk

He won with Keenan as a kid in Oshawa. He won with him as an adult with Team Canada in the Canada Cup. But his decision to join Keenan in St. Louis did not bring much joy and happiness, although it did pay well. Hawerchuk proved ineffective as a free-agent signee, got benched in front of his family in Buffalo, and got shuffled off to Philadelphia shortly after Keenan acquired Wayne Gretzky in St. Louis. Chronic hip problems forced him to retire in 1997.

Ron Hextall

Once Keenan left Philadelphia, life just wasn't the same for this combative goaltender. He had one more solid season, then went belly up. The Flyers traded him to Quebec in the massive Eric Lindros deal, then got him back from the Islanders. Then, and only then, did Hextall finally get his bearings back and play as he did in the glory days. All in all, he enjoyed a splendid career before retiring.

Brett Hull

The Golden Brett finally proved, once and for all, that he really was a winner. But he did it in Dallas. The Blues ownership group sided with Hull during his 1996 power struggle with Keenan, but peace did not last long. Keenan's successor, Joel Quenneville, quickly grew weary of Hull's antics and made no effort to stop his departure in 1998 via free agency. Perhaps the fact Hull once fired a puck at him in practice had something to do with that. The Stars signed him to score big goals and he scored the biggest one of all: the game- and series-winning goal against the Buffalo Sabres that won the 1999 Stanley Cup for Dallas. He also played at a Conn Smythe–level pace in the 2000 playoffs, leading then back to the Cup finals.

Craig Janney

Escaping Keenan made Janney's life more pleasant, but it didn't resurrect his career. His aversion to weight training and general lack of conditioning continued to plague him through stops in San Jose, Winnipeg / Phoenix, Tampa Bay, and with the New York Islanders. After producing a solid 82-point season in 1995–96, Janney went into a downward spiral before a circulatory problem in his leg forced him to retire prematurely.

"He put me through hell. He put a lot of guys through hell," Janney would say some years removed from Keenan. "But I think he's a good hockey man. He runs the best practices of any coach I've seen. He's a proven hockey man and a winner. Someone will take a chance on him."

Curtis Joseph

Banished to free-agent purgatory by Keenan in 1995, Joseph eventually signed with the Oilers and played well enough to earn a monstrous free-agent contract with his hometown Toronto Maple Leafs. Although he still hasn't won the big one — the Canada Cup got away from him and neither the Oilers nor the Leafs reached the Cup finals with him in goal — Cujo is in the process of living happily ever after.

Trevor Linden

Keenan took a lot of heat for trading the long-time Canucks fan favorite, but he was right about this former star. Linden faded before his time, disappointing the New York Islanders and Montreal Canadiens for the same reasons he had ticked off Keenan. He remained one of the best people in the game, but injuries took their toll and he seemed to lose some of his fire.

Jacques Martin

At different points along his hockey trail, Martin hooked up with Keenan. He played with him at St. Lawrence University. He scouted for him at Peterborough. He joined him as an assistant coach with the Chicago Blackhawks after getting fired in St. Louis. Eventually, Martin proved to be an excellent NHL head coach with the Ottawa Senators and he considers his time with Keenan well spent.

"What I probably took away is you have to be yourself when you're coaching," Martin said. "I think that's very important. You can't be somebody else. Probably the thing I learned the most is you have to be very demanding. The more you demand, the more you're going to get. That's the bottom line. When I went to work for Mike, it just re-affirmed what I thought you needed to do to build a championship team."

Stephane Matteau

The hero of the Rangers' 1994 Stanley Cup drive returned to obscurity. Matteau would score only seven more goals for the Rangers before following Keenan to St. Louis. As a Blue, he reached his goal-scoring peak at sixteen. From there, he went to San Jose, which resisted trade overtures from Keenan after Mike got control of the Canucks hockey operation. If Keenan gets another NHL job, Matteau figures to be on his third line. Even if he's in his forties.

John McCaw

The Canucks' owner lost his child-like enthusiasm for the sport in a hurry as his losses exceeded $20 million a year. His thirst for over-the-hill legends waned after Messier failed to revive the team. McCaw sold the NBA Grizzlies, who seem destined to move in three or four years, and the Canucks don't appear to be long for Vancouver, either. McCaw reported his 1999–2000 losses as $34.9 million. Ouch! So what will they put in GM Place in years to come? Curling tournaments?

E.J. McGuire

Keenan's long-time aide in Rochester, Philadelphia, and Chicago finally struck out on his own halfway into Mike's tenure with the Blackhawks. Looking to run his own program and create a non-Keenan identity for himself, McGuire worked as a head coach at the minor league and major junior hockey level. A NHL head coaching job never came his way, but he did join the New York Rangers as a professional scout.

Scott Mellanby

After serving as one of Keenan's whipping boys in Philadelphia, Mellanby moved on to play two productive seasons in Edmonton before landing in Florida for Bobby Clarke's Panthers. There he helped lead Florida's unlikely Stanley Cup finalists and twice scored 30 or more goals. Far from being the spoiled kid Keenan believed him to be, Mellanby became one of the NHL's top power forwards and most respected leaders.

"Mike's way was to get on rookies and I didn't take it well," Mellanby recalled. "It's supposed to get me up, but it just got me down."

Mark Messier

This living legend provided absolutely no positive impact for his $7-million salary with the Canucks. He still has his imposing stare, but his legs are gone. Vancouver played marginally better under Keenan's successor, Marc Crawford, but Messier remained a shell of his former self — and the Canucks remained out of the post-season mix. Now he is back on Broadway with the Rangers.

Joe Murphy

"Joe-Joe" did moderately well in San Jose after the Blues shipped him to the Sharks, eating a chunk of his salary in the process. After vastly over-rating his value on the free-agent market, Murphy finally latched on with the Boston Bruins in mid-season. There he clashed with coach Pat Burns and got sent home. Washington took a flyer on him, but it's safe to say that Murphy's days as a top NHL wage earner are long gone.

Nik and the Nice Guys

The former St. Lawrence party band is now an eight-band entertainment conglomerate operating out of Rochester, New York. With Keenan's former college teammate Gary Webb at the helm, Nik Entertainment books big corporate events (such as Super Bowl week) all over the country. Much of the Nice Guys' stylistic success can be traced to Keenan's early days as a charismatic, interactive "vocalist," although Webb has no intention of putting Iron Mike back on stage.

James Patrick

Keenan couldn't get him out of New York fast enough — for good reason, as it turns out. He lasted less than a season in Hartford, then had one good season in four injury-plagued years with Calgary. His all-star career wound down with him playing a part-time role in Buffalo. For a variety of reasons, Patrick was never the same player after leaving New York.

Dave Poulin
The corporate world never did get its clutches on Poulin. After his NHL playing days ended, the former Flyers captain turned to coaching and built a competitive program at Notre Dame University. He often joked that the biggest thing he learned from Keenan was how not to treat people.

"One thing you can never fault Mike for is wanting to win, no question about it," Poulin said. "I had him when he was young and really raw."

Poulin has seen his name linked to various NHL head coaching and general manager openings. Is he destined to one day coach the Flyers for his old friend Bobby Clarke?

Bob Pulford
Predictably, Blackhawks owner Bill Wirtz never did run off his trusted lieutenant, as Keenan had hoped during his reign there. After firing Keenan, Wirtz put Pulford back in charge of the hockey operation. Pulford attempted to develop Bob Murray as his successor, but Murray did a disastrous job. Not only did Pulford have to return to the general manager's post on an interim basis, he went back behind the bench, too, during the 1999–2000 season. The post-Keenan Blackhawks went to hell in a handbasket.

Jerry Ritter
The man who fired Keenan in St. Louis did what he was paid to do. The Blues' ownership group ordered him to clean up the franchise's economic mess and ready the team for sale. His hirings of president Mark Sauer, coach Joel Quenneville, and general manager Larry Pleau all paid off. The Blues quickly rebuilt with quality young players. Bill and Nancy Laurie, heirs to the Wal-Mart fortune, bought the team and the Kiel Center and vowed to compete for the Cup. Ritter rode off into the sunset.

Jeremy Roenick
Once Keenan left Chicago, life was never the same there for J.R. He ran afoul of Wirtz over his salary demands and got dealt to Phoenix in a franchise-gutting trade for the enigmatic Alexei Zhamnov. As a member of

the Coyotes, he frequently campaigned for Keenan to get the coaching job, but to no avail. For his part, Keenan tried to acquire him for the Blues, also to no avail. Now the franchise faces a major rebuilding task after a series of first-round playoff exits and another ownership change.

Ted Sator

Twice Keenan inherited him as an assistant coach. Twice he left after a year. The first time, he left the Flyers to coach the New York Rangers and did a solid job. The second time, after leaving St. Louis, he couldn't find work in the NHL. He currently coaches New Orleans of the East Coast Hockey League. He was one of many former Keenan employees who didn't respond to interview requests for this book.

Denis Savard

Savard was a winner, regardless of what Keenan thought of him during their time together in Chicago. Denis proved that in Montreal, helping the Canadiens win the 1993 Cup, albeit as a part-time player. He spent some of those playoffs behind the bench as an unofficial assistant coach for Jacques Demers. He later played in Tampa Bay before returning to the post-Keenan Blackhawks to finish his playing career and begin his second career as an assistant coach. He was voted into the Hockey Hall of Fame in June 2000.

Brendan Shanahan

Somehow, some way, Shanahan survived his trade from the Blues to Hartford. The deal devastated him, but he turned the page. With the Whalers languishing as a lame-duck team before moving to North Carolina, Shanahan demanded a trade. Luckily, he landed in Detroit. He helped lead the Red Wings' Stanley Cup charge and disproved any notion that he was just another selfish superstar unwilling to do what it took to win.

"I don't expect to be coddled," Shanahan said, "but I don't like a guy who stabs you in the back. Maybe he didn't like me because I couldn't be intimidated. I'm not going to tell you I'm nostalgic for the man. I wouldn't sit down on an airplane with him and talk about old times."

Neil Smith

After winning his battle with Keenan and maintaining control of the Rangers fiefdom, Smith proved he really didn't know how to build a winner. Without Keenan around to tell him who to acquire, Smith made one catastrophic decision after another to cripple the 1994 Stanley Cup champions. His greatest folly as Rangers general manager came in the summer of 1999, when he committed more than $60 million to free agents Valeri Kamensky, Stephane Quintal, Theoren Fleury, Sylvain Lefebvre, and Tim Taylor. They all floundered, the Rangers missed the playoffs, and Smith finally got fired.

Darryl Sutter

Bill Wirtz was dying to get him behind the bench in place of Keenan in Chicago. Sutter did a solid regular season job for the Blackhawks, but he never took them on a Keenan-like post-season run. After stepping down for family reasons, Sutter later resurfaced in San Jose as coach of the Sharks. There, he coached his brother (and long-time Keenan favorite) Ron Sutter to some moderate success. But again, he was unable to make much post-season noise.

Rick Tocchet

This Keenan favorite stayed true to his rugged Philadelphia Flyers roots and enjoyed a remarkable run, standing out for Pittsburgh, Los Angeles, Boston, Washington, and Phoenix before returning to the Flyers. He broke in as a tough guy and remained a tough guy even after his offensive skills emerged. At his wedding, a lot of former Keenanites gathered to reminisce. Many of those guys even admitted that Mike was the best coach they ever had. Like Roenick, Tocchet tried to campaign for Keenan to get the Coyotes' head coaching job.

"One day you'd feel like killing him, the next day hugging him," Tocchet said. "He's that kind of guy. Me and Mike have always gone at it. I always liked Mike. He made me a better player."

Tom Watt

Keenan's coach during his post-graduate playing days at the University of Toronto went on to bigger and better things. He coached Winnipeg, Vancouver, and Toronto, and worked against his pupil in the latter two stops. He joined Keenan's staff for the epic 1987 Canada Cup quest and gained a world-wide reputation as a hockey teacher and tactician. Most recently, he served as a developmental coach for the Calgary Flames. He would hire Keenan if he ever became a general manager.

"It's sad that he's not coaching now," he said. "People are afraid of that drive. They shouldn't be."

Doug Wilson

Weary of Keenan's browbeatings, Wilson asked for, and got, a trade to San Jose. He walked away from his life in Chicago and the post-Blackhawks career he had lined up for himself there. Wilson didn't last long as a Sharks player — his body finally gave out in 1993 — but he eventually moved into the franchise's front office. After a four-year stint with the NHL Players Association, he was hired as the team's director of pro development in 1997.

Bill Wirtz

The owner of the Blackhawks has never been in touch with the real hockey fans that spent so freely to make his family rich. All those Chicago fans that dutifully attended games in their Stan Mikita sweaters had to be sickened by the demise of their franchise. Euro-friendly general manager Mike Smith took charge of the franchise and installed Alpo Suhonen as coach. Suhonen, arguably the greatest coach in Finnish hockey history, once took a sabbatical to produce plays. More than a few Hawks fans were left longing for the days when Iron Mike ruled with an iron fist and Dirk Graham squashed enemy defensemen into the end boards.

Trent Yawney

After suffering much torment under Keenan in Chicago, he returned for more abuse in St. Louis. He got to relive the old times of sitting out Blackhawks games by sitting out Blues games. He joined Savard, another Keenan whipping boy, as an assistant coach with the Blackhawks. Yawney had no doubt that Iron Mike would get back into the league as a head coach.

"I definitely think so," Yawney said. "He can still coach. His record speaks for itself. He definitely needs the right kind of team. He proved that when he went to New York."

Peter Zezel

There was no way Zezel could fall out of the NHL if Keenan was working in the league. After torturing him as a young player in Philadelphia in the 1980s, Iron Mike extended Zezel's career in the 1990s. He brought him to St. Louis in 1995, then rescued him from the Albany River Rats in 1998, bringing him to Vancouver in February 1998. After Keenan left, Zezel nixed a trade to Anaheim because he wanted to remain close to a gravely ill relative. He sat out the 1999–2000 season, but didn't consider himself retired. Rather, he was just waiting for Keenan to get back into the league and give him a call.

◄ APPENDIX II ►

Be Like Mike

FEW, IF ANY, NHL COACHES TALK LIKE MIKE KEENAN. ALL THOSE managerial treatises he read during his formative years left him prattling on like a business professor. Do you want to sound just like Keenan when you talk to your own sports team or work force? Here is a sampler of Keenan's coaching truisms uttered over the course of his career. Feel free to steal some of these for yourself.

• • •

"You have to learn to embrace change. It's a very difficult thing to learn for some players. Some never accept it."

"Great players have needs that have to be satisfied, but needs of the team come first."

"Hockey is a team game. It is fundamentally based on a player's ability to trust his teammates and be part of a team. He must realize that the growth and maturation of the team depends on his own ability to develop his own style and become a leader."

"You can't win on individual performances in this league, not consistently."

"All the talent in the world without execution and smart work is frivolous."

"The value of the team's attitude has to come from leadership and must be intrinsic amongst the group. Ultimately, the only way for it to succeed is if they want it — if they want it bad enough amongst themselves as players."

"I think there is room for both tough physical play and finesse hockey in the pursuit of excellence. I think to employ any system, you have to evaluate the talent you have and mold that system to it."

"One thing that's been consistent throughout my career is that the best players, when they play with the best players, are better players than they would be if they didn't play with the best players."

"I always feel that your best players should be able to participate in all aspects of the game."

"If you accept the status quo in sports, you're toast. You're finished."

"You're asking for abnormal behavior. It's not normal to win."

"You're asking them to walk down a line or road that they've never been on before and it's treacherous. There's pitfalls everywhere. There's a lot of risk-taking to step out and be a champion."

"Playing 110 games in 240 nights isn't normal. So if you try to make normal demands on your club, you won't be successful. I still believe people are capable of doing more than they think they are. So what you have to do is find a way to make challenges seem intrinsic rather than extraneous. What I love about coaching is seeing players believe in what they're doing and go on to do things they didn't think they could do."

"It could be perceived as a Keenanism, if you like, but in reality, it's to challenge your athletes to a higher level of expectation than they have for themselves and the team. It looks like chaos, but it's not."

"Our whole mentality in pro sports is geared toward winning, but we don't cut all the values to that level."

"I expect a lot from my players. If that means I'm tough on them because I'm challenging them to be better than what they are on a daily basis, I can't apologize for that. And I won't apologize because they are capable of it. And unless you ask and expect it, you don't get it."

"Most players thrive on challenges and are proud of their ability. And because they are proud of their ability, you structure the expectations. If you don't expect it, you can't win it."

"A key element of coaching is that the pride of your best players is probably the most motivating factor."

"You have to appeal to their pride. Whether players are competing in junior, university, or the NHL, they bring certain physical abilities, and you have to find out what they can bring to the table. After that, it's a matter of developing an atmosphere of expectation and an atmosphere where they can bring out the best in each other."

"Players have to have intrinsic values from within the soul. They have to want to be a good player. You try to perpetuate that."

"Psychological preparation makes all the difference. Everybody has talent. Coaching hockey is not a matter of Xs and Os on the ice. It's understanding all aspects of a player's being."

"Everyone tries. Amateurs try. You have to accept more responsibility. If the guys don't accept more responsibility, you have to make changes."

"This is a physical game. Sometimes you have to send a physical message."

"If you're in charge, you should be in charge. If you're the coach, you should be in charge. It's not a democracy."

"We don't take away their individual attributes or skills. But we have to have some kind of kind of structure. We have to have some kind of formation. If that's being a control freak."

"I read something by [NFL coach] Don Shula , and he said any time a team perceives that you are not as emotional about winning as they are, then your relationship won't be as strong."

"You take steps to get into a slump, you take steps to get out of one."

"In business, you have quarterly reports. In hockey, you have eighty reports. Three a week, sometimes four."

"Perfect practices makes perfect, not just practice. I don't know any championship team that hasn't practiced successfully. Our practices are very short and very intense, but that's the way you play the game."

"There's a great saying that goes like this: 'When does the teacher become a good teacher? When the student is ready to learn.'"

"It's like a teacher in the classroom. What do you do with a disruptive group of students? You just have to continue to try to instill basic teaching principles, and hopefully one day they'll enjoy learning."

"Sometimes it's described as fear. Other times it's described as respect. It's like the teacher you had in elementary school or high school. You perceived that teacher to be the most difficult to deal with, but later in life you realize that's the individual you had the highest degree of respect for."

"Players shouldn't be thinking of what the coaches are thinking. They should be thinking of what we need."

"Internal competition raises the level of your team."

"It's human nature: You see someone there waiting to take your job, you stay ready."

"Not everybody is going to fit into a certain system or style of play, and it's best for that individual not to even be with the program because they're not going to be able to make the adjustment. That's not unlike a president going into office or a new CEO going into a corporation."

"The things you can't manage, you have a responsibility to manage better. That's part of having strong leadership skills."

"There's winning and there's misery."